Reason & Revelation:
New Directions in Bahá'í Thought

Studies in the Bábí and Bahá'í Religions
Volume Thirteen

Studies in the Bábí and Bahá'í Religions

(formerly *Studies in Bábí and Bahá'í History*)

ANTHONY A. LEE, General Editor

Studies in Bábí and Bahá'í History edited by Moojan Momen	Volume One
From Iran East and West edited by Juan R. Cole and Moojan Momen	Volume Two
In Iran edited by Peter Smith	Volume Three
Music, Devotion, and Mashriqu'l-Adhkár by R. Jackson Armstrong-Ingram	Volume Four
Studies in Honor of the Late Hasan M. Balyuzi edited by Moojan Momen	Volume Five
Community Histories edited by Richard Hollinger	Volume Six
Symbol and Secret: *Qur'an Commentary in Bahá'u'lláh's Kitáb-i Íqán* by Christopher Buck	Volume Seven
Revisioning the Sacred: *New Perspectives on a Bahá'í Theology* edited by J. A. McLean	Volume Eight
Modernity and the Millennium: The Genesis of the *Baha'i Faith in the Nineteenth-Century Middle East* by Juan R. I. Cole (Columbia University Press)	Volume Nine
Paradise and Paradigm: Key Symbols *in Persian Christianity and the Bahá'í Faith* by Christopher Buck (State University of New York Press)	Volume Ten
Religion in Iran: From Zoroaster to Baha'ullah by Alessandro Bausani (Bibliotheca Persica Press)	Volume Eleven
Evolution and Bahá'í Belief: 'Abdu'l-Bahá's Response *to Nineteenth-Century Darwinism* by Keven Brown and Eberhard von Kitzing	Volume Twelve

Bahá'í World Center

TERRACES LEADING TO THE SHRINE OF THE BÁB
Haifa, Israel

Studies in the Bábí and Bahá'í Religions

Volume Thirteen

General Editor
Anthony A. Lee

REASON & REVELATION:

New Directions in Bahá'í Thought

Edited by Seena Fazel & John Danesh

Kalimát Press • Los Angeles

First Edition

Manufactured in the United States of America

Library of Congress Cataloging-in-Publication Data

Reason and revelation : new directions in Bahá'í thought /
edited by Seena Fazel & John Danesh.
p. cm. -- (Studies in the Bábí and Bahá'í religions ; v. 13)
Includes bibliographical references.
ISBN 1-890688-20-7
1. Bahai Faith--Doctrines. I. Fazel, Seena. II. Danesh, John. III. Series.

BP375.R36 2001
297.9'32--dc21 2001038900

Kalimát Press
1600 Sawtelle Boulevard, Suite 310
Los Angeles, California 90025

www.kalimat.com
kalimatp@aol.com

Contents

Foreword

Perhaps alone among the world's great religions, the writings of the Bahá'í Faith explicitly establish that the religion aspires to be "scientific in its method."[1] The Bahá'í teachings promote rational argument as a way towards seeking spiritual reality. Intellectual inquiry is regarded as "the most praiseworthy power"[2] possessed by human beings, their "most precious gift,"[3] the "discoverer of the realities of things."[4] Rather than being destructive, the clash of different opinions is understood as a catalyst for the emergence of truth.[5]

Most of the essays in the present collection are based on outstanding work published in the *Bahá'í Studies Review* during the past decade.[6] They share a rational approach to the texts and teachings of the Bahá'í Faith and illustrate how academic study can yield fresh insights, often opening entirely new areas to scholarship. Several articles begin with simple—but searching—questions. In "Fundamentalism and Liberalism," for example, Moojan Momen asks why some followers of religion interpret teachings and texts in a systematically different way from their co-religionists. In "Prayer As Remembrance," Christopher White asks: What is the purpose of prayer? In "Theocratic Assumptions in Bahá'í Literature" Sen McGlinn queries the scriptural basis for the widespread (but, in his view, mistaken) idea that the Bahá'í writings anticipate the merging of political and religious institutions in society.

Several essays show how the application of specialist academic skills can enhance an understanding of Bahá'í scripture and belief. In "Scripture as Literature," Franklin Lewis demonstrates how a reading of Bahá'í sacred texts can be seriously handicapped without the perspective of their literary backgrounds and an understanding of their original languages. Sholeh Quinn's essay, "The End of History?" illustrates how the use of formal academic methods can enrich perspectives on events in Bahá'í history. In "Bahá'í Universalism and Native Prophets," Christopher Buck draws on Bahá'í texts and cross-cultural studies to propose a broader understanding of Bahá'í theology that embraces indigenous religions as part of the world's spiritual heritage.

Rational discourse also involves the systematic collection, presentation, and evaluation of relevant evidence on a particular question. Bryan Graham provides the first comprehensive review of secondary Bahá'í literature on economics, highlighting, for example, how previous commentators have neglected aspects of capitalism and competition that are encouraged in Bahá'í writings. Geeta Gandhi Kingdon summarizes recent evidence from development economics in her essay "Women, Education, and Development," showing that there is now a substantial empirical basis to support the longstanding Bahá'í emphasis on the education of women and girls. In "Infallible Institutions?" Udo Schaefer reviews texts about the functions and powers of the supreme body of the Bahá'í Faith, the Universal House of Justice, and he concludes with a challenging analysis of its role.

Despite the status given to reason in the Bahá'í writings, it is regarded as only one of several ways of approaching truth—alongside aesthetics, mysticism, and revelation.[7] So, although the authors of these essays have exercised what Bahá'í writings describe as their "undoubted right" to "self-expression . . . to declare [their] conscience and set forth [their] views,"[8] these personal understandings are, of course, open to debate and revision. Indeed, it is hoped that this publication will encourage such critical dialogue.

Seena Fazel & John Danesh
Oxford & Cambridge
June 2002

NOTES

1. Shoghi Effendi, *The World Religion of Bahá'u'lláh: A Summary of Its Aims, Teachings and History*. Statement to the High Commissioner of Palestine, June 1933, published as *The Faith of Bahá'u'lláh: A World Religion* (Wilmette: Bahá'í Publishing Trust, 1947 ([1980]).
2. 'Abdu'l-Bahá, *The Promulgation of Universal Peace* (Wilmette: Bahá'í Publishing Trust, 1982) p. 31.
3. 'Abdu'l-Bahá, *Paris Talks* (London: Bahá'í Publishing Trust, 1969) p. 41.
4. 'Abdu'l-Bahá, *Promulgation*, p. 417.
5. 'Abdu'l-Bahá, *Selections from the Writings of 'Abdu'l-Bahá* (Haifa: Bahá'í World Centre, 1978) p. 87.
6. See http://bahai-library.org/bsr/. Moojan Momen, "Fundamentalism and Liberalism: Towards an Understanding of the Dichotomy," *Bahá'í Studies Review*, Vol. 2 (1992) pp. 11-24. Christopher White, "Searching for God in Time and Memory: An Examination of Bahá'í Prayer as 'Remembrance'," *Bahá'í Studies Review*, Vol. 7 (1997) pp. 49-60. Franklin Lewis, "Scripture as Literature: Sifting through the Layers of the Text," *Bahá'í Studies Review*, Vol. 7 (1997) pp. 125-46. Sholeh Quinn, "Historical Research and Bahá'í Scholarship," *Bahá'í Studies Review*, Vol. 9 (1999/2000) pp. 163-74. Christopher Buck, "Native Messengers of God in Canada?: A Test Case for Bahá'í Universalism," *Bahá'í Studies Review*, Vol. 6 (1996) pp. 97-133. Bryan Graham, "The Bahá'í Faith and Economics: A Review and Synthesis," *Bahá'í Studies Review*, Vol. 7 (1997) pp. 15-37. Geeta Gandhi Kingdon, "Education of Women and Socio-economic Development," *Bahá'í Studies Review*, Vol. 7 (1997) pp. 39-48. Udo Schaefer, "Infallible Institutions?" *Bahá'í Studies Review*, Vol. 9 (1999/2000) pp. 17-45.
7. 'Abdu'l-Bahá, *Some Answered Questions* (Wilmette: Bahá'í Publishing Trust, 1984) pp. 297-99. Also see Moojan Momen, "Relativism: A Basis for Bahá'í Metaphysics," in *Studies in Honor of the Late Hasan M. Balyuzi, Studies in Bábí and the Bahá'í Religions,* Vol. 5 (Los Angeles: Kalimát Press, 1988).
8. Shoghi Effendi, *Bahá'í Administration* (Wilmette: Bahá'í Publishing Trust, 1968) p. 63.

SEENA FAZEL is a clinical research fellow in psychiatry at the University of Oxford. JOHN DANESH is professor of epidemiology and medicine and head of the Department of Public Health and Primary Care at the University of Cambridge. They are co-authors of *The Bahá'í Faith in Words and Images* (Oneworld, 2002) and editors of *The Bahá'í Studies Review* (1990-2002).

Interpreting Principles

Bahá'í World Center

THE SEAT OF THE UNIVERSAL HOUSE OF JUSTICE
Mt. Carmel, Haifa, Israel

Infallible Institutions?

Udo Schaefer

"Infallibility" is a complex term in Bahá'í scripture that has not been much discussed in Bahá'í secondary literature. The concept, which has analogies in Catholicism and Islam, is historically burdened and has become obsolete in secular thought. This paper analyzes two categories of infallibility: essential infallibility, which is inherent in the messengers of God, and conferred infallibility, which is a characteristic of the institutions of the Guardianship and the Universal House of Justice.

This paper focuses on the Universal House of Justice. Does its infallibility operate to an unlimited extent? Are every one of its decisions infallible, and if not, what are the boundaries? The immanent limits of this charisma are analyzed and a detailed argument provided that supports a defensible restrictive interpretation.

Introduction[1]

Reason (*'aql*) has been called "the first and foremost" among the "favors, which the Almighty hath conferred upon men,"[2] however, it is not an infallible source of knowledge,[3] and is "liable to err."[4] All human thought must be prefaced with St. Jerome's dictum *errare human est*.[5] "Mortal man is prone to err," says Bahá'u'lláh.[6] The question then arises whether there is anything that could unreservedly be called truth, whether there is any infallible source of truth.

Revealed religion is inseparably associated with a claim to truth. If it is the Word of God that is proclaimed, it cannot be but truth, and, indeed, all the prophets claimed to be the "straight Path of Truth."[7] The Qur'an is "a guidance to the God-fearing,"[8] by which "the right way [is] made distinct from error"[9]; "Nay, we hurl the truth at falsehood, and it shall smite it, and lo! it shall vanish."[10] To Bahá'ís, Bahá'u'lláh is "the living Book who proclaimeth the truth," his message "a Truth [which is] not overtaken by error."[11] His book "that judged between truth and falsehood,"[12] is the divine standard of all morality, the "essence of justice,"[13] the "infallible Balance."[14]

Under the premise of faith that he is the "mediator between God and men"[15] and has come with the truth, the messenger of God must be considered an infallible source of knowledge. This is a logical conclusion. Referring to the Gospel of St. John,[16] Christian theology claimed for Jesus Christ not only infallibility but even omniscience.[17] In Islamic dogmatics the doctrine of *'isma* was developed according to which immunity from error and sin is ascribed to the prophets.[18] Whereas the term "infallibility" does not occur in the sacred writings of the past, neither in the Bible nor in the Qur'an, Bahá'u'lláh has dealt with this subject explicitly and, as I will explain below, has confirmed infallibility as an inherent attribute of the Manifestation of God.

However, the claim to infallibility has been raised also for two institutions of the community: the Guardianship and the Universal House of Justice. According to Bahá'í texts both are explicitly "freed from all error."[19] "Whatsoever they decide is of God[20] . . . God will verily inspire them with whatsoever He willeth."[21] Whereas infallibility is an essential attribute of the Manifestation who occupies an ontologically higher station in the hierarchy of creation than human beings and is endowed with innate knowledge, the individuals who serve in these two institutions are human beings. The *charisma*[22] of infallibility has been *conferred* on the institution (not on the persons in office). To secular thought, the concept of *conferred* infallibility has become untenable and unacceptable. In the age of "fallibilism,"[23] "infallibility is an obsolete claim."[24] Moreover, the concept is historically burdened, it conjures up all sorts of negative connotations, provokes fierce rejection and is regarded as an expression of human presumptuousness and hubris, a sign of antiquated thinking.

In Western thought, infallibility is closely associated with the Catholic Church and its disputed dogma of papal infallibility, which was promulgated by the first Vatican council in 1870 under the Pontificate of Pius IX.[25] The dogma[26] defines the Roman bishop to be infallible if he takes a final decision in matters of doctrine or morals and speaks *ex cathedra,*[27] i.e. in performance of his teaching office (*magisterium*). The dogma of papal infallibility was accepted by the Council after many disputes, with the result that a major splinter-group, made up mainly of German bishops, left the Catholic church and founded their own church, the so-called "Old Catholics." The term is still controversial in Catholic theology. Hans Küng has written a sizeable book[28] on this subject in which he radically contests this dogma. The discussion among Catholic theologians on this issue continues and the Curia has been unable to silence the voices of dissidents. Today the concept of infallibility is discredited, inasmuch as a significant number of Christian theologians do not even ascribe infallibility to Christ, since he is presumed to have erred with regard to the question of parousia. Hans Küng has coined a formula for a widespread conviction among Catholics: "*Nemo infallibis nisi Deus ipse*" ("No one is infallible save God").

In the skeptical climate of Western societies, infallibility is a concept that is virtually impossible to impart; that of *conferred* infallibility is even more difficult to explain. Indeed, this concept cannot be validated through rational argumentation. Nevertheless, it ought to be possible to demonstrate that the idea of conferred infallibility is not necessarily irrational under the premise of religious faith. In order to do so, how-ever, it would be necessary to clarify this notion in critical discourse. Bahá'ís will only be able to avoid the accusation of superstition if they manage to show that the infallibility of the institutions is not a magical element in the Bahá'í system, but rather something that is reasonable and acceptable for those who believe in the revelation of Bahá'u'lláh.

In this critical discourse, the discussion of the immanent limits of conferred infallibility would be of crucial significance. The idea that the Universal House of Justice is invested with unlimited infallibility leads to untenable and unacceptable consequences. Unfortunately, experience has shown that in the Bahá'í community a critical discussion on this subject is not an easy thing—so strong are the convictions of many that 'Abdu'l-Bahá's assurance, "Whatever they decide is of God,"[29] is valid for absolutely every kind of decision—the Bahá'í community thus being in possession of a kind of oracle that can be consulted and from whom the community gets infallible guidance in all matters.

As Shoghi Effendi himself has clarified the extent of his infallibility as Guardian and formulated its immanent limitations, the focus of this article is on the Universal House of Justice: does its infallibility operate without limit with the result that absolutely every decision is covered by it? Or, if this question is to be answered in the negative, what exactly is the scope of its infallibility?

At the outset it would be more complete to elucidate the concept of the "essential infallibility" of the messengers of God, but it is beyond the scope of this article to deal with this issue comprehensively. I will neither discuss the issue of omniscience,[30] nor will I go into details (e.g., the question as to whether references in the holy texts to facts or historical events[31] are infallible statements), nor will I discuss the nature of 'Abdu'l-Bahá's infallibility.[32]

The issue of institutional infallibility has already been the subject of a discussion in the context of the refutation of the confused and blatantly erroneous accusations of a Covenant-breaker.[33] An English edition of this rebuttal[34] has recently been published by George Ronald under the title *Making the Crooked Straight: A Contribution to Bahá'í Apologetics* (Oxford, 2000) to which I refer.[35] The present article contains some further arguments.

"Infallibility" (*'isma*)[36] is a complex term which has, according to Bahá'u'lláh, "numerous meanings and diverse stations."[37] In one sense (that of immaculacy) it can be applied "to every soul whom God hath guarded against sin, transgression, rebellion, impiety, disbelief and the like."[38] This gift of grace is "a ray of the bounty of infallibility" and "is granted to every holy soul."[39] Bahá'í scripture distinguishes between *essential* infallibility and infallibility that has been *conferred* through divine bestowal.[40]

Essential Infallibility[41]

Essential infallibility is an inherent attribute and confined to the prophets; it is an exclusive characteristic of the ontological station of the messengers of God, just as the sun's rays are inherent in the sun. This concept can only be understood in the context of Bahá'í prophetology.[42]

In the past, there have been different answers to the question of the nature of the founding figures of the various religions. The starting point of the theophanology of the Abrahamic religions was the dualism existing between God and man. Again and again, the question has been raised as to whether the mediator of the divine will is a human being called upon by God to carry out a special mission, or whether, instead, God has incarnated himself, taking on the human form in the person of the prophet or messenger of God. According to Jewish, Zoroastrian, and Islamic doctrine, Moses, Zoroaster, and Muhammad are human beings who have been called upon to act as the mouthpiece of God.[43] Christian theology, on the other hand, defined the nature of Christ at the Council of Nicaea in the year 325 C.E., giving an ontological interpretation to the dignitary title of the Messiah "Son of God," expressed by the formula "*vere homo, vere Deus*" ("true man, and true God"). According to the doctrine of the Holy Trinity, Christ is the incarnate Son of God, being simultaneously man and God in "hypostatic union."[44]

Bahá'u'lláh's revelation conveys a more differentiated view of the divine messengers. The scripture imparts a conceptual scheme of Bahá'í ontology, a trichotomy according to which there are three worlds: the eternally inaccessible world of God (*'álamu'l-haqq*) which is "exalted beyond the grasp of the minds of men,"[45] the world of creation (*'álamu'l-khalq*), and an intermediate world—the world of the revelation of the divine command (*'álamu'l-amr*). The prophets and messengers of God are part of this intermediate world.

This view has been expressed terminologically: In place of the quranic terms *nabí* (prophet) and *rasúl* (messenger), we find in Bahá'í scripture the frequently occurring term *mazharu'lláh* or *az-zuhúr* (Manifestation of God)[46] by which it is indicated that these figures are exalted above normal human existence and have an ontological station above that of man, that they are beings *sui generis*. A twofold nature has been assigned to them: a human station and a spiritual station which is "born of the substance of God himself" (*iláhí*).[47]

The fundamental ontological difference between human beings and the prophets is pre-existence[48] and their innate knowledge of the world of creation (*násút*) and of the metaphysical world (*malakút, jabarút*): "They are the Treasuries of divine knowledge[49] . . . the Mines of divine knowledge."[50] Their knowledge is not acquired, not gained by reflection or experience. Rather it is "divine knowledge,"[51] the "knowledge of being" (*'ilmu'l-wujúd*)[52] which is "like the cognizance and consciousness that man has of himself."[53] The Manifestations of God "are aware of the reality of things,"[54] of the needs and exigencies of the human world, they are "sanctified Mirrors"[55] that "truly and faithfully reflect the light of God,"[56] "the focal points where the signs, tokens and perfections of that sacred pre-existent Reality appear in their splendor."[57] Their "knowledge of being"[58] has been expressed by Bahá'u'lláh in a metaphor according to which the Manifestation is like a "Divine and Infallible physician"[59] who "has His finger on the pulse of mankind" who "perceiveth the disease and prescribeth, in His unerring wisdom, the remedy."[60]

Thus, the divine messengers are "Manifestations" of God and not his incarnations.[61] In relation to God, the Manifestation appears as utter nothingness, but in relation to the world of creation (*'álamu'l-khalq*; *násút*) he is endowed with all the attributes of God.[62] Only through knowledge of the Manifestations is knowledge of God attainable.[63] Each of them has been the "representative and mouthpiece of God:"[64]

> Whoso recognizeth them hath recognized God. Whoso hearkeneth to their call, hath hearkened to the Voice of God, and whoso testifieth to the truth of their Revelation, hath testified to the truth of God Himself. Whoso turneth away from them, hath turned away from God, and whoso disbelieveth in them, hath disbelieved in God. Every one of them is the Way of God that connecteth this world with the realms above, and the Standard of His Truth unto every one in the kingdoms of earth and heaven.[65]

The charisma of infallibility is a logical precondition, an "essential requirement"[66] for this representation of God, by which he safeguards and protects his word, his laws and ordinances, from all error. God's sovereignty which has been expressed in the verses:

> The Will of God is not limited by the standards of the people, and God doth not tread in their ways . . . Verily He is to be praised in His acts and to be obeyed in His behests. He hath no associate in His judgment nor any helper in His sovereignty.[67]

God's sovereignty is also an attribute of the Manifestation:

> He doeth what He pleaseth, He chooseth, and none may question His choice . . . [68]
>
> Were He to pronounce water to be wine or heaven to be earth or light to be fire, He speaketh the truth and no doubt would there be about it; and unto no one is given the right to question His authority or to say why or wherefore. Whosoever raiseth objections will be numbered with the froward in the Book of God, the Lord of the worlds. 'Verily He shall not be asked of His doings but all others shall be asked of their doings.' He is come from the invisible heaven, bearing the banner 'He doeth whatsoever He willeth' and is accompanied by hosts of power and authority.[69]

Thus, God's sovereignty is represented through his Manifestations. Therefore they are "not under the shadow of the former laws."[70]

Bahá'u'lláh has confirmed the doctrine of *'isma* (infallibility) which has been deduced from the Qur'an and developed in Islam according to which the prophets are *ma'súm*, i.e., sinless, immaculate, morally infallible, and rendered by God immune to error, and infallible in their judgment and decree. He termed this essential infallibility, "the Most Great Infallibility," (*al-'ismatu'l-kubrá*) which is confined to the Manifestation, to:

> One Whose station is immeasurably exalted beyond ordinances or prohibitions and is sanctified from errors and omissions. Indeed He is a Light which is not followed by darkness and a Truth not overtaken by error[71] . . . He Who is the Dawning-place of God's Cause hath no partner in the Most Great Infallibility. He it is Who, in the kingdom of creation . . . is the Manifestation of 'He doeth whatsoever He willeth.'[72]

By virtue of their essential infallibility everything that emanates from the Manifestations "is identical with the truth and conformable to reality . . . Whatever they say is the Word of God, and whatever They perform is upright action."[73]

Bahá'u'lláh has made this principle the touchstone of faith and has formulated its consequences in challenging language:

> Blessed is the man that hath acknowledged his belief in God and in His signs, and recognized that 'He shall not be asked of His doings.'[74] Such a recognition hath been made by God the ornament of every belief and its very foundation. Upon it must depend the acceptance of every goodly deed . . . Were He to decree as lawful the thing which from time immemorial had been forbidden, and forbid that which had, at all times, been regarded as lawful, to none is given the right to question His authority. Whoso will hesitate, though it be for less than a moment, should be regarded as a transgressor. Whoso hath not recognized this sublime and fundamental verity, and hath failed to attain this most exalted station, the winds of doubt will agitate him, and the sayings of the infidels will distract his soul. He that hath acknowledged this principle will be endowed with the most perfect constancy.[75]

This passage is undoubtedly a provocation which should be seen in the light of "the showers of tests from His realm of glory,"[76] the divine purpose of which is that "the true should be known from the false, and sun from the shadow."[77] Bahá'u'lláh elsewhere speaks of the "fears and agitation which the revelation of this law provokes in men's hearts."[78] Similar tests happened in previous dispensations.[79]

Conferred Infallibility[80]

There is a categorical difference to *essential* infallibility: *conferred* infallibility covers only one of the two categories of *'isma*, the inability to fall into error, and the infallibility of judgment. Infallibility conferred to an institution does not imply freedom from sin, sinlessness, or immaculacy.[81] In the Bahá'í Faith, infallibility has been exclusively conferred on the Guardian in his function as the authoritative interpreter of the holy writ and on the Universal House of Justice.[82]

Referring to the Guardian and to the Universal House of Justice, 'Abdu'l-Bahá's Testament proclaims:

> The guardian of the Cause of God as well as the Universal House of Justice . . . are both under the care and protection of the Abhá Beauty, under the shelter and unerring guidance of His Holiness, the Exalted One[83] . . . Whatsoever they decide is of God.[84]

With reference to the Universal House of Justice it is stated that this institution has been made "the source of all good and freed from all error"[85] by God, and that whatever it decides is "the Truth and the Purpose of God himself."[86] Bahá'u'lláh has given the assurance that, "God will verily inspire them with whatsoever He willeth."[87] Hence, the *charisma* of infallibility rests not upon the community as a whole (as in the Catholic Church)[88] and not upon the individual members of the House, but upon the office,[89] which constitutes the objective, inherent limit of infallibility.[90] It is therefore important at this juncture to consider the critical question of the immanent limits of conferred infallibility, in order to clarify the principles involved.

The question is whether absolutely everything written and spoken by the Guardian claims to be free of error, and similarly whether everything decided by the Universal House of Justice, even down to day-to-day administrative decisions or decisions on trivial matters, is governed by 'Abdu'l-Bahá's dictum: "Whatever they decide is of God?[91] . . . Whatever they decide has the same effect as the Text itself."[92] In other words, is the infallibility conferred upon these institutions without restriction or does it have inherent limits?

The Extent of Conferred Infallibility

It is easier to define the extent of the conferred infallibility in the case of the Guardianship than for the Universal House of Justice, because Shoghi Effendi himself defined the limits of the infallibility conferred upon the Guardianship. His infallibility was restricted to the sphere of his interpretative power (*auctoritas interpretationis*)[93] and to his office, i.e. to his authoritative interpretation of the scripture[94] and his role as protector of the Faith. Beyond these functions the Guardian was expressly not infallible,[95] and indeed he made no decisions concerning anything "that is not in the teachings."[96] As far as the recorded facts are concerned, his historical works do not fall within the sphere of his interpretative authority and are therefore not covered by the charisma; however in those parts of his historical writings that constitute "narrative theology," where it is "his interpretation of the theological significance of historical events"[97] that is at the forefront, this charisma is indeed brought to bear.

There is no explicit statement either in the scripture or in the writings of Shoghi Effendi concerning the specific spheres in which the functions of the House of Justice are granted infallibility.[98] No statement on the subject has yet been made by the Universal House of Justice itself. Indeed, it is hardly likely that any official statement will be issued since, as will be seen later, although this is a question with far-reaching psychological implications on the consciousness of the believers and their institutions, it has no relevance for the *legal* authority of that supreme body, which derives simply from the fact that it has been ordained by Bahá'u'lláh. The strict obedience the believers have to pay to this institution, as expressed in 'Abdu'l-Bahá's Testament, "Whoso obeyeth him not, neither obeyeth them, hath not obeyed God,"[99] is not based on their special charisma.

I think that, analogous to Shoghi Effendi's self-restricting interpretation, the infallibility conferred on the Universal House of Justice does not extend to all its acts, but covers only those functions which are explicitly mentioned in 'Abdu'l-Bahá's testament. These are all acts of supplementary legislation on matters that are not expressly recorded in the Book,[100] including decisions on problems which have caused difference, questions that are obscure, and on issues that are of universal relevance.

Reasons for a Restrictive Interpretation

Several factors might support this interpretation of the infallibility conferred on the House of Justice. The starting point of our discourse is the fact that the Universal House of Justice possesses the fullness of *jurisdictional* power, comprising executive (administrative), judicial, and legislative functions, whereas the Guardian has been invested with the power of interpretation. There is a strict separation of the two powers between the two pillars of the order.[101]

From the very beginning the House of Justice was envisioned as a legislature and invested with the function of supplementary legislation. The norms of the Book that constitute the law of God are valid and unchangeable for at least one thousand years,[102] and have therefore been formulated on a more abstract level.[103] The House of Justice has been empowered to elaborate these laws and to provide for subsidiary laws according to the requirements of a steadily changing society through the enactment of supplementary legislation.

The future development of Bahá'í law will not come about, as was the case in Islam, through *authoritative interpretation* by the "learned ones" (*al-'ulamá'*),[104] but rather through *supplementary legislation* by an authorized legislative body that is, moreover, empowered to abrogate its own laws and to adapt its own legislation to the exigencies of a continuously changing world. Thus the Bahá'í law has been provided "with an essential element of flexibility."[105] The Bahá'í sacred law is constituted by both the laws Bahá'u'lláh has given his people in the Kitáb-i Aqdas, which is the kernel of the law of God, and the supplementary laws enacted by the Universal House of Justice.

Another factor supporting this interpretation is the testimony provided in written sources. Whenever the supreme body is mentioned in the holy text or referred to in the writings of Shoghi Effendi it is in the context of matters "which have not outwardly been revealed in the Book,"[106] i.e. matters that are not covered by the holy text and need to be regulated by legislation. This becomes evident from the "eighth leaf" of the Words of Paradise (*Kalímát-i firdawsíyyih)* where Bahá'u'lláh defines the functions and competences of the House of Justice and promises to this body the assistance of the holy spirit:

> It is incumbent upon the Trustees of the House of Justice to take counsel together regarding those things which have not outwardly been revealed in the Book, and to enforce that which is agreeable to them. God will verily inspire them with whatsoever He willeth, and He, verily, is the Provider, the Omniscient.[107]

Also in the Ishráqát, Bahá'u'lláh undoubtedly refers to legislation when, after having paid tribute to the "two pillars, reward and punishment" as the "sources of life to the world" and after having mentioned that "for each day there is a new problem and for every problem an expedient solution," he continues: "Such affairs should be referred to the Universal House of Justice that the members thereof may act according to the needs and requirements of the time."[108] He also refers to legislation when he states shortly afterwards that, "all matters of State should be referred to the House of Justice."[109] The same is true when Bahá'u'lláh, dealing with the subject of interest, says that he "desisted from laying down its limits"[110] and entrusts "the conduct of these affairs" to the "men of the House of Justice."[111]

Whenever 'Abdu'l-Bahá mentions the Universal House of Justice, it is clear that the purpose of this body is future legislation.[112] He defines in his testament the purpose, competencies, and functions of the House of Justice, "the source of all good and freed from all error"[113]:

> Unto this body all things must be referred. It enacteth all ordinances and regulations that are not to be found in the explicit *Holy Text*. By this body all the difficult problems are to be resolved . . . This House of Justice enacteth the laws and the government [*hukúmat*] enforceth them.[114]

> Unto the *Most Holy Book* every one must turn and all that is not expressly recorded therein must be referred to the Universal House of Justice. That which this body, whether unanimously or by a majority doth carry, that is verily the Truth and the Purpose of God Himself.[115]

> . . . It is incumbent upon these members (of the Universal House of Justice) to . . . deliberate upon all problems which have caused difference, questions that are obscure and matters that are not expressly recorded in the *Book*.[116] Whatsoever they decide has the same effect as the *Text* itself . . . The House of Justice is both the Initiator and the Abrogator of its own laws.[117]

Shoghi Effendi's references to the Universal House of Justice leave no doubt that the ultimate purpose of this body is "to fill in those gaps which the author of the Kitáb-i Aqdas has deliberately left in the body of His legislative and administrative ordinances"[118]; that the Universal House of Justice "has been invested with the function of legislating on matters not expressly revealed in the teachings," that it has the "exclusive right and prerogative . . . to pronounce upon and deliver the final judgment on such laws and ordinances as Bahá'u'lláh has not expressly revealed."[119]

As long as the Baha'i Faith is still "in its infancy"[120] and has not yet attained "the plenitude of its power,"[121] there is little need for the House of Justice to exercise its legislative powers. Indeed, there has so far been little in the way of legislation. The only enactments made by the Universal House of Justice which I can discern as constituting acts of legislation were:

- its declaration on 6 October 1963 that there is no way to appoint or to legislate to make it possible to appoint a second Guardian to succeed Shoghi Effendi;[122]
- the establishment of the Continental Boards of Counsellors by its message to the Bahá'í world of 24 June 1968;[123]
- the enactment of the Constitution of the Universal House of Justice on 24 November 1972;[124]
- the establishment of the International Teaching Center by its message of 8 June 1973;[125]
- the enactment of the law of the *huqúqu'lláh* (The Right of God) by its Ridván message 1991;
- the enactment of Regional Bahá'í Councils by its message of 30 May 1997;
- the enactment of the ritual provisions of the Kitáb-i Aqdas referring to the obligatory prayers, fasting and *dhikr* (repetition of the phrase *Alláh-u Abhá*) by its announcement to the Bahá'í world on 28 December 1999.

The activities of the Universal House of Justice have, up to now, been purely administrative in nature, with the exception of those judicial decisions made on the basis of Article VIII of its constitution. Since Shoghi Effendi foresees a time when "officially constituted Bahá'í courts" will be in existence,[126] the question arises as to whether the House of Justice will retain its judicial function as set out in its constitution. In the course of time, the judicial and executive functions of this institution will certainly give way to its main task of legislation, whose importance will steadily increase.

It should be noted that the spheres of competence mentioned in the holy text along with supplementary legislation, i.e. to resolve "all the difficult problems,"[127] to "deliberate upon problems which have caused differences, questions that are obscure,"[128] are to be counted as legislative functions.[129] The context[130] reveals clearly that this refers not to *ad hoc* executive, administrative, or judicial decisions, but to decisions that are of general, universal relevance.

The fact that pneumatic direction, unerring guidance,[131] has been promised by Bahá'u'lláh and 'Abdu'l-Bahá in the context of those scriptural passages that define the legislative competence of this body, and is accompanied on every occasion by a reference to the "Book" or the "Holy Text,"[132] is strong support for the suggested *restrictive* interpretation according to which infallibility covers only acts of legislation.[133] The "Book," the "Holy Text," is of universal validity. From this it can be concluded that only those decisions are "infallible" that are likewise of universal validity, whereas decisions concerning individual cases are not covered by this charisma because they have no legal relevance for the world community.

A third reason to support a restrictive interpretation of conferred infallibility relates to certain logical arguments. Like any other decision-making body the Universal House of Justice is *dependent* on information.[134] But the quality of this information varies according to the level on which the decision is made. At the executive and judicial levels, knowledge of the historical facts of a specific case is required, while at the legislative level what is needed is general knowledge of the matters to be regulated.

As to the first category, the ascertainment of relevant facts, the House of Justice is dependent on others. The factual information necessary for executive and judicial decisions is gathered by subordinate institutions or individuals. An infallible decision would require that, in every case, the factual information provided were absolutely error free. How could that be possible? There can be no guarantee that all the facts relevant to the decision are indeed compiled, or that these are correctly assessed as to their respective importance before being conveyed to the Universal House of Justice. If this cannot be guaranteed, then there can be no guarantee of the absolute correctness of decisions made at these levels. The correctness of any decision in such an instance is *conditional*: it depends on the correctness and absolute reliability of the information provided concerning the matter in hand. *Conditional* infallibility, however, is a contradiction in terms. A decision that is based on fragmentary or wrongly transmitted relevant facts cannot be guaranteed to be correct. The Universal House of Justice's statement that a decision can be "*corrected*" when "new facts emerge"[135] confirms this interpretation.

The situation is different in the case of legislation (that is, the establishment of general abstract norms) and of decisions on specific issues of universal relevance.[136] In these cases, the decision is made at the abstract level of norms; it is independent of any concrete historical case and the ascertainment of its relevant facts. What is required is general information. Here, too, the Universal House of Justice needs to inquire into the conditions of all aspects of the matter to be regulated and to know the legal dogmatic implications[137] of legislation. However, legislation is not dependent on the clarification of historical data and the provision of facts by other institutions or individuals that always remain fallible. The House of Justice is thus independent from the necessarily fallible acts of other institutions or individuals. This *independence* of the supreme body is a logical precondition for a decision that is free of error.

What is the purpose of an infallible legislature? The seal of immunity to error means that the law passed by the Universal House of Justice constitutes sacred law, which is qualitatively different from any *ius humanum* and is ascribed in the hierarchy of law to the divine law (*ius divinum*).[138] Infallibility is expressed in different categories.[139] The sphere of *interpretation* is governed by the categories "true-false." An infallible interpretation is one that is absolutely "true"; it is a manifestation of divine truth. The law enacted by an infallible *legislature* is not "true," but rather absolutely appropriate to the social requirements, and therefore "just." Therefore, infallible legislation means the enactment of legal norms that is in accordance with divine justice. Both the divine law of the revelation and the laws that result from the supplementary legislation of the Universal House of Justice constitute that divine justice, the advent of which Bahá'u'lláh has prophesied: "The reign of justice will assuredly be established amongst the children of men, and the effulgence of its light will envelop the whole earth."[140]

Infallible decisions are "the Truth and the Purpose of God himself,"[141] they are manifestations of the divine will. In principle, such decisions are as unchangeable for human beings as the will of God. Just as the will of God cannot be "corrected," infallible acts are not liable to "correction."

The Guardian's interpretations of the holy writ are infallible and—as they are "of God"—unchangeable until the next divine revelation.

The legislation of the House of Justice is infallible and—as its laws are "the Truth and the Purpose of God Himself"[142]—they would not be liable to abrogation had 'Abdu'l-Bahá not provided an explicit provision in his Testament according to which the Universal House of Justice has not only the power "to enact laws that are not explicitly recorded in the Book," but also "the power to repeal the same."[143] Only by virtue of this *clausula salvatoria* is the House of Justice empowered to abrogate its own legislation and to adapt the law "to the exigencies of the time"[144] so that it is "the Initiator and the Abrogator of its own laws."[145]

If one extends infallibility to decisions of the House of Justice in the sphere of its administrative, executive and judicial powers, this body would not be empowered to correct its own judgments when new facts have emerged, since the text does not contain such an explicit provision for decisions outside the supplementary legislation. This result would be unacceptable. I think this is one more argument for my view that executive and judicial decisions are not covered by infallibility and are therefore liable to change.

In this context it should be noted that the abrogation of an old law given by the Universal House of Justice in order to supersede it by a new law that is appropriate to changed conditions, and the cancellation of a decision in the sphere of executive or judicial power because new facts have emerged, have different qualities. By the abrogation of one of its laws, the House of Justice does not "correct" its former legislation; it is rather adapting it to changed conditions.[146] 'Abdu'l-Bahá has made it clear that only "circumstances having profoundly changed and conditions having altered" legitimates the House of Justice's abrogating and adapting of its own laws to the "exigencies of the time."[147] A relatively long period has been envisioned, as 'Abdu'l-Bahá speaks of "another House of Justice" (perhaps only after a complete change of its membership) and exemplifies this with "a hundred years." There is no contradiction between these two acts of legislation; each one was perfectly appropriate to the conditions of the time.

The change of a decision related to the administrative and judicial power of the House in the same matter after new facts have emerged is of a different quality. However one looks at it, the change due to new facts is a *correction*. There are two contradictory judgments of which only one can be true. If one claims infallibility for all administrative or judicial decisions of the House of Justice, a crucial question arises as to how one can cope in a reasonable way with contradictory decisions of the same House of Justice on the same matter. How is one to escape the logical dilemma? I think the claim to infallibility for both decisions is untenable; it cannot be maintained without violating the principles of logical thinking.

The "infallibility" of an erroneous and therefore corrected decision cannot be upheld by means of the sophistical argument that the (wrong) decision would have been free of error if the facts on which it had been based had been correct. This would amount to a merely *hypothetical* infallibility, whereby it is not the decision itself that is infallible, but rather the process by which it was arrived at. This sort of argument would reduce the principle to an absurdity. Thus the fact that such decisions are liable to correction appears to me to constitute another rational argument that these decisions are not covered by the conferred charisma of infallibility.

A fourth support for this view derives from the implications of a claim to unlimited infallibility. Such a claim would have far-reaching consequences. It would imply that decisions in even the most trivial, daily routine affairs are included and covered by infallibility. Should, for instance, the appointment of a person responsible for certain functions at the Bahá'í World Centre be seen as an "infallible" decision, an embodiment of the will of God with the result that this appointment has "the same effect as the Text itself"?[148] Should such a decision be one of "the ordinances and regulations that are not to be found in the explicit holy text"?[149] What if the individual appointed to the position were to fail to fulfill what was expected? Claiming this charisma for such things would reduce it to absurdity and trivialize the will of God and the august concept of infallibility. This cannot be the intention of the text.

I think it is obvious that infallibility cannot be claimed for decisions in such relatively trivial matters.[150] If one tries to exclude them and to restrict the sphere of infallibility to more essential issues,[151] the question arises as to the criteria for delineating the boundaries for those administrative or judicial decisions for which infallibility should be maintained. I do not see any such criteria.

To claim infallibility for virtually everything that has been decided by the Universal House of Justice, without exception, would be, in my opinion, extremely risky and utterly unwise. Such an interpretation of the infallibility of the House of Justice is untenable and indefensible and could easily become its Achilles heel. There are undoubtedly many people zealously searching and taking great pains in order to find one single evident error which would suffice to disprove empirically and for all time the infallibility of the House of Justice. One single error would suffice for a "falsification" of the claim infallibility.[152] I am sure that an *extensive* interpretation of this concept would lead to never-ending queries and unresolved discussions, and Bahá'ís would constantly feel obliged to refute the ongoing accusations.

Moreover, such a concept of infallibility also has far-reaching psychological implications affecting the consciousness of the believers.[153] An unreflected, even magical vision of the unerring guidance which has been conferred on the House of Justice currently prevails in the community.[154] Some imagine the community to be in possession of some kind of Delphic Oracle, to which everyone can appeal whenever they are in a quandary. This is an utterly unacceptable attitude that fosters the frequently shown inclination to avoid making one's own decisions and to escape one's own responsibility by submitting difficult matters to the Universal House of Justice in order to get "infallible guidance."

This attitude and way of thinking is irrational. Furthermore, it reveals that one presupposes that the Universal House of Justice does not operate in a rational way and that it does not make decisions after having conducted a rational consultation, but rather acts as a mere recipient, transformer, and mouthpiece of the Holy Spirit; that its decisions are *revelational* in character. In reality, decisions do not come about through quasi-prophetic inspiration ("*quasi per inspirationem,*" "*Divino afflante spiritu*"). Instead, they are reached in the course of a rational discursive process in which, subsequent to clarification of the normative guidelines set out in the scripture and the establishment of the relevant facts, a formal process of consultation leads to a *consensus* of opinion and finally to a decision reached by majority vote or by unanimity. This means that the Holy Spirit does not act as a *deus ex machina*. Information on every decision must be prepared and every decision must be the subject of consultation. Shoghi Effendi has expressed this in an incontrovertible statement: "They may, indeed they must, acquaint themselves with the conditions prevailing among the community, must weigh dispassionately in their minds the merits of any case presented for their consideration," then "they are to follow, in a prayerful attitude, the dictates and promptings of their conscience."[155] Thus, infallibility is not, as the Universal House of Justice has expressly stated[156] synonymous with omniscience, nor does it preclude rational consultation and judgment.

According to Bahá'u'lláh, humankind has "attained the stage of maturity,"[157] and I think such expressions of irrationality and obscurantism as mentioned above are not a sign of maturity but rather of self-incapacitation and of contempt for human reason (*'aql*), which—together with wisdom and prudence (*hikmat*[158])—has been so highly praised by Bahá'u'lláh[159] and by 'Abdu'l-Bahá.[160]

The limits of infallibility conferred on the House of Justice should be compatible with reason. The charisma should be reflected upon with the intention of arriving at an understanding that does not imply a *sacrificium intellectus*. To believe in the *conferred* infallibility of an institution with certain immanent limits, to believe that legislative acts are immune to error by virtue of divine guidance, to believe that the will of God is manifested in them according to the promise of infallible guidance is an act of faith that is not in contradiction with human reason.

Aspects of Divine Guidance

The view expressed here is of no consequence for the *legal* authority of the supreme House of Justice. This authority is—as already pointed out—not based on its special charisma, but rather results simply from the fact that this institution has been ordained by Bahá'u'lláh. As it is the supreme body, it has the last word[161] in all spheres of its powers. Everything the House of Justice decides has to be obeyed. This obedience to the two supreme institutions, the Guardian and the Universal House of Justice, has been emphasized by 'Abdu'l-Bahá in unequivocal language:

> Whoso obeyeth him not, neither obeyeth them, hath not obeyed God; whoso rebelleth against him and against them hath rebelled against God; whoso opposeth him hath opposed God; whoso contendeth with them hath contended with God . . . May the wrath, the fierce indignation, the vengeance of God rest upon him![162]

The infallibility conferred on the supreme House of Justice reaches far beyond its authority to have the final say in all matters. By virtue of its unerring guidance the Bahá'í community is permanently in possession of an institution that by its legislation ensures "the continuity of that divinely-appointed authority which flows from the Source of our Faith" and safeguards "the unity of its followers."[163]

One objection could be made: Does this restrictive interpretation not result in a reduction of the divine guidance that is granted to this supreme body, if its decisions in administrative and judicial matters are excluded from the sphere of conferred infallibility? I do not think so.

Divine guidance has different aspects. The Arabic term *hudá* is used in the Qur'an to mean the divine revelation, i.e. the Qur'an itself, of which is said: "That is a book, wherein is no doubt, a guidance for the God-fearing."[164] This book is the divine guidance to the "straight path"[165] for those who believe. Besides that, God grants guidance in all matters to all those who turn to him.[166] Beyond this individual guidance, there is the guidance which has been promised in this dispensation to institutions of the community. I can observe two categories of divine guidance in the scripture:

- a *general* divine guidance that is promised to all elected bodies, which is a relative one, because it necessarily depends on certain preconditions, "prime requisites for them that take counsel together"[167] and;

- a *specific* divine guidance conferred on the twin pillars which is an absolute one, because it is not made dependent on preconditions. This absolute divine guidance is *infallibility*.

In contrast to the *absolute* divine guidance, the *relative* one does not exclude a wrong decision. Hence, decisions of the Universal House of Justice that have been made in the sphere outside its legislation can be cancelled. However, one can presuppose that the members of this supreme institution are highly motivated for meeting these sublime "prime requisites" enumerated by 'Abdu'l-Bahá and that this institution partakes of that *general* divine guidance, undoubtedly in an incomparably higher degree than all the subordinated elected bodies.

Taking this proposition for granted, the practical consequences of restricted infallibility for the believers would be insignificant: they can continue to regard the House of Justice as divinely guided, as a source of divine guidance, and could nevertheless admit that in a special case this (relative) guidance might not operate because the House of Justice was wrongly or not fully informed. This would be an unassailable position against all criticism and all attempts to deny the concept of (conferred) infallibility by empirical argumentation. Instead of saying: "We have an infallible body," one would then say: "We have a divinely guided body that is infallible in the sphere of legislation." The scheme outlined in Figure 1 on the next page might be helpful for a better understanding of my views.

By contrast, all the other decision-making institutions, the local and national "Houses of Justice," are also promised divine guidance, but only under certain, legally unverifiable circumstances that have been defined by 'Abdu'l-Bahá.[168] They have not been granted infallibility. One indication that the local and national bodies do not share in the charisma is the fact that both their governing statutes and the constitution of the Universal House of Justice[169] include rights of review and appeal to ensure that erroneous decisions can be revised. Such rights would be superfluous and meaningless if the decisions of the local and national assemblies were also an expression of the divine will.

The Purpose of a Restrictive Interpretation

My proposal for a restrictive interpretation of the concept of infallibility should not be misconstrued as an attempt to adjust opportunistically a concept that has negative connotations in our secular society and is regarded as a provocation by skeptical people today in order to make it acceptable to the consciousness of people that are "feeble and far removed from the purpose of God."[170] General acceptability is most certainly no seal of truth. Some norms of the Kitáb-i Aqdas (such as

Figure 1

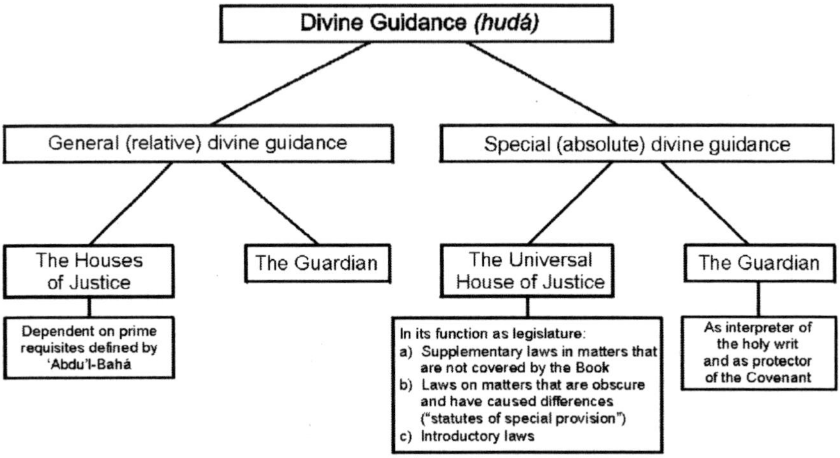

the possibility of capital punishment in cases of murder and arson, the stigmatization of the thief, of prohibition of adultery, of pre- and extra-marital sexual intercourse [*ziná'*], and of acts of homosexuality [*liwát*]) are perceived as a slap in the face by the general public, especially in Europe.

It is not my intention to deny or to reduce anything that has been conferred on the House of Justice by the holy text, thus unintentionally undermining its *spiritual* authority. My aim is rather to examine the sources in order to attain a better understanding of the provisions of Bahá'u'lláh and 'Abdu'l-Bahá and a rationally satisfying answer to a crucial question. My only purpose in touching on the different aspects of this issue was apologetic: to make the Faith and the authority of the House invulnerable against the attacks and the cynical criticism of those contemptuous of religion, and the ridicule of critics, by offering an interpretation that is unassailable and can be accepted as reasonable by people of good will.

We should have a clear vision of a term with such far-reaching implications, so that we are able to explain it to others and defend it against the objections of our skeptical contemporaries. An open exchange of views and opinions on this matter should take place in the community. This contribution is considered a step towards such a discussion. The problems we are facing cannot be solved by making the issue taboo and by leaving the field to the discussions of those who question the whole concept of infallibility and are purposely undermining the spiritual authority of the House of Justice.

A critical discourse is the means to clarify such issues. Such theological discourse should not be misconstrued as "idle disputations,"[171] as "the investigation of useless conceits," or as "empty, profitless debates" and "useless hair-splitting and disputes."[172] 'Abdu'l-Bahá's statement according to which "the shining spark of truth cometh forth only after the clash of differing opinions"[173] is a common truth and not only valid in the context of consultation within assemblies. As the Universal House of Justice has emphasized, Bahá'ís must learn to live with a variety of theological opinions.[174]

Notes

Udo Schaefer, former chief prosecutor at the state court of Heidelberg, is the author of a number of books and articles, most recently co-authoring *Making the Crooked Straight* (George Ronald, 2000).

1. I am much indebted to Dr. Geraldine Schuckelt for checking and making stylistic improvements to my English draft. References to Bahá'í scripture are by section/chapter followed by paragraph.
2. *Gleanings from the Writings of Bahá'u'lláh* (London: Bahá'í Publishing Trust, 1978) 95:1; see also 83:1; *Paris Talks. Addresses given by 'Abdu'l-Bahá in 1911* (London: Bahá'í Publishing Trust, 1995) 11:4; 8:23, 8; *The Secret of Divine Civilization* (Wilmette: Bahá'í Publishing Trust, 1970) 1-2; *Some Answered Questions* (Wilmette: Bahá'í Publishing Trust, 1981) 58:3; 82:3-5.
3. On the limitations of reason see my *Bahá'í Ethics* (in preparation), ch. 6, 4.
4. *Some Answered Questions* 83:4.
5. *Epistulae* 57, 12.
6. *Gleanings* 93:6.
7. *Gleanings* 81. As to the "straight path" (*as-sirátu'l mustaqím*) cf. Qur'an 1:6; 4:70; 5:15; 37:118; *Tablets of Bahá'u'lláh revealed after the Kitáb-i Aqdas* (Haifa: Bahá'í World Centre, 1978) 4:8, 10; 5:17; 6:11; *Gleanings* 81; 82:5; 110; 114:1; 116:3; 128:3; *The Kitáb-i-Aqdas. The Most Holy Book* (Haifa: Bahá'í World Centre, 1992) 14, 186. The terms "path" or "way" are known in all religions: "I am the way, the truth and the life" (John 14:6). In the Buddhist canon and in the scriptures of Hinduism the term is (Páli) "*magga*" (cf. *Iti-Vuttaka. Sayings of Buddha* [New York: AMS Press Inc., 1965] Sutta 62) or (Sanskrit) "*márga.*" In the Chinese religion one of the meanings of *Tao* among others (law, teaching, fundamental principle) is "the way" (cf.

Phyllis Chew, *The Chinese Religion and the Bahá'í Faith* [Oxford: George Ronald, 1993] p. 22ff.); *idem*, "The Great Tao," *Journal of Bahá'í Studies*, Vol. 4, no. 2 (1991) pp. 11-29.

8. Qur'an 2:1.
9. Ibid., 2:256.
10. Ibid., 21:18.
11. Kitáb-i Aqdas 134; *Tablets* 8:17.
12. *Tablets* 14:2. There are numerous passages which equate revelation with truth, i.e., *Gleanings* 17:5; 29:3; 47; 82:2; 133:2; 143:1; 153:8; *Tablets* 4:31: 5:21; 6:15-16; 9:6; 17:45, 106, 115, etc.
13. *Gleanings* 88.
14. *qistas al-hudá* (Kitáb-i Aqdas 183); *qistas al-haqq* (Kitáb-i Aqdas 99), literally "the balance of guidance," "the balance of truth."
15. 1 Tim. 2:5.
16. 1:8; 2:24-25; 5:20; 8:12; 9:5; 14:6; 16:30; 21:17.
17. *Lexikon für Theologie und Kirche* (Freiburg: Herder Verlag, special ed. 1986), Vol. X, 1193, 951.
18. Sunní theologians differ in opinion as to the extent to this immunity. Some apply it in unlimited fashion to Muhammad only, others to all the prophets. Some Sunní authorities differ in the question whether this charisma existed before or only after the vocation of the prophet to his prophetic ministry. The Shí'ís ascribe *'isma* to all prophets (*rusul*) and to the imáms also (on this subject see *Shorter Encyclopaedia of Islam* [*SEI*] by H. A. R. Gibb and J. H. Kramers, Leiden, photomechanic reprint 1961, p. 178).
19. *Will and Testament of 'Abdu'l-Bahá* (Wilmette: Bahá'í Publishing Committee, 1944) 1:25.
20. Ibid., 1:17.
21. *Tablets* 6:29; 3:24; 8:60.
22. The Greek term taken from the New Testament (see Rom. 6:23; I Cor. 7:7) is used in the original sense: a gift of grace, a gift of God.
23. See Karl Popper, *The Logic of Scientific Discovery* (New York: Harper & Row, 1968) p. 78ff.
24. Heiner Barz, *Postmoderne Religion* (Opladen: Leske & Budrich, 1992) p. 136.
25. Even early on, the Church Fathers expressed their conviction that the Church is guided by the "Spirit of Truth" (John 14:16ff.) which Christ has promised to his disciples: "And, lo, I am with you always, even unto the end of the world" (Matt. 28:20). Thomas Aquinas formulated: "*Ecclesia generalis non potest errare*" (S. th. Suppl. 25,1). The criterium of truth has been the general consensus in the Church as it has been expressed by Vincentius de Lérin (d. 450 CE) in his formula "*Magnopere curandum est, ut id teneamus, quod ubique, quod semper, quod ab omnibus creditum est, hoc est enim vere proprieque catholicum*" ("Great care must be taken that we keep to that which has been believed everywhere, always and by all, for that is really and truly Catholic"), *Commonitorium*, Ch. 2, 5, quoted from Mirbt, *Quellen zur Geschichte des Papsttums und des römischen Katholizismus* (Tübingen: J. C. B. Mohr, 1967), Vol. I, no. 432, p. 203. This Catholic principle of the *con-*

sensus omnium has an analogy in Sunni Islam where infallible authority is based also on the consensus of the community (*ijma'*). On this subject see footnote 139.

26. *Constitutio Pater aeternus* (D 1838, 1839).
27. It should be noted that the Catholic church is extremely reluctant in making use of this dogma. In the twentieth century it has happened only once, in 1954 when Pius XII proclaimed the dogma of the bodily Assumption of the Virgin Mary. None of the papal doctrinal encyclicals such as *Humanae vitae* by Paul VI (on birth control) claim infallibility. They demand obedience, but they are open to revocation.
28. *Infallible? An Inquiry* (London: William Collins, 1972).
29. See footnote 20.
30. On this subject, see John Hatcher, "The Doctrine of the Most Great Infallibility," in John Hatcher and William Hatcher, *The Law of Love Enshrined* (Oxford: George Ronald, 1996) pp. 83ff.
31. For example, statements in the Lawh-i Hikmat on Empedocles and David, Pythagoras and Solomon as contemporaries (*Tablets* 9:25).
32. The "Most Great Infallibility" is confined to the Manifestations. 'Abdu'l-Bahá was not a Manifestation. Nevertheless, the question arises whether he was in possession of innate knowledge or whether his knowledge was acquired. If his infallibility was conferred, then it was inherent to his office as Bahá'u'lláh's successor (cf. Kitáb-i Aqdas 121, 174; Kitáb-i 'Ahd) which began with the ascension of Bahá'u'lláh. Then the question arises whether 'Abdu'l-Bahá's oral and written utterances before the inception of his office are free from error. Moreover, "conferred infallibility" is immunity against error, it does not comprise immunity against sin. However, 'Abdu'l-Bahá, the "Mystery of God" (*sirru'lláh*) is exalted in his rank, he is "the stainless Mirror of His light, the perfect Exemplar of His teachings . . . The embodiment of every Bahá'í virtue" (*The World Order of Bahá'u'lláh* [Wilmette: Bahá'í Publishing Trust, 1974] p. 134). "Stainlessness" indicates sinlessness. All these questions are still in need of reflection and discussion.
33. F. Ficicchia, *Der Bahá'ismus—Religion der Zukunft? Geschichte, Lehre und Organisation in kritischer Anfrage* (Stuttgart: Quell-Verlag, 1981).
34. Udo Schaefer, Nicola Towfigh, Ulrich Gollmer, *Desinformation als Methode. Die Bahá'ismus-Monographie des F. Ficicchia* (Hildesheim: Olms-Verlag, 1995).
35. See pp. 166-194.
36. From *'asama, yas'imu* (to protect, save from).
37. Bahá'u'lláh, *Tablets* 8:17, p. 108.
38. Ibid.
39. 'Abdu'l-Bahá, *Some Answered Questions* 45:3-4, p. 172.
40. Cf. Ibid., 45:2, pp. 171–172.
41. Essential infalllibility (*al-'isma adh-dhátiya*). The terms of "essential infallibility" and "conferred infallibility" (*al-'isma al-sifátíya*) are not Western denominations but are taken from the original texts.
42. On this subject see Juan R. Cole, "The Concept of Manifestation in the Bahá'í Writings," *Bahá'í Studies*, Vol. 9 (1982). A summary of the Bahá'í

doctrine on the nature and station of the Manifestation can be found in *Kitáb-i Aqdas*, note 75, p. 200. On this subject see U. Schaefer, *Beyond the Clash of Religions* (Stockholm: Zero Palm Press, 2nd edn. 1998) p. 124ff.

43. Nevertheless, in Islam they have been elevated above the rank of mortals by assigning to them immunity from error and sin (*'isma*).
44. On the doctrine of the Holy Trinity see the *Catechism of the Catholic Church* (Mahwah, N. J.: Paulist Press, 1994) nos. 249-56. This doctrine has become an insurmountable obstacle in interfaith dialogue with Jews and Muslims.
45. Bahá'u'lláh, *Gleanings* 26:1, 3; 78:2; 94:3; 160:1 (pp. 60, 61-62, 150, 193, 335-36). *Tablets* 8:26, p. 113.
46. Cf. Nicola Towfigh, *Schöpfung und Offenbarung* (Hildesheim: Olms Verlag, 1989) p. 172ff.
47. *Gleanings* 27:4, p. 66.
48. "The soul or spirit of the individual comes into being with the conception of this physical body. The Prophets, unlike us, are pre-existent. The soul of Christ existed in the spiritual world before His birth in this world." (Shoghi Effendi, quoted in Helen Hornby, ed., *Lights of Guidance* [New Delhi: Bahá'í Publishing Trust, 1994] p. 505, no. 1699) John 17:5; 8:58 refer to Christ's pre-existence (cf. 'Abdu'l-Bahá's commentary on this verse in *Some Answered Questions* Ch. 28, sections 3-5 [pp. 116–17]). According to Catholic doctrine, Christ is the pre-existent, eternal Word of God. Bahá'u'lláh alludes to the pre-existent nature of the prophets in the *Epistle to the Son of the Wolf* [Wilmette: Bahá'í Publishing Trust, 1998] 226, p. 155 and in Kitáb-i Aqdas 177, p. 84).
49. *Kitáb-i-Íqán* (Wilmette: Bahá'í Publishing Trust, 1983) 106, p. 100.
50. Ibid., 265, p. 237.
51. *Some Answered Questions* 40:6, p. 158.
52. Ibid., 40:4, p. 157.
53. Ibid., 151, p. 142.
54. Ibid., 40:7, 58:4, pp. 159, 218–219.
55. Bahá'u'lláh, Kitáb-i Íqán 106, p. 99.
56. Ibid.
57. *Selections from the Writings of 'Abdu'l-Bahá* (Haifa: Bahá'í World Centre 1978) 21:12, p. 50.
58. Cf. *Some Answered Questions* 40:4, 6.
59. *Gleanings* 106:2; 34:6; 120:3.
60. Ibid., 106:1.
61. The concept of incarnation (*hulúl*) has been decidedly rejected by Bahá'u'lláh (cf. *Gleanings* 20, p. 49, Kitáb-i Íqán 104, p. 98).
62. Bahá'u'lláh testifies: "When I contemplate, O my God, the relationship that bindeth me to Thee, I am moved to proclaim to all created things 'Verily I am God!'; and when I consider my own self, lo, I find it coarser than clay!" (quoted in Shoghi Effendi, *The World Order*, p. 113).
63. Kitáb-i Íqán 106, pp. 99–100.
64. *Gleanings* 28:2, p. 70.

65. Ibid., 21, pp. 49–50.
66. *Some Answered Questions* 45:2, p. 171.
67. *Tablets* 8:19, p. 109, cf. also *Prayers and Meditations* (London: Bahá'í Publishing Trust, rev. ed. 1978) 103:1, 139:1, 176:46; 184:22 (pp. 172, 227, 286, 339).
68. Kitáb-i Aqdas 7, pp. 21–22.
69. *Tablets* 8:17, p. 108.
70. *Some Answered Questions* 45:5, p. 173.
71. *Tablets* 8:17, p. 108.
72. Kitáb-i Aqdas 47, p. 36. The quranic formula *yaf'alu má yashá'* (3:40, 14:27, 22:18) is frequently recurring in the scripture (Kitáb-i Aqdas 7, 20, 47, 131, 157 [pp. 21, 26, 36, 66, 76], Kitáb-i Íqán 103, 182, 184, 271 [pp. 97, 170, 171, 243], *Gleanings* 59:3, 101, 102, 129:12, 134:3, 136:1 [pp. 116, 206, 284, 291, 295], *Tablets* 5:13; 6:56; 7:40; 8:12, 17, 19, 71, 74; 12:12, 14:14 [pp. 51, 80, 96, 105, 108, 109–110, 132, 133, 184, 216]).
73. *Some Answered Questions* 45:5, p. 173.
74. *lá yus'al 'ammá yaf'al* (Qur'an 21:23), a frequently occurring formula in scripture (*Tablets* 8:17, p. 108, Kitáb-i Íqán 182, pp. 170–171, *Gleanings* 37, 114:8 [pp. 86, 239]).
75. Kitáb-i Aqdas 161-3, pp. 77–78.
76. Kitáb-i Íqán 56, p. 53.
77. Ibid., cf. also ibid., 55, p. 51, Qur'an 2:143.
78. *Gleanings* 88.
79. For instance, when Jesus taught in the synagogue in Capernaum it happened that "many therefore of his disciples, when they heard this, said, 'This is a hard saying, who can hear it?' " (John 6:60). And it is reported that "from that time many of his disciples went back, and walked no more with him." (John 6:66)
80. Conferred infallibility (*al-'isma al-sifátíya*). *Some Answered Questions* 45:4, pp. 172–173.
81. "No Guardian of the Faith . . . can ever claim to be the perfect exemplar of the teachings of Bahá'u'lláh or the stainless mirror that reflects His light . . . he remains essentially human." (*World Order* 151)
82. As to 'Abdu'l-Bahá, refer to footnote 32.
83. That is, the Báb.
84. *Will and Testament* 1:17, p. 11.
85. Ibid., 1:25, p. 14.
86. Ibid., 2:7, p. 19.
87. *Tablets* 6:29, p. 68.
88. See footnote 25.
89. The individual members of the Universal House of Justice have no share in its infallibility.
90. In comparing this with the infallibility of the Pope (Cf. can. 749 CIC; *Catechism of the Catholic Church* nos. 891, 2035), which even "extends to the individual commandments of the natural moral law" (Ibid., no. 2036), it is evident that there are differences not only in content but also in legitima-

tion: papal infallibility is legitimized by means of deductions. According to canon law, the Pope's jurisdictive primacy, which implies doctrinal authority, is based on the calling of Peter to his station as leader of the apostles (Matt. 16:18, John 1:42, 21:15, Luke 22:32) and on the apostolic succession of the Bishop of Rome to the station of Peter. The infallibility of the Pope in his "teaching office" (*magisterium*) is deduced from the promise of the Holy Spirit: "And lo, I am with you always, even unto the end of the age" (Matt. 28:20), and the promise of the "Spirit of truth" (John 14:16ff.), through which the purity and authenticity of the faith preached by the apostles and their successors is guaranteed forever (cf. Luke 10:16; for more detail on this subject see *Lexikon für Theologie und Kirche*, Vol. 10, col. 482ff.). These deductions are disputed by the non-Catholic churches and are controversial even within the Roman Church (cf. Hans Küng, *Infallible?* pp. 53ff., 64ff., 88ff).

The institutions of the Guardianship and the Universal House of Justice, on the other hand, are directly legitimized explicitly by scripture, namely Bahá'u'lláh's Kitáb-i Aqdas and 'Abdu'l-Bahá's Will and Testament. The promise of the charisma of immunity to error is, as shown above, an explicit component of Bahá'í scripture.

91. *Will and Testament* 1:17, p. 11.
92. Ibid., 2:8.
93. Cf. Udo Schaefer, *Die Grundlagen der 'Verwaltungsordnung' der Bahá'í*, Heidelberg 1957 (Diss.), 138ff., U. Gollmer, *Gottesreich und Weltgestaltaung. Grundlegung einer politischen Theologie im Bahá'ítum* (unpublished dissertation), Ch. 11.2.2.
94. The question arises whether the Guardian's infallibility extends also to his judgments on issues of morality, as it is claimed for the teaching authority of the Pope (see above, footnote 89). I think this question has to be answered affirmatively. It is true that the revelation of Bahá'u'lláh does not give support to the concept of natural law (*ius divinum naturale*), on which Catholic doctrine is based (Thomas Aquinas called it *lex aeterna, lex indita non scripta* [S. th. 1, 2 q. 91 a.2]). Bahá'í ethics is *theonomous* (from Greek, *theos*: God; *nomos*: law) and voluntaristic in the sense that all moral values have their origin in the decisions of God's arbitrary will ("He doeth whatsoever He willeth and ordaineth whatsoever He pleaseth" [*Tablets* 8:19, pp. 109–110, cf. Kitáb-i Aqdas 7, pp. 21–22]. "He shall not be asked of His doings" [Kitáb-i Aqdas 161, p. 77]). This concept of ethical voluntarism leaves no room for the idea of natural law. However, if all morality is based on God's sovereign will, as it is expressed in his revelation to humankind, it must be concluded that the Guardian's teaching power (and with it his infallibility) also covers all issues of morality. As to the origin and derivation of ethical norms, refer to my *Bahá'í Ethics* (in prep.) Ch. 4; see also *Making the Crooked Straight*, pp. 403ff.
95. "The infallibility of the Guardian is confined to matters which are related strictly to the Cause and interpretation of the teachings; he is not an infallible authority on other subjects, such as economics, science etc. . . . The Guardian's infallibility covers interpretation of the revealed word, and its

application. Likewise any instructions he may issue having to do with the protection of the Faith, or its well-being must be closely obeyed, as he is infallible in the protection of the Faith" (letter dated 17 October 1944, written on behalf of Shoghi Effendi, cited in: Loni Bramson-Lerche, 'Some Aspects of the Establishment of the Guardianship', in Moojan Momen, ed., *Studies in the Bábí and Bahá'í Religions*, Vol. 5 [Los Angeles: Kalimát Press, 1988] p. 257 with reference to the literature cited on p. 284).

96. Letter written by Shoghi Effendi dated 29 September 1953.
97. Loni Bramson-Lerche, "Some Aspects," p. 258, where it is pointed out that Shoghi Effendi, despite his extremely careful research, made some insignificant errors in his book *God Passes By* (Bramson-Lerche, ibid., p. 285, footnote 20). Robert Stockman, too, states that: "The same observations are true of 'Abdu'l-Bahá and Shoghi Effendi who quote information that appears to be historically inaccurate in their books. Shoghi Effendi's secretary stated the Guardian was not infallible in matters of economics and science and apparently he did not claim infallibility in matters of history (though his historical writing clearly reflects a very high level of precision and accuracy)" (quoted from Abstracts of lectures delivered at the 'Fourth H. M. Arjmand Conference on Scripture' 4–6 November 1994, in Nijmegen, the Netherlands).
98. In my doctoral thesis, published in 1957 before the death of Shoghi Effendi, I left open the question as to whether this institution's immunity to error extended to other spheres beyond that of its legislative power, while at the same time expressing my preference for a restrictive interpretation of the scripture (*Grundlagen,* p. 174). In the relevant literature, this question has more recently been discussed by Gollmer (*Gottesreich*, Ch. 12.4.3).
99. *Will and Testament* 1:17.
100. Ibid., 2:8, p. 20.
101. " . . . each operates within a clearly defined sphere of jurisdiction . . . Neither can, nor will ever, infringe upon the sacred and prescribed domain of the other. Neither will seek to curtail the specific and undoubted authority with which both have been divinely invested" (*World Order,* pp. 148–150).
102. Cf. Kitáb-i Aqdas 37, p. 32.
103. For instance: crimes such as murder, arson, theft, adultery and sodomy (Cf. Kitáb-i Aqdas 19, 62; pp. 26, 41; Questions and Answers, no. 49, p. 121) have not been legally defined; the degrees of the offences, the details of the punishments and the manner in which they are to be carried out is left to the Universal House of Justice to decide "in light of prevailing conditions when the law is to be in operation" (*Kitáb-i-Aqdas,* note 86, p. 204).
104. The '*ulamá' fi'l Bahá'* (Cf. Kitáb-i Aqdas 173, p. 82) have no authority, "unless they are endorsed by the House of Justice" ('Abdu'l-Bahá, in *Kitáb-i-Aqdas*, p. 5).
105. Universal House of Justice, in *Kitáb-i-Aqdas*, Introduction, p. 5.
106. *Tablets* 6:29, p. 68.
107. Ibid., see also 8:78, p. 134.
108. Ibid., see also 8:61, p. 129.

109. Ibid. By continuing "but acts of worship (*'ibádát*) must be observed according to that which God hath revealed in His Book," Bahá'u'lláh makes clear that the House of Justice is not empowered to legislate in the sphere of worship, such as devotional acts, prayers, etc.
110. Ibid., 8:77, p. 134.
111. Ibid.
112. For instance: "The Universal House of Justice, likewise, wardeth off all differences and whatever it prescribeth must be accepted and he who transgresseth is rejected. But this Universal House of Justice which is the *Legislature* hath not yet been instituted" (*Selections* 187:2, p. 215 [my emphasis]). "All must consider themselves to be of the order of subjects, submissive and obedient to the commandments of God and the laws of the House of Justice" (ibid., 33:6, p. 68).
113. *Will and Testament* 1:25, p. 14.
114. Ibid. (my emphasis).
115. Ibid., 2:7, p. 19 (emphasis added).
116. The "Book" is the whole canon of revealed texts.
117. Ibid., 2:8, p. 20 (emphasis added).
118. *World Order,* p. 148.
119. Ibid., p. 150, cf. also p. 153.
120. Ibid., p. 156.
121. Ibid., p. 7.
122. *Messages from the Universal House of Justice 1963-1986. The First Epoch of the Formative Age* (Wilmette: Bahá'í Publishing Trust, 1996) no. 5, p. 14.
123. Ibid., no. 59, pp. 130 ff.
124. *The Constitution of the Universal House of Justice. Declaration of Trust* (Haifa: Bahá'í World Centre, 1972).
125. *Messages,* no. 132, p. 246.
126. *World Order*, p. 200.
127. *Will and Testament* 1:25, p. 14.
128. Ibid., 2:7, 8, p. 20.
129. An example of "problems which have caused difference" might be the decision of the Universal House of Justice (6 October 1963) that "there is no way to appoint or to legislate to make it possible to appoint a second Guardian to succeed Shoghi Effendi" (see footnote 121). This decision on a vital issue of the world community was an act of legislation. The decision has the character of a law, because it is an authoritative clarification of the question whether one of the two pillars of the constitutional order will continue or not. This clarification is of permanent legal relevance for the entire world community. Its public announcement meets another prerequisite of legislation, that a law must be brought to the attention of the people by its publication. It is not a classical law in the sense of general abstract norms but rather a so-called "statute of special provision" (*Maßnahmegesetz*). Cf. footnote 207 of Schaefer, Towfigh, Gollmer, *Making the Crooked Straight,* p. 180.
130. Namely, the explicit recourse to the holy text in each case and the reference

to these additional functions as "matters that are not expressly recorded in the Book," (*Will and Testament* 2:8, p. 20) combined with the express statement that all decisions made as part of this sphere of competence "have the same effect as the Text itself" (Ibid.).

131. "freed from all error" (ibid., 1:25, p. 14).

132. There is only one exception, a passage in 'Abdu'l-Bahá's Testament, where the Universal House of Justice is mentioned for the first time, named together with the Guardian: "The guardian of the Cause of God as well as the Universal House of Justice . . . are both under the care and protection of the Abhá Beauty, under the shelter and unerring guidance of His Holiness, the Exalted One . . . Whatsoever they decide is of God. Whoso obeyeth him not, neither obeyeth them, hath not obeyed God . . . " (ibid., 1:17, p. 11). Here, indeed, no reference is made to what kind of decisions the statement "whatsoever they decide is of God" refers. However, it cannot be concluded from this passage that everything one of the two institutions decides is under the shelter of the unerring guidance. Statements Shoghi Effendi made concerning matters that are not in the scripture are, as he declared himself, not covered by this promise. This relatively long passage focuses on the obedience, the submissiveness and subordination every believer has to pay to these supreme institutions. The passage must be understood in the context of the other statements in the Testament. I think it is clear that "whatsoever they decide" presupposes decisions which are later on specified in the Testament.

133. Cf. *Tablets* 6:29, p. 68, *Will and Testament* 1:25, 2:7, 2:8, pp. 14, 19-20. See the texts referring to notes 113-116.

134. "The Universal House of Justice in arriving at a decision needs to have before it all the facts involved in the matter. If, after making a decision, new facts emerge, it may well be changed." (Letter on behalf of the Universal House of Justice, dated 13 August 1981) "With regard to decisions taken by the Universal House of Justice itself, instructions it issues, and the relationship of these to the information supplied, it is obvious that the nature of a decision or instruction is affected by the information on which it is made." (Letter on behalf of the Universal House of Justice, dated 26 May 1993)

135. Letters dated 22 August 1977 and 13 August 1981 (my emphasis).

136. Universal relevance is a decision that has legal relevance for the "people of Bahá," i.e., for the Bahá'í world community.

137. Legal dogmatics and legal techniques are among the necessary foundations of any type of legislation. This legal dogmatic groundwork, which is a prerequisite for the clarity and reliability of the law laid down, will be conducted by the "scholars" or the "learned ones in Bahá" (*al-'ulamá' fi'l Bahá'*), who are at "the focal center of the legislative (power)" (cf. Kitáb-i Aqdas 173, p. 82, 'Abdu'l-Bahá, *The Secret of Divine Civilization* 37) but whose legal views "have no authority unless they are endorsed by the House of Justice." ('Abdu'l-Bahá, quoted in *Wellspring of Guidance*, p. 85) On the whole subject see also U. Gollmer, *Gottesreich* Ch. 11.2.3, 12.4.3.

138. Cf. *Grundlagen,* p. 174.

139. Cf. ibid., p. 74ff.

140. *Tablets* 11:6, p. 164, cf. *Will and Testament* 2:5, p. 18. As 'Abdu'l-Bahá elucidated in a tablet (cf. *Kitáb-i Aqdas*, p. 5 [introduction]), the significance of the provisions made by Bahá'u'lláh and by himself for the future development of Bahá'í law becomes apparent if it is considered in the context of Islamic law. For this reason a comparison shall be made which will reveal some parallels, but more cardinal differences.

Both religions claim to possess a divine law, but even the primary sources of that law are different. In Islam, it is the Qur'an *and* the Sunna (the sayings, actions and customs of the Prophet Muhammad as reported in the *hádíth*). In the Bahá'í Faith, it is only the scripture: the canon of the tablets of Bahá'u'lláh and the writings of 'Abdu'l-Bahá. Tradition is not recognized as an authoritative source in the Bahá'í Faith, neither for doctrine nor for law. (As to the *sola scriptural*-principle see *Grundlagen,* pp. 66-70; *Making the Crooked Straight,* pp. 682-83 and note 27). In both religions, the revealed law had and has to be developed.

In Islam this process took place through the interpretation of the sources by the *'ulamá'* who claimed authority, although the Qur'an contains no legitimation for such an authority. The development of the law (*fiqh*) has been worked out in Sunni Islam by the four legal schools (*madháhib*), in Shí'ih Islam by the Usúlí school. In Sunní Islam, the authority is ultimately based on the *ijmá'*. From a *hádíth* reported by Ibn Mádja, "My people will never agree on an error" (*SEI* 157), it was deduced *per argumentum e contrario* that a consensus (*ijmá'*) on a question of faith or law would always be based on truth. An *ijmá'* was held to exist when the recognized religious scholars of a period, the *mujtahids*, agreed on a question of faith. Anything that had once been decided by *ijmá'* was regarded as the truth and deemed binding for all time (on this subject cf. Bergsträsser, *Islamisches Recht* [Berlin-Leipzig: de Gruyter 1935] p. 131ff., Goldziher, *Introduction to Islamic Theology and Law* (Princeton/New Jersey: Princeton University Press, 1981) pp. 50ff., *SEI* p. 157). The sharí'a, the Islamic code of duties is regarded as divine. A human legislation is unimaginable for Islamic thought. Therefore, Islam never had a legislative body.

In contrast to Islam, the Bahá'í community is in possession of an infallible legislature so that in the fullness of time the "people of Bahá" will be governed by a universally applied sacred law, beyond which there will be wide scope for the legislation of human law according to the different conditions and exigencies on earth. A major difference in comparison with Islamic law is the fact that the Universal House of Justice can repeal its own legislation and adapt it to changed social conditions, as will be further elucidated below.

An analogy (Ficicchia, *Der Bahá'ismus*, pp. 162, 283; Hermann Römer, *Die Bábí-Behá'í. Eine Studie zur Religionsgeschichte des Islams* [Potsdam: Verlag der Deutschen Orient-Mission, 1911] p. 118) between the infallibility of the Universal House of Justice and the Islamic principle of consensus (*ijmá'*) is not convincing as the following cardinal differences demonstrate:

- *ijmá'* is neither an institution nor a decision made and proclaimed at a particular point in history, but is rather a statement that, at a particular point in the past, there was a unanimous consensus of the *mujtahids*;
- legal issues and questions of faith are authoritatively clarified by *ijmá'*. The Universal House of Justice is a body that makes decisions that are not concerned with matters of doctrine. It is a legislative organ that has never existed in Islam;
- this legislation is preceded by consultation, whereas *ijmá'* was not based on consultation between all the recognized *mujtahids* because the institution of a council never developed in Islam. *Ijmá'* could only ever be ascertained with the passage of time (*postero tempore*);
- an *ijmá'* requires unanimity, whereas the Universal House of Justice makes its decisions on the basis of a majority vote following consultation.

141. *Will and Testament* 2:7, p. 19.
142. Ibid., 2:7, p. 19.
143. Ibid., 2:8, p. 20.
144. Ibid.
145. Ibid.
146. Cf. ibid.
147. Ibid.
148. Ibid.
149. Ibid., 1:25, p. 14.
150. For example, on such details of administration as the decoration of the holy places, the design and construction of the buildings at the World Centre, the publication of the holy texts in English, etc.
151. The publication of an English edition of the Kitáb-i Aqdas was undoubtedly a significant act of the Universal House of Justice. However, this body did not raise such a claim for the text of the book, although it had consulted upon and approved it, but rather states that the translation "represents an acceptable rendering of the original" (*Kitáb-i Aqdas*, p. 11 [Introduction]).
152. I refer to Sir Karl Popper, *The Logic of Scientific Discovery* (New York-London: Harper & Row, 1968); *Objective Knowledge. An Evolutionary Approach* (Oxford: Clarendon Press, 1981), according to whom we approach truth not by verification of a hypothesis, but rather by its "falsification." A thesis "all swans are white" is valid as long as no black swan has ever been seen. As soon as one black swan is discovered, the thesis is falsified and no longer valid. Thus, one single error would suffice for the falsification of the claim to infallibility. It should be noted that one of the main arguments brought forth against the papal infallibility is that a great number of papal decisions made over the course of time have evidently been erroneous. The concept of conferred infallibility without any limits is, I feel, indefensible.
153. Perhaps that of the members of this body as well.
154. In seminars on the Kitáb-i Aqdas, when the arguments against capital pun-

ishment were analyzed, I sometimes came across the argument that an error of the judiciary and the irreparability of an execution would cause no problem in a Bahá'í society, since the House of Justice would have to approve such a verdict and confirm only those in which the convicted is guilty—and this without knowing the files, without consultation on facts, just by virtue of meditation and prayers! Meditation and prayers would, by virtue of the Holy Spirit, directly result in an infallible decision. If that were true, the question arises, why is the House of Justice dependent in its decisions on facts at all, and why is consultation required if prayers and meditation suffice for its illumination by the Holy Spirit?

155. *World Order,* p. 153.
156. Letter dated 22 August 1977.
157. *Gleanings* 33:2, p. 77; Kitáb-i Aqdas 185.
158. Cf. *Tablets* 6:52, 7:7, 7:32, 11:41, 13:5, 17:43 (pp. 77, 85, 93, 175, 196, 242).
159. "First and foremost among these favors which the Almighty hath conferred upon man, is the gift of understanding . . . This gift giveth man the power to discern the truth in all things, leadeth him to that which is right, and helpeth him to discover the secrets of creation." (*Gleanings* 95:1, p. 194)
160. "He has chosen the reality of man and has honored it with intellect and wisdom, the two most luminous lights in either world. This supreme emblem of God stands first in the order of creation and first in rank, taking precedence over all created things. Witness to it is the Holy Tradition, 'Before all else, God created the mind.' " (*The Secret of Divine Civilization,* pp. 1, 2)
161. One could modify the famous dictum of Augustine "*Roma locuta, causa finita*" (*Sermones* 131.10) to say "*Haifa locuta, causa finita*" ("Haifa has spoken, the matter is closed").
162. *Will and Testament* 1:17, p. 11.
163. *World Order,* p.148.
164. Qur'an 2:2, cf. also 2:97, 2:120, 2:285, 3:73, 6:71, 18:89, etc.
165. Ibid., 1:6.
166. Among the prayers revealed by the Báb and by Bahá'u'lláh there are many for this purpose.
167. "The prime requisites for them that take counsel together are purity of motive, radiance of spirit, detachment from all else save God, attraction to His Divine Fragrances, humility and lowliness amongst His loved ones, patience and long-suffering in difficulties and servitude to His exalted Threshold. Should they be graciously aided to acquire these attributes, victory from the unseen Kingdom of Bahá shall be vouchsafed to them." (*Selections from the Writings of 'Abdu'l-Bahá* 43, p. 87, *Bahá'í Administration* [Wilmette: Bahá'í Publishing Trust, 6th ed. 1953] p. 21ff.) "The first condition is absolute love and harmony amongst the members of the assembly. They must be wholly free from estrangement and must manifest in themselves the Unity of God . . . Should harmony of thought and absolute unity be non-existent, that gathering shall be dispersed and that assembly be brought to naught . . . They must, when coming together, turn

their faces to the Kingdom on high and ask aid from the Realm of Glory. They must then proceed with the utmost devotion, courtesy, dignity, care and moderation to express their views. They must in every matter search out the truth and not insist upon their own opinion, for stubbornness and persistence in one's views will lead ultimately to discord and wrangling and the truth will remain hidden . . . Should they endeavor to fulfil these conditions the Grace of the Holy Spirit shall be vouchsafed unto them, and that assembly shall become the center of the Divine blessings . . . " (Ibid., p. 45, pp. 87–89). Thus, 'Abdu'l-Bahá makes clear that the guidance of the Holy Spirit will be granted only to those assemblies whose consultation is conducted under the conditions he has set out in these passages.

168. See footnote 166.
169. *Constitution of the Universal House of Justice*, Art. VII (The right of review), VIII (Appeals).
170. Bahá'u'lláh, quoted in *Kitáb-i Aqdas*, p. 6 (Introduction).
171. Kitáb-i Aqdas 77 and note 110. On this subject see also Schaefer, Towfigh, and Gollmer, *Making the Crooked Straight,* p. 289ff.
172. *The Secret of Divine Civilization* 186, p. 106.
173. *Bahá'í Administration,* p. 21.
174. Letters dated 20 October 1977 and 28 May 1991.

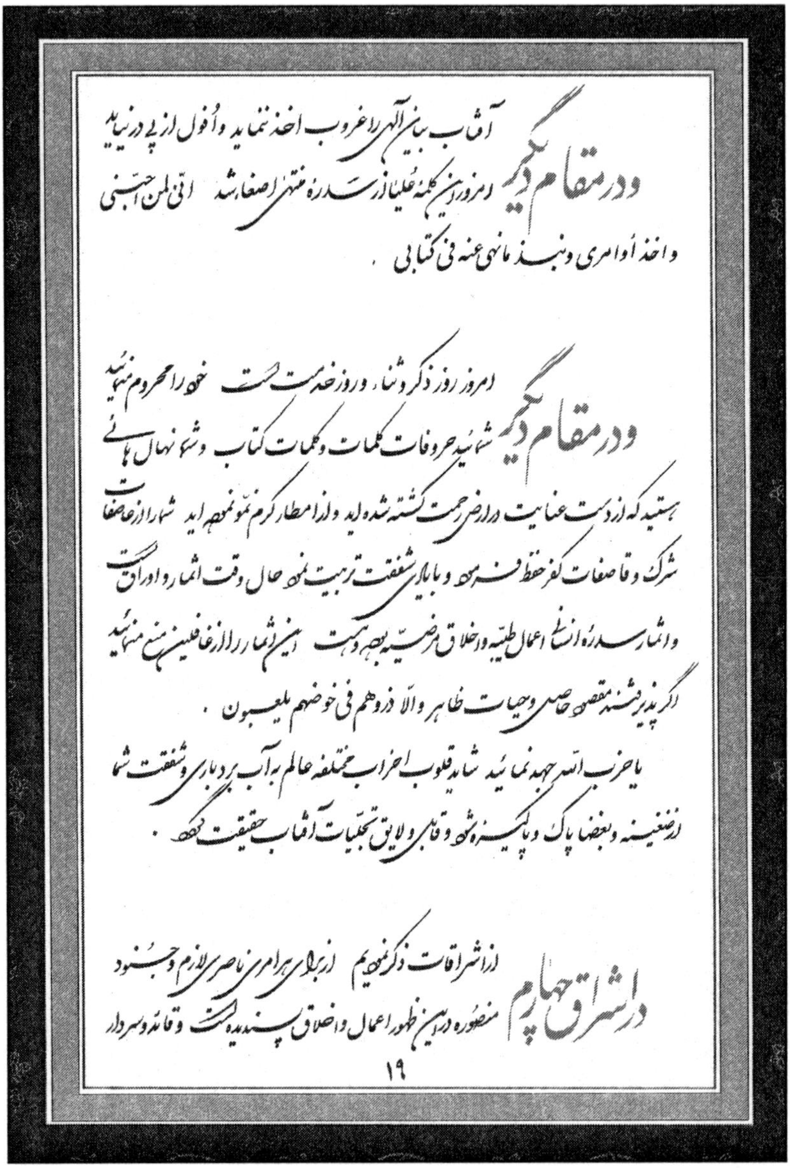

CALLIGRAPHIC RENDERING
of a page from Bahá'u'lláh's Epistle to the Son of the Wolf

Theocratic Assumptions in Bahá'í Literature

Sen McGlinn

A survey of Bahá'í secondary literature in major European languages indicates that most commentators have supported the idea that Bahá'ís do not accept the separation of church and state. In contrast, this essay presents scriptural support that suggests that the institutional differentiation of the religious and political orders is a central Bahá'í doctrine. This essay examines one passage from the writings of Shoghi Effendi that might plausibly be interpreted in a theocratic sense, and one phrase interpolated into The Promulgation of Universal Peace, *and then argues against the theocratic theory by criticizing one form of argument that has been used to support it. Beyond this, it points to three challenges facing the Bahá'í community: the need to provide explicit scriptural foundations to support ideas presented as Bahá'í teachings; the need to clarify certain attitudes toward politics; and the need for moral self-examination. If Bahá'ís are to present Bahá'u'lláh's remarkably modern teachings to the world, they will need to detach themselves from some inherited ideas and from their emotional associations.*

> The instruments which are essential to the immediate protection, the security and assurance of the human race have been entrusted to the hands, and lie in the grasp, of the governors of human society. This is the wish of God and His decree. . . .
>
> — *Bahá'u'lláh*
> Lawh-i Ashraf[1]

In February 1995, I presented a paper on "Church and State in the World Order of Bahá'u'lláh" at the Bahá'í Studies Colloquium.[2] The "church" part of the title is inaccurate, since the Bahá'í Faith is a religion, not a church, and the institutional structure of the Bahá'í community is not a single organization but an interlocking set of institutions with distinct functions. Nevertheless, "church and state studies" is the accepted name for such studies, whether the society concerned is Christian, Muslim, Hindu or, in this case, the prospective Bahá'í society as we find it in the Writings. My paper argued that institutional differentiation of the political and religious orders is a basic, and therefore a permanent, doctrine of the Bahá'í Faith.

During the question time that followed the presentation, I was asked why I had not dealt with the counterarguments, since Bahá'ís have generally supported a theocratic model (that is, the government of the state by Bahá'í religious institutions) for a future world order. My answer then was that I had not found any published presentation of the Bahá'í theocratic position that cites scripture or gives arguments. I hoped that my paper would at least show that the theocratic model is not self-evident, and that this might prompt others to make explicit what has merely been assumed. The counterarguments could then be addressed and theories modified accordingly.

Church and State in the Secondary Literature

The direct response I had hoped for has not been forthcoming. There is still, to my knowledge, no coherent published statement of the notion that the Bahá'í teachings advocate theocracy.[3] But I have, in the meantime, collected twenty-five books and articles by Bahá'ís that mention a theocratic model of government. These are listed in the bibliography, with brief comments on some of them. Others are discussed in the text below.[4] The results of this literature search were also negative in terms of uncovering the texts and arguments on which theocratic ideas in the Bahá'í community are based: I found many references to the church-state relationship or to Bahá'í theocracy, but these were neither supported by arguments nor based on what Bahá'u'lláh, 'Abdu'l-Bahá, and Shoghi Effendi have written on the topic. The few that do cite any scriptural source cite one that is not authentic, or one that contradicts their conclusions, or they do not explain the connection between the citation and the conclusion.[5] The reasons why Bahá'ís hold theocratic beliefs remain unclear, but there is no doubt that a considerable portion do.

Many of the works that mentioned political teachings took a theocratic position, mostly by implication, some explicitly. But this is not unanimous. In one early Bahá'í pamphlet (1925), Charles Mason Remey argues against the theocratic model, and in favor of a pious society, involving "not a union of church and State, but a union of religion and State." Remey presents only his conclusions, without indicating their basis, and he seems to have been alone among the authors of his generation. Juan Cole's 1992 article, "Iranian Millenarianism and Democratic Thought in the Nineteenth Century" marks a renewed interest by Bahá'ís in Bahá'u'lláh's political thought. His focus is mainly on Bahá'u'lláh's advocacy of democracy and parliamentary government, but he also says that Bahá'u'lláh "clearly envisioned the Baha'i houses of justice as coexisting alongside secular parliaments and rulers" (p. 15). He has expanded considerably on this in *Modernity and the Millennium*, which I have reviewed elsewhere.[6] Christopher Sprung, in his essay "Bahá'í Institutions and Human Governance" (1996), addresses the question but comes to no conclusion. He does insist that there is "a solid ambiguity linked to the question: is it completely correct to suggest that the Bahá'í system means and implies 'rule by God'?"[7] Most recently, Nader Saiedi has taken an anti-theocratic stance, which is outlined in the bibliography.

Leaving aside the last decade, however, we must conclude that the secondary Bahá'í literature has almost unanimously endorsed theocratic concepts. One example from this literature might serve to illustrate what I mean by "theocratic" thought in the strict sense in the Bahá'í context. It appears in the *Encyclopaedia of Islam*, in the lemma

"Bahais," and was written in 1958 by Alessandro Bausani. He says that:

> The Bahá'ís do not accept the separation of Church and State, but maintain that in the absence of priests and sacraments the Bahá'í fusion of religion and administration will take on a different character from that of the traditional theocracies.

The last two words here suggest that Bausani is thinking of a letter written on behalf of the Guardian, which says: "What the Guardian was referring to was the Theocratic systems, such as the Catholic Church and the Caliphate, . . . The Bahá'í theocracy, on the contrary, is both divinely ordained as a system and, of course, based on the teachings of the Prophet Himself . . ."[8] This letter describes the Bahá'í "system" as a theocracy. But a little further research shows that the letter is not referring to the system of *government* in a Bahá'í state: it is an explanation of some words of Shoghi Effendi, who had written that: "the *Administrative Order* of the Faith of Bahá'u'lláh [does not] conform to . . . any of the various theocracies, whether Jewish, Christian or Islamic which mankind has witnessed in the past."[9] No one would dispute that the *Bahá'í Administrative Order* could be called theocratic, although it is unlike previous systems in detail and because its principle features are set out in the Bahá'í scriptures. But this is not theocracy in the political sense, where the state is governed by the religious order. The letter says only that the Bahá'í Administrative Order—the religious order in itself—is theocratic. But in this limited sense, any free religion is theocratic, for it is governed by a religious order: itself.

Theocratic *political* theories are an entirely different thing: these advocate that *the state* should be ruled by the religious order. It appears that Bausani began with an assumption, that the Bahá'í Administrative Order is also intended to be a government. That is, he has assumed a political theocratic theory. He has then observed that the Bahá'í Administrative Order itself is called "theocratic," and has concluded that a Bahá'í government would also be theocratic. This is circular reasoning—it only says something about the Bahá'í teachings regarding government if we have already assumed that the Administrative Order is intended to serve as a government. Such circularity is quite typical of the references to a theocratic order, and of claims that the Bahá'í

Faith does not recognize the separation of church and state, that I have found in the literature by Bahá'ís. It is because the reasoning is circular that my efforts to discover the roots of such thinking have proven inconclusive.

In the course of this search of the literature, I also found many references to the theocratic model of Bahá'í government in works not written by Bahá'ís. These range from more or less well-informed academic studies to (sometimes) virulent attacks. The most destructive of these to date has been the claim by Shaykh Mohammad Taghi Falsafi, on Iranian radio programs in 1956, saying that there was a Bahá'í plot to take over the country. This resulted in mob violence and government action suppressing the Bahá'í Faith.[10] Other claims that the Bahá'ís aim at establishing a theocracy have damaged the prestige of the Bahá'í Faith in the West.[11] Some of these non-Bahá'í works do give sources in the Bahá'í writings, or a coherent argument. But since they have no bearing on the reasons why Bahá'ís themselves have believed in theocracy, I have not considered these authors here.

In the hope of prompting a discussion that is based on texts and arguments (and accepting the risk that I may be accused of setting up a straw man), this paper will focus on one text from Shoghi Effendi, one saying that has been attributed to 'Abdu'l-Bahá, and one type of argument that I have called "dispensationalism." I will attempt to demonstrate that none of these is adequate to support a theocratic model against the weight of the scriptural evidence to the contrary. The scriptural evidence, it will be argued, supports the proposition that

the institutional differentiation of the religious and political orders is a central and permanent doctrine of the Bahá'í revelation.

Setting Up a Straw Man

Let us imagine that I did find a Bahá'í author who wrote: The Bahá'í teachings regarding government present a theocratic model, in the sense that the institutions of religion and government are to merge, with the institutions of the Bahá'í administrative order taking over the functions of local and national governments. This can be seen from the following two sentences from Shoghi Effendi:

> Not only will the present-day Spiritual Assemblies be styled differently in future, but they will be enabled also to add to their present functions those powers, duties, and prerogatives necessitated by the recognition of the Faith of Bahá'u'lláh, not merely as one of the recognized religious systems of the world, but as the State Religion of an independent and Sovereign Power. And as the Bahá'í Faith permeates the masses of the peoples of East and West, and its truth is embraced by the majority of the peoples of a number of the Sovereign States of the world, will the Universal House of Justice attain the plenitude of its power, and exercise as the supreme organ of the Bahá'í Commonwealth all the rights, the duties, and responsibilities incumbent upon the world's future superstate.[12]

And suppose our author continues: While there are also many passages in the Bahá'í writings that do mandate a civil state governed by human governments, and some specifically endorsing the separation of church and state and condemning the interference of religious institutions in government, these must refer to preliminary stages as the world evolves towards a full theocracy. 'Abdu'l-Bahá says that the institution of the Universal House of Justice represents "the consummate union and blending of church and state."

My imaginary author presents us with a definition, two proof texts, and a strategy for resolving apparent contradictions with other scriptures. This argument is, of course, a "straw man" in the sense that it is my own creation. No theocratic authors have been so explicit about the roots of their theocratic beliefs.[13] But, it is at least an honest straw man. There is some evidence that the words attributed to 'Abdu'l-Bahá have in fact influenced some Bahá'ís, and the other points are the strongest, not the weakest, arguments that I can imagine that might underlie theocratic thought.

Definitions

The fact that my imaginary author includes a definition of theocracy is important. Some of the Bahá'í authors in my literature survey use the word *theocracy*, but they are really speaking of a society permeated by religion, rather than of government by religious institutions. For example, John Hatcher, in *The Law of Love Enshrined*, refers in passing to "a spiritually based society, essentially theocratic in form," as if the two are necessarily the same thing.[14] Others use the word theocracy, but in reference to the Bahá'í administrative order rather than to a Bahá'í government. Yet others simply assume that anything that is divinely ordained, as both the civil government and religious institutions are ordained in the Bahá'í writings, is by definition theocratic. But this is clearly not true: monarchy, mosquitoes, marriage, and my own progressive baldness are all in different senses ordained by the Creator and have their place in the grand scheme of things. But they are not theocratic. The question here is not whether God rules. In the debate about Bahá'í theocracy, the question is: To whom has God delegated authority as regards earthly government—to the "Kings and Rulers" or to Spiritual Assemblies and Houses of Justice?

Most Bahá'í authors cannot be described as promoting theocracy as a political theory, for they have no political theory. Theocracy appears rather as a background assumption, unelaborated and without an explicit basis. Their views should be attributed to asking inexact questions, using terms imprecisely, or to circular reasoning. Other authors work with a model of society that is so simple that politics itself would be impossible. One form of imprecision is to take a scriptural passage referring to the Bahá'í Administrative Order, assume that this is the same thing as a Bahá'í government, and conclude that the Bahá'í government would be theocratic. A variation is to take a passage referring to the Bahá'í Commonwealth (the '*umma*, or religious community) and suppose that this is the same thing as the world commonwealth of nations (the political federation of states). In both cases, the Bahá'í writings are read within an *a priori* assumption that the Bahá'í teachings do not support the separation of church and state.

I do not mean to denigrate the intelligence or sophistication of the literature, but rather to emphasize the low ideological "heat" around this issue within Bahá'í communities. There appear to be few, if any, Bahá'ís who have thought about the issue systematically and worked out a theocratic theory of government or who have any personal commitment to theocracy as an ideology. This is important because it contrasts Bahá'í ideas starkly to contemporary Islamist movements. The latter do have elaborated political theories, with lines of argument and scriptural sources to justify them. Despite the similarity between Islamist and Bahá'í theocratic ideas, they are completely different sociological phenomena.[15]

The "Establishment" of Religion

The first sentence of the quotation from *The World Order of Bahá'u'-lláh* above provides an opportunity to clear up some terminological misunderstandings. It says that the Bahá'í Faith will be recognized as "the State Religion" of at least one country. In other works, Shoghi Effendi refers to the Faith's "establishment and recognition as a State religion."[16] We need therefore to be clear about what is meant here. The establishment of religion (having an "established church") has some negative associations, especially for Americans, because of the role of England's established church in the founding myths of the United States. These associations need to be made explicit and so cleared away.

In the first place, the establishment of religion does not mean theocratic government. Establishment is a constitutional agreement between the state and one or more religious organizations to place the relationship between them on a long-term footing, and thus beyond the vagaries of day-to-day politics. Second, the establishment or disestablishment of religion does not entail—or even foster—the restriction of religion to the private sphere. Religion plays a more visibly intrusive role in American politics than it does in either England or Denmark, both of which have established churches. Third, establishment is not compatible with a church-state. Establishment is only possible if the church and the state are two separate and distinct institutions, so that they can recognize and affirm one another. For this reason, the Islamic Republic of Iran, where the religious institutions define the limited role that is permitted to politics and closely supervise political life, is properly seen as a theocracy—*not* as a state with an established religion. In the Iranian model, the political order does not have the power or freedom to establish or disestablish religion; whereas in England

and Denmark the state as a sovereign entity has chosen to establish particular national churches. Fourth, while establishment *may* privilege one religious group over others, it does not necessarily do so: England and Denmark do not discriminate between citizens on the basis of religion. Nor is establishment necessarily confined to a single church or religion. In a pluralist society such as the United Kingdom, the state could invite confessions other than the Church of England to provide members to sit alongside the bishops in the House of Lords, not because they represent a certain proportion of the population (the Lords is not meant to be representative in that sense), but because their religious traditions represent a source of wisdom that can contribute to the process of governance. Fifth, establishment does not in itself say anything about the religious quality of the state: the state may regard religious institutions in a purely pragmatic fashion as a means of inculcating desirable ethics and providing necessary social services, or it may be motivated by religious conviction and bind itself to follow religious teachings. Shoghi Effendi presents these as successive stages in the relationship, when he refers to "the stage of establishment" being followed by "the emergence of the Bahá'í state itself."[17] In Roman history too, we can see a considerable gap between the "establishment" of Christianity and the Christianization of the Roman state, and also that this was not achieved once-for-all.

Having set aside what establishment does not mean, or does not necessarily mean, we are left with a minimal definition. The establishment of religion requires only that there be a constitutional understanding between a state and one or more religious institutions: it is a contract between government and religion as partners.

Church and State in the Bahá'í Scriptures

Before addressing the crucial second sentence from *The World Order of Bahá'u'lláh* cited by my imaginary author, we should briefly consider other relevant passages from the Bahá'í writings; for no reading of a single passage can be relied upon unless it is placed in the context of the broad sweep of Bahá'í scriptures.

Working chronologically, we must start with the doctrine of the two sovereignties that is one of the major themes of the Kitáb-i Iqán. The first kind of sovereignty is spiritual:

> . . . by sovereignty is meant the all-encompassing, all-pervading power which is inherently exercised by the Qá'im whether or not He appear to the world clothed in the majesty of earthly dominion. . . . That sovereignty is the spiritual ascendancy . . . which in due time revealeth itself to the world . . . [18]

The sovereignty of the prophets resides in the power to attract devotion and to change hearts, to reform morals, call forth sacrifices, and to create a new form of human community. While it is clearly differentiated from the worldly sovereignty, and superior in as much as it is long-lasting, Bahá'u'lláh does not say that it also entails temporal government. On the contrary:

> Were sovereignty to mean earthly sovereignty and worldly dominion, were it to imply the subjection and external allegiance of all the peoples and kindreds of the earth—whereby His loved ones should be exalted and be made to live in peace, and His enemies be abased and tormented —such [a] form of sovereignty would not be true of God Himself, the Source of all dominion, Whose majesty and power all things testify.[19]

In the opening section of the Súriy-i Mulúk, it is true, Bahá'u'lláh commands the kings to "Fling away . . . the things ye possess, and take fast hold on the Handle of God."[20] However, this submission to the will of God, through acceptance of the revelation of Bahá'u'lláh, clearly does not require that the kings should abdicate their thrones. Bahá'u'lláh goes on to command them to rule justly; to care for the poor; to form international agreements; to moderate their armaments, expenditure, and taxation; and to punish wrong-doers:

> God hath committed into your hands the reins of the government of the people, that ye may rule with justice over them, safeguard the rights of the down-trodden, and punish the wrong-doers. If ye neglect the duty prescribed unto you by God in His Book, your names shall be numbered with those of the unjust in His sight.[21]

In the Kitáb-i Aqdas, Bahá'u'lláh recognizes and honors the institution of human government, in the forms of monarchy, democracy, and republican government, and he enjoins all people to obey "those who wield authority." Given the importance attached to this book, no alteration to these principles is conceivable. Bahá'u'lláh announces himself using messianic political titles ("the Desire of the nations" and "the King of Kings") so that the reader has no doubt that this is the Qá'im speaking. But he combines this with an equally forthright renunciation of any claim to earthly sovereignty:

> He Who is the sovereign Lord of all is come . . . from the heart of Zion there cometh the cry: "The promise is fulfilled" . . . Ye are but vassals, O kings of the earth! He Who is the King of Kings hath appeared, . . . Arise, and serve Him Who is the Desire of all nations, Who hath created you through a word from Him, and ordained you to be, for all time, the emblems of His sovereignty. . . . By the righteousness of God! It is not Our wish to lay hands on your kingdoms. Our mission is to seize and possess the hearts of men. . . . To this testifieth the Kingdom of Names, could ye but comprehend it. . . . Forsake your palaces, and haste ye to gain admittance into His Kingdom. This, indeed, will profit you both in this world and in the next.[22]

The Aqdas also contains a similar passage addressed to republican governments in America, and another promising that Tehran will have both a monarchy and a democratic government.[23] Without entering into a discussion of Bahá'u'lláh's ideas about forms of government, it is important to note that, while he frequently addresses monarchs in the Aqdas, his theology and ethic of government apply to governments of whatever form.

Another text from the same period as the Aqdas, Bahá'u'lláh's letter to Pope Pius IX (1869), gives an indication of the church-state relationship he favored. Bahá'u'lláh advises the Pope to: "Abandon thy kingdom unto the kings, . . . Exhort thou the kings and say: 'Deal equitably with men. Beware lest ye transgress the bounds fixed in the Book.' "[24] From this it is clear that religious institutions are not intended to withdraw to an apolitical cloister, but to work in the body politic within the ethical sphere, with full respect for civil government, and without laying claim to the authority that God has delegated to "the kings."

In the Lawh-i Dunyá, Bahá'u'lláh proposes a specific role for the Iranian clergy and senior government officers in a body that appears to be a constitutional convention to frame reforms for Iran (although it might also be a permanent legislature).[25] The argument for a consultative role for the clergy is repeated at more length in his Epistle to the Son of the Wolf,[26] citing Mark 12:17 ("Render unto Caesar") and Qur'an 4:62. He goes on to apply the same model of separated but cooperating church and state institutions to the Bahá'í institutions:

> According to the fundamental laws which We have formerly revealed in the Kitáb-i Aqdas and other Tablets, all affairs are committed to the care of just kings and presidents and of the Trustees of the House of Justice. . . . The system of government which the British people have adopted in London appeareth to be good, for it is adorned with the light of both kingship and of the consultation of the people.

It may well be that it is not only English constitutional monarchy that Bahá'u'lláh admires, but also the constitutional position of the church in England. The Church of England is within the state, broadly defined, but it is not in the government. It is in a position to be consulted, to criticize, and to provide religious services to the state, but not to rule or to coerce belief.

As it happens, the United Kingdom also provides us with an analogy of the relationship between religious and political orders, for it is called "united" because it consists of two separate kingdoms, England and Scotland, having different laws but united under one crown. If we substitute the political order for "Scotland," and the religious order for "England," and God for the sovereign over them both, we have a good model of the teachings regarding the church-state relationship in the writings of Bahá'u'lláh: church and state are two allied kingdoms under the sovereignty of God.

This constitutional settlement—of cooperating religious and state orders—is implied again by Bahá'u'lláh in the Lawh-i Maqsúd:

> Our hope is that the world's religious leaders and the rulers thereof will unitedly arise for the reformation of this age . . . Let them . . . take counsel together and, through anxious and full deliberation, administer to a diseased and sorely-afflicted world the remedy it requireth.[27]

Much the same points are repeated in later writings.[28] There seems to be almost a plaintive tone as Bahá'u'lláh writes again, probably towards the end of his life:

> Most imagine that this Servant hath the intention of establishing a full-blown government on earth—even though, in all the tablets, He hath forbidden the servants to accept such a rank. . . Kings are the manifestations of divine power, and our intent is only that they should be just. If they keep their gaze upon justice, they are reckoned as of God.[29]

In summary, the separation of church and state, as distinct but interdependent organs within the body politic, is one of the key themes running through Bahá'u'lláh's life work, and he takes a single position, from his first major doctrinal work to his Will and Testament, the Kitáb-i 'Ahd.[30]

The Writings of 'Abdu'l-Bahá

Many of 'Abdu'l-Bahá's letters are relevant to the question of theocracy, but only one of his book-length works, the *Risáliy-i Siyasiyyah* (1893)[31] will be mentioned here. This draws extensively on Iranian and Ottoman political history to demonstrate that the separation of church and state, and freedom of conscience, are prerequisites for good government, while the interference of religion in government, or vice versa, has always brought disaster. Similar points are made in *The Secret of Divine Civilization* and *A Traveller's Narrative*.[32]

'Abdu'l-Bahá relates the separation of church and state to two fundamental forces, or metaphysical principles (*quvvih*): the first, the principle of governance "which bestows external happiness on the human realm . . . safeguards human life, property and honor"; the second "represented by the spiritual, holy authority, heavenly, revealed books, divine prophets, celestial souls, and the learned in the All-Merciful." Religious leaders, including "divine prophets," do not enter the political sphere because:

> . . . the affairs of leadership and government, of kingdom and subjects, already have a respected object of authority, an appointed source, whereas a different holy center and distinct wellspring exists with regard to guidance, religion, knowledge, education, and the promulgation of good morals and of the virtues of true humanity. These latter souls have nothing to do with affairs of civil leadership, nor do they seek to interfere in them. Thus, in this most great cycle of the maturity and adulthood of the world . . . it is written [by Bahá'u'lláh] in the Book of the Covenant . . . whose decree is decisive . . .: "O ye the loved ones and

> the trustees of God! Kings are the manifestations of the power, and the daysprings of the might and riches, of God. Pray ye on their behalf. He hath invested them with the rulership of the earth, and hath singled out the hearts of men as His Own domain. Conflict and contention are categorically forbidden in His Book. This is a decree of God in this Most Great Revelation. It is divinely preserved from annulment . . ."[33]

Religious leaders, he says, can only advise:

> These souls are the authorities in establishing the purport of divine laws, not with regard to their implementation. That is, whenever the government questions them about the exigencies of the revealed law and the reality of the divine ordinances . . . they must communicate the conclusions to which their jurisprudential reasoning has led them about the commands of God . . . Otherwise, what expertise do they have in political matters . . .?

A similar description of religion and the state as distinct and cooperating spheres is found in his Will and Testament:

> This House of Justice enacteth the laws and the government enforceth them. The legislative body must reinforce the executive, the executive must aid and assist the legislative body so that through the close union and harmony of these two forces, the foundation of fairness and justice may become firm and strong . . ."[34]

Thus, in the writings of both Bahá'u'lláh and 'Abdu'l-Bahá, we find that the political and religious orders should be distinct but not hermetically separated. They are organs of one body, whose distinct natures are required so that they can work together. The world and its political institutions are not to be abolished in the Kingdom of God, but rather baptized with the spirit and thus strengthened.

The World Order of Bahá'u'lláh

Now, equipped with a general concept of how this topic is treated in the Bahá'í writings, we can return to the specific passage from Shoghi Effendi cited in our "straw man" argument. The first of the sentences from *The World Order of Bahá'u'lláh* said that the Bahá'í Faith will be recognized as "the State Religion" of at least one country. He continues:

> And as the Bahá'í Faith . . . is embraced by the majority of the peoples of a number of the Sovereign States of the world, will the Universal House of Justice attain the plenitude of its power, and exercise as the supreme organ of the Bahá'í Commonwealth all the rights, the duties, and responsibilities incumbent upon the world's future superstate.

Taking this passage in isolation, one possible reading is that the Universal House of Justice will exercise the rights of the government of the superstate. But is that the most likely way to read the text? We have seen above that this would be contrary to the principles found in the Bahá'í scriptures. It would also involve an unexplained contradiction because of the different memberships and electoral methods for the Universal House of Justice and the institutions of world government.[35] Beyond this, however, I think that there are reasons in the text itself to believe that Shoghi Effendi did not intend any reference to the Universal House of Justice as a world government when he wrote this passage.

In the first sentence, the Faith attains the stage of becoming "the State Religion of an independent and Sovereign Power." What has changed in the second sentence? The Faith has become more widely accepted, and by a number of sovereign states, and the Universal House of Justice has come into being as the supreme institution of a Bahá'í Commonwealth. (Shoghi Effendi was writing in February 1929, before the Universal House of Justice existed.)

We should note that Shoghi Effendi differentiates consistently between the Bahá'í Commonwealth and a commonwealth of nations. The first refers to the believers in solidarity with one another, analogous to the Islamic *'umma*, or to Gibbon's use of the term "Christian commonwealth" to refer to the Christian community before the age of Constantine. The second refers to a commonwealth whose members are nations, united in an analogous, but political, bond of solidarity. The Universal House of Justice is said to be the supreme organ of the first, but never of the second. The Universal House of Justice has in fact been the "supreme organ of the Bahá'í Commonwealth" from the day it was first elected.

Now if Shoghi Effendi was intending to say that the Bahá'í administrative institutions should become the governments of nations, the decisive change in the role of the Universal House of Justice would come when a National Spiritual Assembly had become the government in one nation. But what is said is that the Faith will first become the state religion of one power and then, when more countries have Bahá'í majorities, the Universal House of Justice will come to exercise some function in the superstate. One might understand this to be the role of government, but it seems more logical, in the light of the progressive structure of the paragraph, to suppose that Shoghi Effendi expected us to understand that it would be the "State Religion." The Bahá'í Faith becomes the state religion first of one country, then of more, and finally the Universal House of Justice has rights, duties, and responsibilities in the world superstate because it is the supreme organ of the Bahá'í Commonwealth. This seems to imply that the Universal House of Justice occupies the position of an established religious institution at a global level, in relation to the separate institutions of world government.[36]

In relation to this passage, I would also like to caution against an attitude that leads readers to search the Writings diligently to find a single passage that can support a preestablished view, rather than examining the Writings as a whole to see what they say. We need to consider the broader implications of our readings of particular texts and always read them in the context of the body of Bahá'í scripture and interpretation.

In addition to reading our "problem text" in relation to the Writings of Bahá'u'lláh and 'Abdu'l-Bahá, we should also place this text from Shoghi Effendi alongside clearer texts by the same author. The first parallel text is found just two months earlier, in a letter dated December 6, 1928, and published in *Bahá'í Administration.* With regard to events in Persia, Shoghi Effendi then welcomed "the slow and hidden process of secularization" as one of the "symptoms that augur well for a future that is sure to witness the formal and complete separation of Church and State."[37] In passing, it should be noted that secularization means literally the withdrawal of religious institutions from the control of other social spheres, such as politics, economics, science, and law. But the word is often used to refer to the profanation or disenchantment of the world, to a society in which religion itself is irrelevant. These are two different processes, the first positive and the second negative. What Shoghi Effendi is welcoming is secularization in the first sense, the gradual demarcation of distinct spheres of religion and politics, reducing both interference by the Iranian government in matters of conscience and the political and judicial power of the Shí'í clergy.

The next passage is three years later, in the letter "The Golden Age of the Cause of Bahá'u'lláh," where he writes:

> Theirs is not the purpose, while endeavoring to conduct and perfect the administrative affairs of their Faith, to violate, under any circumstances, the provisions of their country's constitution, much less to allow the machinery of their administration to supersede the government of their respective countries.[38]

This is very strong: the "much less" construction seems to mean that allowing the Bahá'í administrative institutions to supersede national governments would be worse than a violation of the constitution. It certainly rules out the suggestion that the Bahá'í institutions could accept temporal power if it were freely offered to them. It does not seem unreasonable to assume that this passage should be read as correcting misunderstandings that had arisen from the passage in *The World Order of Bahá'u'lláh* that has been discussed above. We must at any rate recognize that it is the same Shoghi Effendi writing both pieces, and read the first in the light of the latter.

By 1936, in "The Unfoldment of World Civilization," Shoghi Effendi is describing the state mechanisms of a world commonwealth that is "sustained by its allegiance to one common Revelation,"[39] without even mentioning the existence of a Universal House of Justice (although religion is mentioned alongside other aspects of life, such as science, commerce, the media, etc.). And at about the same time he must have been selecting the tablets for inclusion in his 1939 translation, *Gleanings from the Writings of Bahá'u'lláh*, including the Lawh-i Ashraf (CII), Súriy-i Mulúk (CXVI), Lawh-i Maqsúd (CX), Lawh-i Nabíl-i A'zam (CXXXIX), and Lawh-i Dhabíh (CXV). This activity would be consonant with a concerted effort on his part, between 1932 and 1939, to make it clear to the Bahá'ís that the Bahá'í teachings do not permit any religious institutions to assume temporal power.

We have now dealt with the scriptural source, in *The World Order of Bahá'u'lláh*, which I believe is most likely to be responsible for sustaining theocratic ideas in the contemporary Bahá'í community. This is the only passage of authentic Bahá'í scripture that I know of which is open to a theocratic reading. But we have seen that such a reading would be inconsistent with the main lines of Bahá'í teachings, and with Shoghi Effendi's other writings, and that there are alternative ways to read it that do not produce problems of consistency.

The Promulgation of Universal Peace

Before passing on to discuss the type of argument which I have called dispensationalism, I would like to look at an earlier passage which might, in part, explain the popular Bahá'í beliefs on this topic. These are the words attributed to 'Abdu'l-Bahá in *The Promulgation of Universal Peace*, in which he appears to refer to the "House of Justice" as "the consummate union and blending of church and state."[40]

This might appear to be a very weak argument, put up only to be knocked down, since most Bahá'ís would be aware that reports of 'Abdu'l-Bahá's statements are not authentic Bahá'í scripture. Can they really have had any influence on Bahá'í thinking? A survey among Bahá'ís would be required to provide a clear answer, but it is striking to me that the only Bahá'í author using a theocratic model who cites any source to explain these beliefs, cites this one. This is Loni Bramson-Lerche, in her 1991 essay "An Analysis of the Bahá'í World Order Model."[41] Moreover one reviewer of an earlier version of this essay objected to my saying that this passage is not authentic, citing a letter on behalf of the Guardian which states that: "It is permissible to use selections from *The Promulgation of Universal Peace* in compilations."[42] It appears salutary, therefore, to review the standards by which we should judge the authenticity and degree of authority of words attributed to 'Abdu'l-Bahá, and also to look at the history of this particular phrase.

In a 1930 letter, the Guardian's secretary wrote on his behalf:

> The early translations are far from being accurate, no matter who the translator may be. Shoghi Effendi firmly believes that only Tablets with the Master's signature and in the original tongue should be recognised. Any translations or copies of them fail from having real authority.[43]

If this is true of translations of tablets, where the translator has at least had an authentic written copy from which to work, it is doubly true of ad hoc translations of 'Abdu'l-Baha's talks. In these situations, the interpreter has worked without preparation, and a note-taker has done his or her best to record the simultaneous translation. This record is no different in principle to table talks, where 'Abdu'l-Bahá would speak to pilgrims, an interpreter would do his best to convey his meaning, and the pilgrims would take notes.

As regards the reports of talks, the Guardian's secretary wrote in 1947 that: "Nothing can be considered scripture for which we do not have an original text. A verbatim record in Persian of His talks would of course be more reliable than one in English because He was not always accurately interpreted . . ."[44] 'Abdu'l-Baha himself, referring to these talks, speaks of "errors and deviations committed by previous interpreters."[45] Thus it goes against a very strong principle of Bahá'í hermeneutics to use such reports as a basis for defining Bahá'í law or belief.

If the original reports of these talks have a rather minimal status, analogous to pilgrim's notes, the revised versions of these reports in *The Promulgation of Universal Peace* and *Paris Talks* must be given an even lower status: they are often indicative of the editor's opinions rather than what 'Abdu'l-Bahá said. The passage in *The Promulgation of Universal Peace* in which 'Abdu'l-Bahá refers to the "House of Justice" as "the consummate union and blending of church and state" is a striking example of this. As Jennifer McNair pointed out on Talisman9 on 7 Jan 2001, this phrase is an editorial insertion into the English notes of the talk published in *Star of the West*, Vol. 4, no. 15 (December 12, 1913). The original reads:

> The eleventh teaching is the organization called, The House of Justice, which is endowed with a political as well as a religious aspect. It embodies both aspects, and it is protected by the Preserving Power of Baha'o'llah [sic] Himself.

In 1925 the editor of *The Promulgation of Universal Peace*, Howard MacNutt, revised this to read:

> He has ordained and established the House of Justice, which is endowed with a political as well as a religious function, the consummate union

> and blending of church and state. This institution is under the protecting power of Bahá'u'lláh Himself.

Thus the key phrase concerning "church and state" is a corruption of the text. The original continues:

> A Universal or World House of Justice shall be organized. That which it orders shall be the Truth in explaining the Commands of Baha'o'llah, and that which the House of Justice ordains concerning the Commands of Baha'o'llah shall be obeyed by all.

Which MacNutt revises to read:

> A universal, or international, House of Justice shall also be organized. Its rulings shall be in accordance with the commands and teachings of Bahá'u'lláh, and that which the Universal House of Justice ordains shall be obeyed by all mankind.

By removing the phrase "in explaining the Commands of Baha'o'-llah," MacNutt makes it appear that the Universal House of Justice has an unlimited authority, whereas the original says only that it has the authority to elucidate Bahá'í laws.

Howard MacNutt was taught the Faith in Ibrahim Kheirella's lessons, was appointed by him as the "teacher" for New York, and remained close to him for some time after Kheirella had split with 'Abdu'l-Bahá and broken the Covenant.[46] Kheirella's views of Bahá'í teachings were theocratic, owing more to Christian eschatology than the Bahá'í scripture. From notes taken during Kheirella's lessons,[47] we know that Kheirella taught in his eleventh lesson that Bahá'u'lláh's Tablets to the Rulers called on the rulers "to throw their kingdoms at his feet." In fact, it was only the Pope whom Bahá'u'lláh called upon to abandon his kingdom (and he was to pass it to the kings, not to Bahá'u'lláh).[48]

This suggests that at least one of the roots of theocratic belief in the Bahá'í community can be traced from Christian eschatology to Kheirella's teachings, through his Bahá'í students, and then—as a result of this remarkable exercise of editorial freedom by MacNutt—to an influential Bahá'í book. Once established as being "a Bahá'í teaching," the theocratic idea has been transmitted and sustained through deepenings and Bahá'í summer schools from which Bahá'í youth and new believers gain their understandings of the Faith (as illustrated, for example, in David Hofman's lectures on theocracy at the Maxwell Bahá'í School).[49]

I have made similar comparisons of the *Paris Talks* and *Star of the West* versions of other passages, in one case also with the Persian notes of the same talk. The same conclusions follow. These books should not be used except as handy references to locate the date of the talk in question, from which one can then locate the Persian notes (ideally) or the original notes of what the interpreter rendered of what 'Abdu'l-Bahá had said.[50] Any paper or book that uses either *The Promulgation of Universal Peace* or *Paris Talks* uncritically, as though these sources record the actual words of 'Abdu'l-Bahá, is not a work of rigorous scholarship and should be dismissed in any serious study of Bahá'í law or teaching. But, this is relatively easy. What will be difficult is the eradication of the ideas that have spread in this way through the Bahá'í secondary literature and through what is taught in summer schools and discussed in local community deepenings. An evaluation of the extent to which the Bahá'í secondary literature has relied on weak texts is sobering. We may have to question and revise a considerable part of what has been taken at a popular level in the Bahá'í community to be "the Bahá'í teachings."

Dispensationalism

Dispensationalism is a strategy for resolving the contradictions that arise from a theocratic reading of Bahá'í scripture, if one supposes that all of the Bahá'í teachings about religious and civil governance refer to the same institutions. It is a way of explaining away the many passages found in the Bahá'í writings which emphatically endorse the civil state and the project of human governance, and dismissing the texts that condemn the involvement of the political order in matters of religion or vice versa. Dispensationalism allows the reader to regard the Bahá'í teachings on civil government and on the Bahá'í administrative order as referring to two consecutive stages in future development, rather than to two different things. In effect, a temporal separation of church and state takes the place of a constitutional separation of church and state.

John Hatcher's treatment, in *The Arc of Ascent* (1994), can serve as a fairly recent example of the way these stages are envisioned:

> . . . for an indefinite period at the beginning of this process, the secular and sacred institutions will evolve separately . . . The final and complete stage in this process will occur when, through some process we can only imagine, the secular system of federated governance merges with the Bahá'í administrative order. This event will simultaneously signal the arrival of the Most Great Peace, the wedding of the bride with the bride-groom, the new heaven with the new earth, and the emergence of the Bahá'í Commonwealth as the Kingdom of God come on earth in all its plentitude.
>
> Perhaps as piece by piece the secular system comes to appreciate and emulate ever more completely the systems and procedures of the Bahá'í administrative order, the distinction between the two will eventually become so nebulous that it will be seen as unnecessary to maintain two systems . . . Yet it is clear in the Bahá'í writings . . . that this convergence will not produce a third entity from the two distinct systems, nor will the Bahá'í institutions become subsumed by secular governance.[51]

One interesting feature here is that power is transferred from the political federation of states to the Bahá'í administrative order by a peaceful transition, rather than through an apocalyptic upheaval. But without an apocalyptic change, how is the transition to be achieved? And why would it be desirable in any case? The theocratic premise, that the "Kingdom of God on earth" must mean that government power is exercised by the Bahá'í administrative order, is not substantiated in any way. But the Bahá'í writings quite plainly speak of the need to build up institutions of world governance and of national governance, institutions that are not the same as the Bahá'í administrative order. Does it make sense to build them up, if they are to be abolished?

In his book, Hatcher rejects two alternative ways of making the two systems one: the Bahá'í administrative institutions are not to be absorbed by the state, and the two are not to give way to a new creation. The third logical possibility is that the Bahá'í administrative institutions absorb the state, but Hatcher does not explore the implications of his line of reasoning. Nevertheless, if one concedes the premise that it is desirable for "the two systems to become one" (p. 282), this is all that remains, and we must suppose that this is what he intends us to deduce.

Hatcher himself touches on an alternative model when he uses the metaphor of the wedding of the bride and the bridegroom. But what happens after the wedding? The well-told story says that the couple lived together happily ever after, and not that one partner was swallowed by the other (unless the couple are praying manti!). There are forms of unity that do not require either that the parties become identical, or that one absorbs or imposes its will on the other. These forms of unity, known as "unity in diversity," "organic unity," "mystic union" and, more simply, "love" are expounded at length in the Bahá'í scriptures. Indeed, the Bahá'í revelation might be described as a midwife intended to aid the birth of social structures which transcend the unities of dominance and uniformity. On this point, Hatcher's Bahá'í world order model has been developed, not only without references to the Bahá'í writings, but also without referring to some of the finest and most characteristic of Bahá'í beliefs.

The Weakness of Dispenationalism

The first thing we should note about dispensationalism is that it is a seductively easy strategy for the interpreter to adopt. Any texts that do not fit can simply be wished away by supposing that they refer to an earlier stage and are therefore not the real Bahá'í ideal. The real Bahá'í ideal is the idea already in the interpreter's mind. We can see how this works in Loni Bramson-Lerche's paper "An Analysis of the Bahá'í World Order Model." She resolves some obvious contradictions in her model by dividing the period known as the Most Great Peace into one period governed by a world government characterized by a separation of powers (world legislature, executive, and judiciary), and a later period in which the Universal House of Justice is the supreme body. The way her interpretation is imposed onto the text is evident where she treats a well-known passage from Shoghi Effendi in "The Unfoldment of World Civilization" which begins:

> The unity of the human race, as envisaged by Bahá'u'lláh, implies the establishment of a world commonwealth . . . This commonwealth must, as far as we can visualize it, consist of a world legislature . . . [52]

In this passage, Shoghi Effendi envisions the institutions of world government and the glories of a world civilization in an idyllic future when war has ended, hatred is no more, and the world's "life is sustained by its universal recognition of one God and by its allegiance to one common Revelation." It does not contain any reference to the Universal House of Justice as a world government institution, or to National Spiritual Assemblies as national governments. Bramson-Lerche solves this problem by introducing this passage as Shoghi Effendi's "vision of a future Bahá'í world commonwealth, *at least in its early stages*."[53] But, there is nothing in the passage cited to suggest an early stage is intended. On the contrary, Shoghi Effendi says that the model he describes is "the goal towards which humanity . . . is moving" and that the institutions he outlines are to be established "once for all." The reference to early stages has been inserted to cover the gap between what Shoghi Effendi says and what the author proposes.

There is a similar clear use of the dispensationalist strategy in the 1980 edition of J. E. Esslemont's *Bahá'u'lláh and the New Era* (the fifth edition), in the section on "government."[54] It should be noted that this section bears no resemblance to Esslemont's original text or to his ideas. The whole passage is an editorial insertion, absent from the original text of the book. As such, it gives us a picture of what one group of Bahá'ís believed in the 1970s, when this edition was being prepared. Where Bramson-Lerche divides the Most Great Peace into two dispensations, the 1980 *Bahá'u'lláh and the New Era* supposes that the change in the Bahá'í teachings regarding government coincides with the change from the Lesser to the Most Great Peace.

The second weakness in the dispensational type of argument is that it supposes that quite central Bahá'í teachings may change over time. An observer would have every reason to ask, if the principles concerning government can change as the Bahá'í community takes its place in the world, what about those concerning tolerance and the treatment of minorities, or the equality of men and women?

The answer is that such a change is impossible. We have seen in the passage cited from Hatcher's *The Arc of Ascent* that he is unsure about how the world could move from the system of world federal government outlined in the Bahá'í writings to a system in which the Houses of Justice would take over the task of government. What would be the mechanism of transition? A coup is unthinkable, and even passive acceptance of a power "thrust upon them" is ruled out by Shoghi Effendi's dictum that Bahá'ís must not "*allow* the machinery of their administration to supersede the government of their respective countries."[55] Apart from the mechanics of change, where would the authority for change come from? The principles regarding the right of civil government are embedded in the sacred texts, including both the Kitáb-i Aqdas and the Kitáb-i 'Ahd, as well as the writings of 'Abdu'l-Bahá. The details of the institutions of the world federal government are explained by Shoghi Effendi, whose interpretations "become part of the sacred text." It is doctrinally impossible for any authority to arise within the Bahá'í community that could authorize us to abolish these institutions and change these principles, unless it be a new Manifestation of God. And that, according to Bahá'u'lláh will not happen "ere the expiration of a full thousand years."

These problems apply to dispensationalist thinking in general, and not just to the question of church and state. Wherever we see an author using it, we should immediately suspect that some element of the Bahá'í writings that does not fit the author's scheme is being swept under the rug of "earlier stages." However the illegitimate appeal to dispensationalist arguments should be distinguished from references to historical change as such. Shoghi Effendi for example refers to a historical process:

> . . . which will carry the steadily evolving Faith of Bahá'u'lláh through its present stages of obscurity, of repression, of emancipation and of recognition . . . to the stage of establishment . . . a stage which must later be followed by the emergence of the Bahá'í state itself, functioning, in all religious and civil matters, in strict accordance with the laws and ordinances of the Kitáb-i Aqdas . . . a stage which . . . will culminate in the establishment of the World Bahá'í Commonwealth, functioning in the plenitude of its powers, and which will signalize the long-awaited advent of the Christ-promised Kingdom of God on earth . . .[56]

Some have suggested that the existence of stages beyond that of establishment of the Faith as a state religion implies that the principles of the church-state relationship may also change. In other words, that a "Bahá'í state" is necessarily a theocratic state.[57] But what is this assumption based upon? Shoghi Effendi has defined the Bahá'í state here as one that functions in accordance with the laws of the Kitáb-i Aqdas, and that book states:

> [God] ordained you to be, *for all time*, the emblems of His sovereignty . . . It is not Our wish to lay hands on your kingdoms. Our mission is to seize and possess the hearts of men. Upon them the eyes of Bahá are fastened. To this testifieth the Kingdom of Names, could ye but comprehend it.[58]

The reference to the "Kingdom of Names" in the Aqdas passage indicates, I think, that this teaching reflects the innermost nature of the creation. I have already developed this line of argument in another article,[59] which also discusses the other references to kings, rulers, and democratic government in the Aqdas. Those arguments need not be repeated here. We can see that a theocratic state would be contrary to "the laws and ordinances of the Kitáb-i Aqdas," since the Aqdas endorses a civil state distinct from the religious order. Conversely, a Bahá'í state as Shoghi Effendi defines it could not be theocratic.

For the dispensationalist argument to be successful as a way of resolving a contradiction one must not only point to the existence of various stages, eras, and ages in the Bahá'í view of the future. One must also show that the relevant principle embodied in the initial state can be changed at the various subsequent stages, and furthermore demonstrate that the undesired outcome represents an earlier stage, and the desired outcome a later stage. The mere reference to stages of development is not helpful and explains nothing.

Two Sovereignties

In the particular case of the differentiation of political and religious orders (the separation of church and state), Bahá'u'lláh appears to have ruled out any change at all, even—it would seem—a change made by some future Manifestation of God. He writes:

> Give a hearing ear, O people, to that which I, in truth, say unto you. The one true God, exalted be His glory, *hath ever regarded*, and *will continue to regard*, the hearts of men as His own, His exclusive possession. All else, whether pertaining to land or sea, whether riches or glory, He

> hath bequeathed unto the Kings and rulers of the earth. *From the beginning that hath no beginning* the ensign proclaiming the words "He doeth whatsoever He willeth" hath been unfurled in all its splendor before His Manifestation. What mankind needeth in this day is obedience unto them that are in authority, and a faithful adherence to the cord of wisdom. The instruments which are essential to the immediate protection, the security and assurance of the human race have been entrusted to the hands, and lie in the grasp, of the governors of human society. This is the wish of God and His decree . . . [60]

> Out of the whole world He hath chosen for Himself the hearts of men . . . Thus hath it been ordained by the Fingers of Bahá, upon the Tablet of God's *irrevocable* decree . . . [61]

> Kings are the manifestations of the power . . . of God. Pray ye on their behalf. He hath invested them with the rulership of the earth and hath singled out the hearts of men as His Own domain. Conflict and contention are categorically forbidden in His Book. This is a decree of God in this Most Great Revelation. *It is divinely preserved from annulment* and is invested by Him with the splendor of His confirmation.[62]

Bahá'u'lláh not only refers to irrevocability in several of the verses that provide the mandate for civil government, but also, in the first of the passages above, states that this has always been God's will. We can see that this is not simply hyperbole from his use of quranic and New Testament passages to support his argument in Epistle to the Son of the Wolf. The biblical passages he uses are too well-known to require a full citation: "render to Caesar the things that are Caesar's" from the Gospels,[63] and two verses from Paul ". . . the powers that be are ordained of God," and "For he [the ruler] is the minister of God, a revenger to execute wrath upon him that doeth evil."[64] The verse from the Qur'an that Bahá'u'lláh uses is also a well known one: "Obey God and obey the Apostle, and those among you invested with authority."[65]

It appears then that Bahá'u'lláh considers that the distinction between the authority of religion and of human governance has always been part of the ancient Faith of God. In that case, we should classify the doctrine of the two sovereignties not as one of the social teachings revealed for the Bahá'í era, but rather as an essential spiritual teaching that may be reformulated by future Manifestations of God but cannot be annulled. It is, as C. S. Lewis would say, part of the "deep magic," a truth at the level of "God is Good," "love conquers all," or "do unto others."

The Challenge

We have seen that much of the secondary Bahá'í literature has assumed that a theocratic model of governance is the Bahá'í ideal, and that it is not at all clear what arguments and scriptural texts underlie this idea. The simplest of the challenges that face us is to draw out the reasonings that have led many Bahá'ís over several generations to champion an idea which is not supported by their own scriptures, and to lay these arguments to rest. We must also suppose that there may be other substantial areas of the Bahá'í teachings that we are still misinterpreting. This calls for a sustained and critical review of all that we think we know, as a community, about the Bahá'í Faith and the shape of the Bahá'í community. We need to develop a habit of relating every claim about the Bahá'í teachings to authentic scriptural sources.

A second challenge is to revise our attitudes to politics and to government institutions in the light of Bahá'u'lláh's unequivocal endorsement of the claims of human governance. We are called to full citizenship of this world and the next. We are not only to "know and worship" God, but also to "carry forward an ever advancing civilization."[66] Citizenship of this world involves duties that we cannot ethically leave to others. `Abdu'l-Bahá writes:

> Thou hast asked regarding the political affairs. In the United States it is necessary that the citizens shall take part in elections. This is a necessary matter and no excuse from it is possible. My object in telling the believers that they should not interfere in the affairs of government is this: That they should not make any trouble and that they should not move against the opinion of the government, but obedience to the laws and the administration of the commonwealth is necessary. Now, as the government of America is a republican form of government, it is necessary that all the citizens shall take part in the elections of officers and *take part in the affairs of the republic*.[67]

We are called to be genuine well-wishers of government.[68] This requires much more than simply not disobeying its laws. It demands active, responsible, and spiritual participation. We cannot indulge in sneering at politics from the sidelines. Since democracies depend on broad participation for survival, a consistent refusal to participate is a passive subversion of the governing system. But participation presents a real challenge: how can we participate as believing individuals, while respecting the separation of the religious and political orders? Where can we participate without becoming involved in divisive partisanship that might do more harm than good?[69]

Fortunately, we know that a democratic system depends at least as much on broad public participation in the institutions of civil society and non-partisan governmental institutions (quasi-non-governmental organisations and NGOs) as on participation in its party electoral system. We may concentrate for now on "civil society" politics, but these challenging questions will one day have to be addressed.

The Moral Weight of Theocratic Ideals

Thus far, I have treated Bahá'í theocracy as if it were simply a structure of incorrect ideas or bad readings of particular texts, as if it were part of the conceptual structure of the Faith and did not affect our experience of faith. But a greater challenge is, I think, for the Bahá'í community to examine itself—for example, in the mirror of the secondary Bahá'í literature—and ask whether its adhesion to these ideas does not have a moral weight as well. For instance, when we come across John Robarts writing that "the Bahá'í spiritual assemblies will be the local government and the national spiritual assemblies the national government,"[70] what sort of emotional picture do we form of the future? Is there not a certain satisfaction in contemplating our own eventual triumph? A bolstering of our sense of self-importance? And the possibility, perhaps, of indulging in survivalist fantasies, in which Bahá'ís reconstruct a ruined world and start anew? The ideas that we have, even in our daydreams, help to shape the people we become: ideas have a moral significance.

The contemporary world is hard to understand: globalization, individualization, and the differentiation of social spheres (politics, economics, science, religion) mean that more is demanded of each of us. There are conflicting claims, and the only place they can be resolved is within "the spirit of the true believer," as Shoghi Effendi said.[71] Is the hope of an ultimate reversion to a simpler, undifferentiated, premodern society a psychological crutch? Has the Faith, which should be a path leading the peoples of the world into the postmodern era, been made instead into a refuge where the Bahá'ís can shelter themselves from its demands?

Church and State in Contemporary Crises

Finally, and supposing that the other challenges can be met, the Bahá'ís face the challenge of bringing the Bahá'í teachings to the world. The relationship between the religious and political institutions of society is one of the oldest questions in human society. Yet it has taken particular and pressing forms in recent years, with divisive and even violent church-state conflicts in a variety of countries from Tibet to Algeria, Poland to Afghanistan.

The rise of political Islam in many countries has brought with it a questioning of whether the state, as a thing in itself, has any right to exist apart from the (true) religious community and its laws. The assertion that "the separation of church and state has no justification in Islamic teaching" is like a flag planted by Islamists to mark out the field on which the clash of civilizations will be fought. Few other doctrines can awaken such unanimous rejection among the inheritors of the "Western" liberal tradition (in East and West). Thus the separation of church and state becomes a slogan and an emblem for deeper anxieties and wider hopes. It is not a technical question for the constitutional lawyers, but a touchstone for how we see ourselves and how we view the world. It has often taken the form of a struggle between parties with differing visions of the nation and its future: Islamists versus the governments of Islamic countries, or Nativists versus globalizing elites. But this is not primarily a struggle between parties and factions, it is an historic struggle for an understanding wide enough to embrace the religious and the political aspects of our own natures.

For those who consider religion a superstitious vestigial organ, the problem of church and state is external. But for the believer, it is an intimate dilemma and, if it is not resolved, a pain in the heart. How can we say, as we must: "Sovereignty is God's," and *not* say: "Therefore politics, science, and economics fall under the control of religion"? The solution that I have found in the Bahá'í writings may be of interest to all believers, of whatever faith. For, I think, it shows that adherence to fundamental values derived from religion and faith does not entail a denial of the prerogatives of the state, of the dignity of statecraft, and of our duties to both. It is indeed possible to be a citizen of the city of God and of a modern nation too, providing one can establish that God so wills it. The question is how we can take this gift of Bahá'u'lláh to the world.

One of the attractions of Bahá'u'lláh's model to me is that it is beautiful—a dance of complementary pairs, rather than the totalitarianism of monist models or the artificiality of those secular models that seek to rule religion and culture out of the public sphere. If aesthetics is a valid argument in mathematics, it may certainly be admitted in theology. And if Bahá'ís were really to teach and explain this model to the world, perhaps its beauty would attract those who are torn between the unattractive option of a state that denies a role for faith, on the one hand, and the fear of a decline into theocracy on the other. Religion and the state can only be reconciled if they recognize and respect one another. While many states appear willing to enter into a partnership with organized religion where they consider it safe to do so, the Bahá'í Faith is the only religion I know of which has the unambiguous theological underpinnings that would enable religion to recognize the state as an expression of its own fundamental and unchangeable religious principles.

Notes

Sen McGlinn is a student of Persian and Islamic Studies at the University of Leiden, the Netherlands.

1. Bahá'u'lláh, Lawh-i Ashraf, in *Gleanings from the Writings of Bahá'u'lláh*, translated by Shoghi Effendi, second revised edition (Wilmette: Bahá'í Publishing Trust, 1939 [1976]) CII, pp. 206-207.
2. Unpublished, but available at www.bahai-library.org/unpubl.articles/church.html. A Dutch translation was published in *Vizier*, Vol. 34, no. 5/6 (1995) and Vol. 35, no. 1/2 (1996).
3. Theocracy is used in the specific sense of government by religious bodies.
4. See the bibliography. The Bahá'í literature available to me in the Netherlands is limited, but I believe the sample is fairly representative.
5. This last saving clause refers primarily to the various versions of Esslemont's *Bahá'u'lláh and the New Era*, which form an interesting study in themselves but have not been dealt with here for reasons of brevity.

6. See my review on H-Bahai Reviews at http://www2.h-net.msu.edu/~bahai/reviews/modrev.htm; and *Iranian Studies*, Vol. 32, no. 4 (1999) pp. 580-82.
7. Christopher Sprung, "Bahá'í Institutions and Human Governance" in *Law and International Order* (London, Bahá'í Publishing Trust, 1996) pp. 154-55.
8. *Directives of the Guardian*. Compiled by Gertrude Garrida (New Delhi: Bahá'í Publishing Trust, 1973) pp. 78-79.
9. *God Passes By* (Wilmette: Bahá'í Publishing Trust, 1944 [1974]) p. 321. Emphasis added.
10. Cf. *The Bahá'í World 1954-1963,* Vol. 13 (Haifa: Bahá'í World Centre, 1970) pp. 292-96. Fischer, Michael M. J. *Iran: from religious dispute to revolution* (Cambridge, Mass.: Harvard University Press, 1980). See pp. 186-87 and p. 275, note 16, citing *New York Times* (July 10, 1956, and July 17, 1956) p. 3; and the Tehran daily *Keyhan* (17 Mordad 1334/1956) p. 70.
11. Francesco Ficicchia, *Der Baha'ismus, Weltreligion der Zukunft?* (Stuttgart: Evangelische Zentralstelle für Weltanschauungsfragen, 1981). See "theokratie" in the index.

    D. MacEoin (under pseudonym of Daniel Easterman), *New Jerusalems, Reflections on Islam, fundamentalism and the Rushdie affair* (London: Harper Collins, 1992), see p. 184.

    William McElwee Miller, *The Baha'i Faith: Its history and teachings* (South Pasadena, Calif.: William Carey Library, 1974). See e.g., pp. 160, 290. Sayyid Ali Raza Naqavi, "Bábism and Bahá'ism: A study of their history and doctrines" *Islamic Studies*, Vol. XIV, no. 3 (1975) pp. 185-217, see especially pp. 205, 212.

    Margit Warburg, "Baha'i: A Religious Approach to Globalization," *Social Compass*, Vol 26, no. 1 (1999) pp. 47-56.
12. *The World Order of Bahá'u'lláh,* (Wilmette: Bahá'í Publishing Trust, second revised edition, 1974) pp. 6-7. Punctuation has been altered to match Shoghi Effendi's manuscript.
13. See, e.g., John Hatcher's treatment, in *The Arc of Ascent* (Oxford: George Ronald, 1994) pp. 281-82. (Also cited on page 60)
14. *The Law of Love Enshrined: Selected Essays* (Oxford: George Ronald, 1996) p. 176.
15. Likewise, the general population has very little idea of what economics and the economy is, or what politics and government is and how it works, as we can see from a series of movements ranging from anarchism and the "do away with money" idealism of the 1960s to the anti-globalization riots of recent times.
16. Shoghi Effendi, *The Advent of Divine Justice* (Wilmette: Bahá'í Publishing Trust, 1939 [1984]) p. 14. See also, *God Passes By*, Ch. 24.
17. *Messages to the Bahá'í World, 1950-1957* (Wilmette: Bahá'í Publishing Trust, 1958 [1971]) p. 155. (Also cited on p. 63)
18. Bahá'u'lláh, *The Kitáb-i-Íqán* (Wilmette: Bahá'í Publishing Trust, 1989) pp. 107-108.
19. Ibid., p. 125.
20. Translated in Shoghi Effendi, *The Promised Day is Come* (Wilmette: Bahá'í Publishing Trust, 1980) p. 20.

21. *Gleanings,* CXVI, p. 247.
22. Bahá'u'lláh, *The Kitáb-i-Aqdas* (Haifa: Bahá'í World Centre, 1992) extracts from K78 to K83.
23. K88 and K91-93 respectively.
24. Extract translated in Shoghi Effendi, *Proclamation of Bahá'u'lláh* (Wilmette: Bahá'í Publishing Trust, 1978) p. 85.
25. *Tablets of Bahá'u'lláh, revealed after the Kitáb-i-Aqdas*, translated by Habib Taherzadeh (Haifa: Bahá'í World Centre, 1978) pp. 92-93.
26. Translated by Shoghi Effendi, revised edition (Wilmette: Bahá'í Publishing Trust, 1979) pp. 89-92, see also pp. 30-31, 33, 104, 137.
27. *Gleanings*, CX, pp. 215-16.
28. For example in a letter to Nabíl-i A'zam, in *Gleanings*, CXXXIX, p. 304; Lawh-i Dhabih, in *Gleanings*, CXV, pp. 241-42; Kitáb-i 'Ahd, in *Tablets of Bahá'u'lláh,* pp. 220-21.
29. Undated passage translated in Cole, *Modernity and the Millenium* (New York: Columbia University Press, 1998) p. 35, citing *Iqtidarat va Chand Lawh-i Digar*, Tehran, n.d. A similar denial of any claim to world domination is found in the Tablet to Násiri'd-Dín Sháh, published in *The Bahá'í World 1930-1932*, Vol. 4 (Wilmette: Bahá'í Publishing Trust, 1933) p. 103, and in E. G. Browne, *A Traveller's Narrative* (Cambridge: Cambridge University Press, 1975 [reprint]) p. 396.
30. *Tablets of Bahá'u'lláh,* pp. 220-21. The relevant passage is included by 'Abdu'l-Bahá in his "Treatise on Leadership" and is cited on p. 52 of this essay.
31. 'Abdu'l-Bahá, *Risálih-ye Siyasiyyah* (Treatise on Leadership, La Politique), Persian text with English and French translations by Juan Cole and Hippolyte Dreyfus respectively. See http://h-net.msu.edu/~bahai/trans.htm. (Translations of Shayhki, Babi and Bahai Texts, Vol. 2, 1998).
32. Regarding the separation of church and state, in *The Secret of Divine Civilization*, pocket-sized edition (Wilmette: Bahá'í Publishing Trust, 1990), the point made at p. 37 concerning the "two potent forces" that uphold the state is obscured by the translation. The Persian is on p. 44 of the *Risáliy-i Madiniyyih* (Bahá'í-Verlag, 1984). The meaning of these "two forces" is explained at length by 'Abdu'l-Bahá in his *Risáliy-i Siyasiyyah*, (see the previous note) from which it is clear that what is translated here as "the legislative" (*tashriyy'ah*) refers to the function of the religious order in propagating and explaining the significance of religious law, while "the executive power" (*tanfídhiyyah*) refers to the function of government as such, and not simply to the executive as one arm of government in Western democracies. 'Abdu'l-Bahá also refers to these "two forces" in his *Will and Testament* (U.S., 1990 reprint, p. 15 and cited on p. 52 of this essay), where the parallelism makes it clear that by *tashriyy'ah*, in the Bahá'í case, he means the Universal House of Justice, and by *tanfídhiyyah* he means the government. In *A Traveller's Narrative* 'Abdu'l-Bahá states that the Bahá'ís "have no worldly object nor any concern with political matters. [Their aim] . . . is restricted to spiritual things and confined to matters of conscience; it has nothing to do with the affairs of government . . . " (U.S., 1980 edition, p. 86).

Regarding the complementary principle, that government should not interfere with the "consciences and beliefs of peoples," see, for example, *A Traveller's Narrative*, pp. 89-92.

33. Here Cole cites the published translation of the Kitáb-i 'Ahd in *Tablets of Baha'u'llah*, pp. 220-21.
34. *Will and Testament*, pp. 14-15.
35. We have details on the methods of election of the tribunal, the Universal House of Justice and the World Legislature, from which it is clear that these cannot be the same institutions.

As for the tribunal, when 'Abdu'l-Bahá wrote to the Central Organization for a Durable Peace at The Hague in 1919 he said "that the national assemblies of each country and nation—that is to say parliaments—should elect two or three persons . . . The number of these representatives should be in proportion to the number of inhabitants of that country. The election of these souls who are chosen by the national assembly, that is, the parliament, must be confirmed by the upper house, the congress and the cabinet and also by the president or monarch so these persons may be the elected ones of all the nation and the government. The Supreme Tribunal will be composed of these people, and all mankind will thus have a share therein, for every one of these delegates is fully representative of his nation . . . " (*Selections from the Writings of 'Abdu'l-Bahá*, p. 306, except that I have used the revised translation of this Tablet from the World Center in 1985, in which "men" has been changed to "persons.")

As for the legislature, Shoghi Effendi has said that the members of the legislature should be "elected by the people in their respective countries and whose election shall be confirmed by their respective governments." (*The World Order of Bahá'u'lláh*, pp. 40-41.) However Bahá'u'lláh says, in respect to the gathering which is to establish (and presumably maintain) world peace, that it would be "preferable and more fitting that the highly honored kings themselves should attend such an assembly." (*Epistle to the Son of the Wolf*, p. 31.) This looks rather like a two-chamber structure, with one chamber elected directly by the people and the other consisting of government representatives.

Regarding the election of the National Assemblies and the Universal House of Justice, on p. 84 of *Bahá'í Administration* (Wilmette, Bahá'í Publishing Trust, 1928 [1974]), Shoghi Effendi writes:

"Regarding the method to be adopted for the election of the National Spiritual Assemblies. . . . In one of His ['Abdu'l-Bahá's] earliest Tablets . . . addressed to a friend in Persia, the following is expressly recorded: 'At whatever time all the beloved of God in each country appoint their delegates, and these in turn elect their representatives, and these representatives elect a body, that body shall be regarded as the Supreme Baytu'l-'Adl (Universal House of Justice).' These words clearly indicate that a three-stage election has been provided by 'Abdu'l-Bahá for the formation of the International House of Justice, and as it is explicitly provided in His *Will and Testament* that the 'Secondary House of Justice (i.e., National Assemblies) must elect the members of the Universal One,' it is obvious that the members of the National Spiritual Assemblies will have to be indirectly elected by the body of the believers in their respective provinces."

36. Another plausible reading of this passage has recently been suggested by Juan Cole on an internet discussion list. (31 January 2001. Archives are available at Talisman9-subscribe@onelist.com.) He proposes that the passage means that it is incumbent upon the world's future super-state that the Universal House of Justice should exercise all the rights, duties, and responsibilities attendant upon the fact that the Universal House of Justice is the supreme organ of the Bahá'í commonwealth. The two readings produce the same result: mine supposes that Shoghi Effendi intended us to carry over the phrase "the State Religion" from the previous sentence.
37. *Bahá'í Administration* (New York: Bahá'í Publishing Committee, 1928 [1974]) p. 149.
38. *World Order of Bahá'u'lláh*, p. 66.
39. Ibid., p. 204
40. 'Abdu'l-Bahá: *The Promulgation of Universal Peace: Talks delivered by 'Abdu'l-Bahá during His visit to the United States and Canada in 1912,* Compiled by Howard MacNutt (Wilmette, Bahá'í Publishing Trust, 1922-1925 [1982]) p. 455.
41. Loni Bramson-Lerche, "An Analysis of the Bahá'í World Order Model," in Charles Lerche, ed., *Emergence, Dimensions of a New World Order*, (London: Bahá'í Publishing Trust, 1991) see p. 40.
42. Letter dated 30 August 1955, published in *Unfolding Destiny: The Messages from the Guardian of the Bahá'í Faith to the Bahá'ís of the British Isles* (London: Bahá'í Publishing Trust, 1981) p. 357.
43. *Unfolding Destiny*, p. 90.
44. *Unfolding Destiny*, p. 208.
45. *The Promulgation of Universal Peace*, p. xx.
46. R. Stockman, *The Bahá'í Faith in America*, Vol. 1 (Bahá'í Publishing Trust: Wilmette, 1985) pp. 125, 177. So far as I know, MacNutt had broken off contact with Kheirella long before the early 1920s, when he would have been editing the third part of *The Promulgation of Universal Peace*. There is no suggestion that the two were working in concert, simply that the ideas MacNutt inserts here are a logical extension of the teachings he had first learned from Kheirella two decades earlier.
47. E. G. Browne, *Materials for the Study of the Bábí Religion* (Cambridge University Press, 1918) p. 138.
48. *The Proclamation of Bahá'u'lláh*, p. 85.
49. Available on tape from Live Unity Productions, 23 Toronto St., Toronto, Ontario (www.liveunity.org).
50. Two exceptions can be noted, and there may well be others: each section of these books must be treated skeptically, but on its own merits. In *The Promulgation of Universal Peace*, the talk beginning on p. 44 has been retranslated by Amin Banani from the Persian notes for the 1982 edition. Although it remains a report, the fact that the notes were taken in Persian and

that the text has not been subjected to MacNutt's editing gives it a high degree of authenticity. In *Paris Talks*, there is one section beginning on p. 182 in which the original is a tablet written by 'Abdu'l-Bahá rather than a talk. The original in this case is authentic Bahá'í scripture, but the version in Paris Talks is a free interpretation of this by an editor, and has caused considerable misunderstanding in the community. The original English translation in this case is published in M. A. Sohrab, *'Abdu'l-Bahá in Egypt* (New York: New History Foundation, 1929) p. 249. (Although Sohrab later became a Covenant-breaker, this book was "approved by the Publishing Committee of the National Spiritual Assembly of the Bahá'ís of the United States and Canada").

51. *The Arc of Ascent,* pp. 281-82.
52. *World Order of Bahá'u'lláh,* pp. 203-204
53. L. Bramson-Lerche, "An Analysis," p. 35, emphasis added.
54. Pages 135-37.
55. It has been suggested to me that this dictum does not apply indefinitely, but only "while" the Bahá'ís are "endeavoring to conduct and perfect the administrative affairs of their Faith" (see the passage from *The World Order of Bahá'u'lláh* quoted above), and that this might be the basis of dispensationalist views. I have not seen any further explanation of when or why, according to this line of argument, the Bahá'ís might at some future date cease to "conduct and perfect the administrative affairs of their Faith," so those supporting this reading may have further arguments which need to be considered.
56. Shoghi Effendi, *Messages to the Bahá'í World,* p. 155.
57. These are the comments of the anonymous reviewer of an earlier draft of this paper.
58. K82-83, emphasis added; see also K78-83, 88, 91-93.
59. "A theology of the state from the Bahá'í writings," *Journal of Church and State*, Vol. 41 (1999) pp. 697-724.
60. *Gleanings,* CII. Emphasis added.
61. *Gleanings*, CXXX, p. 279.
62. Kitáb-i 'Ahd, in *Tablets of Baha'u'lláh*, pp. 220-21.
63. Matthew 22:15-22; Mark 12:13-17; Luke 20:20-26.
64. Romans 13:1 and 13:4.
65. Surah 4:62.
66. *Gleanings,* CIX.
67. *Tablets of Abdul-Baha Abbas* (New York: Bahá'í Publishing Committee, 1909, 1930; 3 vols. with consecutive page numbering) pp. 342-43, emphasis added.
68. *Gleanings,* XLIII; *Epistle to the Son of the Wolf* (Wilmette: Bahá'í Publishing Trust, 1988) pp. 122, 137; etc.
69. For that matter, is the party-based approach to politics always unhealthy? Perhaps there is an analogy to healthy competition in the economic sphere: neither a partisan nor a competitive approach would be healthy in the religious sphere, but religion—as we have seen—is not all. Since they are sepa-

rate spheres, politics, commerce, science, and religion may function according to different principles, and the system of political parties may be appropriate in the political sphere, as a means of institutionalizing input from various interests in society.

We have learned as Bahá'ís to participate in a competitive entrepreneurial economy, while being cautious to keep the commercial affairs of individuals separate from our Bahá'í community life. We do not use the Feast to promote our sales schemes or careers, or at least we should not. We should also be able to keep our individual political involvement distinct from Bahá'í community life.

70. John Robarts in *The Vision of Shoghi Effendi: Proceedings of the Association for Bahá'í Studies ninth annual conference, November 2-4, 1984* (Ottawa: Association for Bahá'í Studies, 1993) p. 174.
71. *Bahá'í Administration*, pp. 63-64.

Bibliography

An annotated bibliography of references relevant to the issue of church and state in Bahá'í secondary literature

Bausani, Alesandro. *Encyclopaedia of Islam*, second edition, article on "Bahais," 1958. This reference is discussed in the text of this essay.

Bramson-Lerche, Loni. "An Analysis of the Bahá'í World Order Model," in Charles Lerche, ed., *Emergence, Dimensions of a New World Order* (London: Bahá'í Publishing Trust, 1991) pp. 1-70. See my review published in *The Bahá'í Studies Review*, Vol. 3 (1993) pp. 87-92.

Cole, J. R I. "Iranian Millenarianism and Democratic Thought in the 19th Century," *Int. J. Middle East Stud.*, Vol. 24 (1992), and *Modernity and the Millennium: The Genesis of the Baha'i Faith in the Nineteenth-Century Middle East* (New York, Columbia University Press, 1998).

Dreyfus, Hippolyte. *Essai sur le Bahá'ísme; Son Histoire, Sa Portée Sociale*, 1st edition, 1909; 3rd edition, revised and enlarged (Paris: Presses Universitaires de France, 1962). See 1909 edition, p. 55. This may be one of the more influential of the works discussed, since it was translated into English. Dreyfus begins his chapter on the Bahá'í Faith and the State by saying that "The separation of church and state can only be temporary—a momentary stage in the march of societies" (p. 55, translation as cited by Rabbani, 1940, p. 5), but what he means is not that the state and religious orders will be collapsed into one "machinery," but that "the state will be religious; not that it must give to all its acts a mystical appearance, which could not be in keeping with their material object . . . But religion being put into practice in all acts of life, from the minister of state down to the humblest official, each one will be penetrated by the sacred character of his responsibility . . . " (Ibid). Dreyfus is writing quite particularly out of the situation in France at that time, when the widespread Roman Catholic support for the royalist cause on the one hand,

and anti-clerical feeling and a positivist philosophy among the leaders of the Third Republic on the other hand, had led to an extreme distrust of the political motives of French Catholics, to the extent of excluding practising Roman Catholics from senior posts in key ministries. The "separation of church and state," especially in the Combes government of 1902-1905, had almost come to mean that state institutions could not in any way accommodate either belief or believers. Dreyfus is not saying that societies will eventually revert to the situation in which church and state were not separate organs, or to a situation in which the prince decides and supervises the religion of his subjects. Rather he is saying that irreligion in public life is a side-effect of a particular stage in the evolution of the state, at which the state and religious orders must differentiate themselves one from another to make the development of the modern state possible, and to ensure freedom of conscience.

Esslemont, J. E. *Bahá'u'lláh and the New Era* first publication in 1923. Fifth revised edition (Wilmette, Bahá'í Publishing Trust, 1980, reprinted 1990) pp. 135-37. This section is entirely different to Esslemont's original and its ideas should not be attributed to him. Brief, vague and incoherent, this is nevertheless the most extensive and best grounded presentation of Bahá'í political teachings available in the current Bahá'í secondary literature. Unusually, it cites scriptural texts, but this has not been treated as a presentation of the scriptural basis for theocracy, because the reasoning by which the authors have proceeded from the texts to their conclusions is unclear.

Hatcher, J. *The Arc of Ascent: The Purpose of Physical Reality II* (Oxford: George Ronald, 1994) pp. 281-82. A dispensationalist approach, which having described the Bahá'í administrative institutions and the institutions of world federal government, then envisions that "The final and complete stage in this process will occur when, through some process we can only imagine, the secular system of federated governance merges with the Bahá'í administrative order." No references are provided.

Hatcher, J. S. and Hatcher, William S. *The Law of Love Enshrined: Selected Essays* (Oxford, George Ronald, 1996). Refers in passing to "a spiritually based society, essentially theocratic in form," as if the two are necessarily synonymous.

Hofman, David. *Commentary on the Will and Testament of 'Abdu'l-Bahá*, Fourth revised edition, (Oxford: George Ronald, 1943 [1982]) pp. 10-11. Hofman uses the term theocracy, but it is not clear from this passage whether he means a godly society, or a religious order that rules the state.

Hofman, David. *The Renewal of Civilization*, Revised edition (Oxford, George Ronald, 1945 [1972]) see Chapter 8. One interesting aspect of this chapter is that Hofman identifies Christ's saying "Render to Caesar the things that are Caesar's, and to God the things that are God's" as underlying the separation of church and state in Christian history and theory (which he calls a "schism," "from which Christendom has never recovered"). He seems unaware that this is precisely the biblical verse that Bahá'u'lláh, in *Epistle to the Son of the Wolf* (pp. 89-90) used and endorsed in upholding the theological legitimacy of the authority of the shah and other rulers. This endorsement in turn was cited by 'Abdu'l-Bahá and Shoghi Effendi in works that Hofman would certainly have known (e.g., in *The Promised Day Is Come*, p. 71). Moreover, Hofman claims that "in the World Order of Bahá'u'lláh there is no cleavage between religion and other human activities . . . there is no professional priesthood and no professional politics . . . " (pp. 121-22) although both Bahá'u'lláh and 'Abdu'l-Bahá do in fact assume that there will be professional politicians, from kings and heads of state to ministers and representatives of the people, and have written extensively to them and about them. This book has been widely used in the Bahá'í community: the passage I quoted comes from the fourth edition and at least the ninth printing. Each of these editions has presumably been approved by literature review boards. This suggests that Bahá'u'lláh's teachings, which endorse the principle of "render unto Ceasar" and the high rank and special responsibilities of "kings and rulers," have not been widely accepted in the Bahá'í community.

Holley, Horace, introduction to Shoghi Effendi's *World Order of Bahá'u'lláh*, and *Religion for Mankind* (Oxford: George Ronald, 1956 [1976]). Holley claims (p. vii) that the command, "Render unto God that which is of God, and unto Caesar that which is of Caesar," has been annulled by the law of the oneness of humanity revealed by Bahá'u'lláh. But Holley cannot have been ignorant of Bahá'u'lláh's citation and endorsement of this verse in *Epistle to the Son of the Wolf* (pp. 89-90).

Huddleston, John. *The Search for a Just Society* (Oxford: George Ronald, 1989). The Bahá'í administrative order is referred to as an "alternative system of government" (pp. 425, 426) which is to replace obsolete democratic institutions (pp. 425, 448) in a peaceful transition. He does not explain how he can interpret the development of democracy as one of the main steps towards "a just society" in his historical section, and call for a union of "progressive forces" who are committed to "a free society with a democratic form of government" (pp. 396, 399), while also advocating the abandonment of democracy in the future.

Kheiralla, Ibrahim. "Early Lessons in America," printed by Browne in *Materials for the Study of the Bábí Religion* (Cambridge: 1918); see especially the eleventh lesson. Kheiralla had a limited knowledge of Bahá'í writings and teachings, and draws mainly on millenialist readings of Biblical passages.

Moayed, Vafa. "La Separation des pouvoirs spirituel et temporel: une formule provisoire?" in *Valeurs Religieuses, Valeurs Laïques: Recherche d'une*

Éthique Üniversele, (Switzerland: Association Européenne Francophone pour les Études Bahá'íes [Recueil des Conférences], 1988). Although the entire article is devoted to the church and state question, it tells us little about why some Bahá'ís have believed in a theocratic order. He seems uncertain himself (p. 55). Moayed writes exclusively from a contemporary French perspective. By "separation" he means "separation as it is in France now," and so naturally concludes that this is a French phenomenon and a "provisional formula." He further says that "in a Bahá'í society, the domination of the spiritual over the temporal would be permanent and absolute . . . The Bahá'í Faith has a monist conception of human society." But nothing could be further from the truth: the Bahá'í writings present us with an organic conception of human society. The inadequacy of Moayed's paper reinforces the point made by Sprung, that the question of the Bahá'í attitude to the church-state relationship cannot be approached without first turning to the Bahá'í writings to form a clear idea of the theology of the state, and indeed of human society.

Rabbani, Hussein. "The Church and the World," *World Order*, Vol. 3 (1938) pp. 415-24, especially p. 419, and "Religion and Society: A Unified Society Requires Elimination of Conflict between Church and State," *World Order*, Vol. 6 (1940) pp. 1-8. In the first of these articles he recognizes that ours is a "highly . . . complicated social order," compared to that in which Jesus appeared (p. 421), but he nevertheless supposes that there cannot be more than one source of authority in modern society, and this should be "a Church which seeks to establish upon earth the Government of God, and thus usher in His Divine Kingdom." This "Church," it emerges, is the Bahá'í Administrative Order. Two years later he again addresses the issue. He mentions views such as his own previous views and also other views "that church and state—both being essential and divine in character—should stand on an equal basis." (p. 1) Since Hussein Rabbani was based in Haifa, and since the latter view is an accurate summary of Bahá'u'lláh's teachings as translated in *Gleanings*, one wonders whether Rabbani might have been discussing the question with his brother, Shoghi Effendi, in the intervening two years. If so, the discussions did not entirely convince him, because he declines to "enter into a detailed study of these different theories."

Remey, Charles. *The Bahá'í Teachings Regarding Worship* (1925), in "A series of twelve articles introductory . . . ," (New York: Bahá'í Publishing Committee, 1925) pp. 113-20. Remey does not argue for a theocratic model, but for a pious society, involving "not a union of church and State, but a union of religion and State." It is noteworthy that Remey's pamphlet was published in the same year as Howard MacNutt published his claim that the Universal House of Justice represents "the consummate union and blending of church and state." For other works of Remey on this topic see Chapter 8 of his *The Bahá'í Movement*, 1912 and his 1908 pamphlet, *The Message of Unity*.

Robarts, John in *The Vision of Shoghi Effendi: Proceedings of the Association for Bahá'í Studies Ninth Annual Conference, November 2-4, 1984* (Ottawa: Association for Bahá'í Studies, 1993). Robarts says that "the Bahá'í spiritual assemblies will be the local government and the national spiritual assemblies the national government" (p. 174). He bases himself here on his own shorthand notes of remarks made to him by Shoghi Effendi in 1955, but the words contradict what Shoghi Effendi had written in 1932: "Theirs is not the purpose, . . . to allow the machinery of their administration to supersede the government of their respective countries." (*The World Order of Bahá'u'lláh*, p. 66).

Ruhe, David. "Religion for Adults," *World Order*, Vol. 14, no. 8 (1948) pp. 253-57. Ruhe claims that the Bahá'í Faith "declares the need for fusion of church and state without equivocation" but does not provide any evidence that this is so.

Saiedi, Nader. *Logos and Civilization: Spirit, History and Order in the Writings of Bahá'u'lláh* (University Press of Maryland, 2000). Saiedi rejects theocratism, and the American model of a complete separation of church and state (p. 361), which he sometimes calls "modern" and "Western" rather than American. He also conflates the American model with "the complete separation of religion from public life," which is clearly incorrect. His model of the church-state relationship is of two "relatively autonomous" spheres that "constitute an organic, cooperative and interactive unity." (p. 364) Bahá'u'lláh, he says, called for the "interaction and cooperation of religious and political authorities." (p. 364) He presents some of the passages from the writings of Bahá'u'lláh that I have cited in the main text, and concludes "there is a contrast between dominion in the realm of the heart and dominion in the realm of the earth. The former is the sole interest of God and His Manifestation, while the latter has been entrusted to the kings and rulers of the world." (p. 367) As a presentation of Bahá'í teachings on church and state this is accurate and scripturally based. It is marred by the terminological confusions just mentioned and his habit of presenting his reading of Bahá'í teachings as a contrast to Cole's work (they are in fact almost identical) and in contrast to other social and political philosophies, using simplistic characterizations. The reader must be prepared to look past the polemical use of straw man arguments to those sections in which Saiedi engages with Bahá'u'lláh's own thought.

Sala, Emeric. "New Hope for Minority Peoples," *World Order*, Vol. 12, no. 8 (1946) pp. 267-68. Although it is not stated, it seems clear that Sala is assuming that the Bahá'í administrative order is also to be the temporal government of a Bahá'í state. He transfers the principles which govern the election and operation of the Bahá'í administrative order to the political order.

Shook, G. A. "A Divine Administrative Order," (Section V of "Youth in the Modern World"), *World Order*, Vol. 12, no. 6 (1946) pp. 180-85, especially pp. 181-83. A circular approach, gliding from a discussion of church government, where Shook has shown the Bahá'í model to be different from Christian models, to government per se, which his argument has not addressed at all. It appears, in fact, that it has not occurred to Shook that these might be two different things, either in the Christian past or in the future.

Sprung, Christopher. "Bahá'í Institutions and Human Governance" in *Law and International Order* (London: Bahá'í Publishing Trust, 1996). While he declines to come to any conclusions, Sprung's essay is useful in several respects. It recognizes that the church-state relationship in the Bahá'í world order model cannot be separated from the theology of the state in the Bahá'í writings, and it argues with reference to the Bahá'í writings. While he does not cite any of the many passages in Bahá'í scripture which mandate the civil state, this seems not to be a deliberate bias, since he does not use the absence of these texts to promote the contrary (theocratic) thesis. It seems more likely that the author was not familiar with the writings of Bahá'u'lláh and 'Abdu'l-Bahá on politics. Note that the statement concerning the separation of church and state which Sprung has quoted on pp. 158-59 is not from the Guardian, as he claims there. In note 5, p. 164, Sprung correctly attributes this passage to the National Spiritual Assembly of the United States (1937), but then claims that it was approved by the Guardian in 1935. From the dates, and the fact that the 1937 NSA statement cites the 1935 letter from the Guardian, this is impossible. He also relies, with some reservations, on the words "consummate blending of church and state" attributed to 'Abdu'l-Bahá in *The Promulgation of Universal Peace*, which have been discussed in the main text. Sprung does not define the term "Commonwealth," which he seems to think is a sort of state but refers to at one point (p. 159) as a "world society."

Taherzadeh, Adib. *The Revelation of Bahá'u'lláh* (Oxford: George Ronald, 4 vols., 1974, 1975) see Vol. 3, p. 314. This is a dispensationalist approach, in which the world federal system is only an interim stage pending the maturation of the Faith. However Shoghi Effendi, in *The World Order of Bahá'u'lláh*, provides a vision of the world federal machinery which which he says must be established "once for all" (p. 202) and which does not include the Universal House of Justice.

Townshend, George. *Christ and Bahá'u'lláh* (London: George Ronald, 1957 edition) pp. 100-101. For Townshend, Shoghi Effendi is "the nearest approach on earth to the Divine exaltation" and fulfills the prophecy of Isaiah 9: 6: "For unto us a child is born, unto us a son is given: and the government shall be upon his shoulder: and his name shall be called Wonderful, Counsellor, The mighty God, The everlasting Father, The Prince of Peace." The relevant passage has been changed in later editions of the book.

Bahá'í World Center

PRAYING NEAR THE SHRINE OF THE BÁB
Haifa, Israel

Prayer As Remembrance

Christopher White

This essay attempts to describe practices of Bahá'í prayer in a way that will help both Bahá'ís and scholars of religion better understand and interpret these practices. I begin by borrowing from the Bahá'í scriptures what appears to be an important way of talking about Bahá'í prayer: that is, prayer is a process of "remembering." I then move on to an extended reflection on prayer as "remembrance," examining several ways that understanding Bahá'í prayer as remembrance might help interpreters of Bahá'í worship better understand Bahá'í conceptions of God, human nature, and the divine-human relationship. I suggest that prayer in the Bahá'í tradition is a process of first understanding and then overcoming the problematic gap between the human and divine worlds. In the final part of the paper, I point out that the obligatory prayers can be understood as a particularly efficacious practice of (literally) "re-membering" self, God, and the divine-human relationship. Obligatory prayers are, in Bahá'í language, of "special potency and significance" because they enlist both mind and body in a discipline of remembering.

It is almost impossible to overstate the importance of prayer to the Bahá'í tradition. While the requirements for prayer and other forms of worship are somewhat relaxed in comparison with the Islamic and the

Bábí traditions, the Bahá'í religion upholds prayer and meditation as "the best of all [human] conditions," as the source of the "spiritual nourishment" needed for individual and social progress and, because all human beings have been created to "know and love" God, as one of the main ways to fulfill the purpose of human life.[1] It comes as no surprise that daily prayer is required of all Bahá'ís, who, more specifically, have been told to recite "the verses of God every morn and eventide."[2] Though Bahá'ís can worship together in groups if they wish, there is only one prescribed congregational prayer (the prayer for the dead); prayer is generally considered an individual affair. Even the obligatory prayer (*salát*), considered by Muslims to be more meritorious when said in congregation, is generally performed by Bahá'ís in private, perhaps because it is in private that individuals can give their "best attention to the remembrance of God."[3] In general, then, Bahá'í teachings dwell on the interior aspects of praying—that is, on the importance of proper inner attitudes and dispositions. Human beings should pray to God because they want to express their love for him or want to know and understand him and his purpose for their lives, not because they fear his wrath or crave his grace. Prayer is about remaking one's self, not reorienting God.

Bahá'ís pray every day because they believe prayer brings them closer to the source of all life. Like adherents of most other religions, Bahá'ís pray in order to overcome—if only temporarily—the gap between the divine and human worlds, between Creator and created. In the Bahá'í scriptures this problematic gap often is glossed simply as a "separation" from God. Themes of separation and reunion, of estrangement and reconciliation with God, are conspicuous in Bahá'u'lláh's prayers and in his more mystical writings. At first glance, the separation between us and God does not seem too great: God is closer to the human reality, Bahá'u'lláh writes in a well-known passage, than the jugular vein.[4] In another passage Bahá'u'lláh confirms that God is closer than we might think: "Turn thy sight unto thyself," he says, "and you will find Me standing within thee, mighty, powerful and self-subsisting."[5] Moreover, while spiritual seekers may not find belief easy or instantaneous, Bahá'u'lláh assures us that the sincere will be aided in their search for God by that God-given "trust" which instinctively yearns for its Creator, the human heart.[6] Human beings, we might say, are hardwired for God.[7]

This is not, unfortunately, the whole story. God is not simply resident within us, easy to perceive, to know, and to love. The immanent God of the Bahá'í scriptures has a transcendent side to be sure: God is "immeasurably exalted," Bahá'u'lláh repeatedly stresses, "above all created things"—so much so in fact that, in the final analysis, God's reality can never be known by human beings. Bahá'u'lláh describes God's remoteness concisely: "Every way" to the adequate comprehension of God and his creative word "is barred."[8] At this point, the gap between Creator and created suddenly appears more problematic. How is it that God can be both immanent in the human heart and hidden, distant, and unknown? Why is it that, in Bahá'u'lláh's words: "At all times I am near unto thee, but thou art ever far from Me"?[9]

The paradox of a God who is both astonishingly near and frustratingly hidden is expressed in Bahá'í prayers in language that returns our attention to what it means to be human. As it turns out, the human heart, that "seat of the All-Merciful," also has one quite grievous shortcoming: it has a short memory. All too often it is, Bahá'u'lláh confirms with apparent regret, "forgetful of its Creator."[10] Here then is the reason that the God who has his home within us seems so far away: we have forgotten he is there. We have forgotten our closeness to him. Overcoming this forgetfulness, I will argue, is the main task of Bahá'í prayer.[11] Stated more positively, the purpose of Bahá'í prayer is to "remember."

While there are several reasons to think about Bahá'í prayer as remembrance or remembering, the best reason to do so is simply that Bahá'í prayers themselves describe worship in this way. Bahá'u'lláh's prayers are loaded with words like "remembrance" and "forgetfulness." To take one suggestive example, in *Prayers and Meditations* by Bahá'u'lláh, "remember" and "forget" and their variants appear 110 times in the prayers translated there by Shoghi Effendi.[12] Reading from this collection, worshippers can affirm that God's "remembrance" is their companion in times of loneliness, their healer in times of sickness, their succor in times of anxiety or sadness.[13] It comes as no surprise then that believers might ask God to help them "remember him," "at all times and under all conditions," hoping, in the words of another prayer, that their hearts would be remade into "a receptacle of Thy love and of remembrance of Thee."[14] Of course, remaking one's heart into a place that contains "naught except the treasures of [God's] remembrance and praise" requires hard work and, quite possibly, good role models.[15] Fortunately, the prayers in this same collection speak of spiritual heroes worthy of imitation—faithful believers whose hearts "were so carried away by the sweet savors of Thine inspiration that every single member of their bodies intoned Thy praise and vibrated to Thy remembrance"—and villains who, despite God's lamentations, had "forgotten the wonders of [his] mercy."[16] Bahá'ís really moved by the spirit of these prayers might also promise that "nothing whatsoever" would withhold them from "remembering" God, "though all the tribulations of the earth were to assault [them] from every direction."[17] In general, this collection of prayers leaves little doubt about the importance of "remembering."

The word translated as "remember" or alternately "mention" of God is the Persian (and Arabic) term *dhikr*, a word well known to scholars of Islamic mysticism. For Muslim mystics or Sufis, *dhikr* stands for a range of spiritual practices intended to put believers in a constant state of divine awareness. *Dhikr* practices vary considerably, depending on the particular beliefs and practices of each Sufi order. In some orders, novices learn and repeat different formulae of divine names, until, in Annemarie Schimmel's words, the *dhikr* so permeates the student's being that he or she forgets everything else but God.[18] *Dhikr* can be performed silently (*dhikr* of the heart) or out loud (*dhikr* of the tongue), in public and in private. God should be remembered at all times and in all places, for the believer who "remembers God permanently is the true companion of God."[19] *Dhikr* also can involve chanting, singing, dancing and—yes—even getting drunk. While it is safe to say that Bahá'u'lláh rejected this latter method of "remembrance," recent commentators have debated the extent to which Bábís and early Bahá'ís followed other Sufi *dhikr* practices like repetitive chanting.[20] My sense is that while many, if not most, of the specific Sufi *dhikr* practices were rejected or simplified in Bahá'u'lláh's writings, Bahá'u'lláh does retain the word *dhikr* to describe the process (perhaps it is better to say the discipline) of worship. The question is why? Why is prayer a discipline of remembering? Who or what are we remembering in prayer?

There are several meanings of "remember" as it is used in Bahá'í prayers, many of which I cannot explore here. My brief review of Sufi *dhikr* reminds us of one of them: that remembrance of God is about repeatedly calling God to mind, praying to him, mentioning his names. We remember God in this sense when, as is the case in the short obligatory prayer, we speak of him as mighty, wealthy, helpful, and self-subsisting. In the medium and long obligatory prayers we call to mind and also physically enact God's sovereignty, his mercy, and his greatness through coordinated verses and postures. By the end of any of the obligatory prayers, worshippers know their God and have called him to mind several times. They have also remembered their own place in the universe; God is mighty and humans are by comparison powerless, God is wealthy and humans are impoverished, God is helpful and forgiving, and humans are the recipients of that assistance, forgiveness, and love. So remembrance of God on one level is simply calling God to mind and trying to live with an awareness of that knowledge.

There may be other, less apparent meanings of "remembrance" however. What if prayer actually is about remembering a kinship to God that we once knew but have since forgotten? In a passage reminiscent of the Platonic tradition, Bahá'u'lláh asks all of us: "Have you forgotten that true and radiant morn when in these hallowed and blessed surroundings ye were all gathered in My presence beneath the shade of the tree of life, which is planted in the all-glorious paradise?" As if anticipating our response—yes, we did indeed forget—he continues to recall a very distant past that few of us could claim to remember:

> Awestruck ye listened as I gave utterance to these three most holy words: O friends! Prefer not your will to Mine, never desire that which I have not desired for you, and approach Me not with lifeless hearts, defiled with worldly desires and cravings. Would ye but sanctify your souls, ye would at this present hour recall that place and those surroundings, and the truth of My utterance should be made evident unto all of you.[21]

Whether we interpret this passage as a literal account of our beginnings or merely a metaphor of our kinship to God, the language of remembering and forgetting is striking. We are asked to remember that in a time before time (*illo tempore*) when, upon gathering us together in "paradise," God whispered to us the secrets of life. Is this passage, and indeed all scripture, intended as a kind of mnemonic device? Is it intended to jog our memories, encouraging us to "sanctify our souls" in order to recall our "true and radiant" origins and our kinship with God? Other scriptures make it clear that the passage of time and our own absorption in the "changes and chances" of the contingent world have indeed left us forgetful of the deepest truths about self and God. "The True One possesseth invisible worlds," 'Abdu'l-Bahá explains, worlds which can be sensed only if we "purify and clarify" our "spiritual nostrils from every worldly moisture."[22] This is not the only time the Bahá'í scriptures instruct believers to purify their hearts and minds in order to remember a long-forgotten meeting with God.[23]

This passage also reminds us that while "the world" is not bad *per se* (only undue attention to it is considered blameworthy), it does force upon us one thing that unfailingly separates us from our creator: time. Time makes forgetfulness possible. "In the sight of God the past, the present and the future are all one and the same," 'Abdu'l-Bahá explains, "whereas, relative to man, the past is gone and forgotten, the present is fleeting, and the future is within the realm of hope."[24] While for God all contracts and covenants made with human beings in the contingent world exist simultaneously, for human beings these same events drift out of consciousness into that "gone and forgotten" past, that wastebasket of experiences that are never repeated, called to mind, or otherwise strengthened in memory. Only in moments of sanctification and prayerful remembrance are we able to escape a consciousness of time. The daily practice of prayer, however, reminds us of the spiritual truths forgotten in a lifetime (or, for that matter, in a day) by strengthening our memory of God and his teachings through practice and repetition. In this way, remembering collapses time, making us, as a result, more God-like. (For, isn't God in a constant state of remembrance?) "Remembrance of Thee is eternal," Bahá'u'lláh proclaims;[25] remembrance overcomes our embeddedness in time by returning us to a consciousness of events, ideas, and values that endure.

Searching for God in memory is, of course, nothing new. For Plato and other classical thinkers, the search for truth involved "recollecting the world of primordial forms which the soul had contemplated in between this and its previous earthly existence." "Contemplative knowledge was pure and perfect, but the reincarnated soul drank from the spring of Lethe and forgot the knowledge it had obtained from direct contemplation of the Ideas." Here, learning rather than worship is recollection of "the real, the archaic forms, the transpersonal and eternal truths."[26] Much later, a young Christian bishop struggling to find himself turned inward and in the process made famous the connections between memory, identity, and God. "Ascending by steps to him who made me," Augustine writes in his autobiographical *Confessions*, "I come into the fields and spacious palaces of my memory." In memory this fourth-century thinker found his true self and his God, both of them "various," "manifold," and "immense."[27] For their part, Muslim thinkers have exfoliated the connections between memory and divine knowledge in countless theological and mystical works—so much so that one recent commentator has claimed that the duty of human beings in Islam "is simply to 'remember' (*dhikr*)."[28]

Taking their cue from mystics and theologians, a number of contemporary scholars of religion have begun examining exactly how memory functions for individuals and societies. Lawrence Sullivan recently has pointed out that forgetfulness usually leads to negative consequences: forgetfulness can cause disorientation, broken relationships, and a fractured sense of self. We can see how this might be the case, e.g., with someone afflicted with memory loss or Alzheimer's disease in old age. Without memories sustaining the web of relationships that bind us to others and to our community, our sense of identity unravels. On a communal level, societies recognize the importance of memory by memorializing historical events in ritual, art, and culture. Paul Connerton points out for this reason that religion and society are themselves forms of memory.[29] Examples are legion: Societies memorialize personalities in statues and art, commemorate defining battles by reenacting them, and remember founding principles by institutionalizing them in their legal and judicial systems. Religions memorialize key events and personalities in similar ways. The Christian Eucharist is a good example of this, though there are many others. At communion, each Christian remembers Jesus's archetypal sacrifice by actually partaking of that sacrifice—that is, by eating Jesus's body and drinking his blood. Through this act, each Christian not only remembers Christ's sacrifice but comes to understand its relation to their lives: Christ died so we could live. This ritual places the individual Christian life into a wider context of meaning and, in the process, life in the present takes on the meanings of the past. Like the Christian Eucharist, Bahá'í worship practices connect believers with the wider meanings of their religion. Performing Bahá'í prayers gives believers a basic map of the world and reveals how they fit into it.

Probably no other Bahá'í prayer sets up this basic "map" of the world better than the obligatory prayers, prayers which, according to Bahá'í scriptures, are "by their very nature of greater effectiveness" and "endowed with a greater power than the non-obligatory ones."[30] Unlike all other Bahá'í prayers, these prayers of "special potency and significance" coordinate bodily postures and prescribed verses in a discipline of attentiveness that involves both mind and body. These are the only prayers that come with specific instructions about how and when to perform them. (In other words, these are the only prayers with what we could call ritual requirements.) They typically are recited by individual Bahá'ís on a daily basis; they must be preceded by ablutions, or ritual washings of hands and face; they must be said at prescribed times; and they must be said while facing Bahjí, the place in Israel where Bahá'u'lláh is interred. Unlike other Bahá'í prayers, the obligatory prayers also incorporate bodily postures and gestures. Believers wash their hands and faces while asking God to purify their bodies and minds, believers bow to the ground while affirming God's sovereignty, believers stand with raised arms and entreat God to see and hear their prayers.

This carefully prescribed prayer environment is, as I have said, unusually powerful: "Through such prayer," 'Abdu'l-Bahá explains, "man holdeth communion with God . . . converseth with the true Beloved of one's heart, and attaineth spiritual stations."[31] Unfortunately, other than this short explanation of the power of the obligatory prayers and 'Abdu'l-Bahá's mysterious comment that "in every word and movement of the obligatory prayer there are allusions, mysteries and a wisdom that man is unable to comprehend,"[32] we know little about the obligatory prayers. Why are they "by their very nature of greater effectiveness"? What are the "allusions" and "mysteries" that are enshrined in their "every word and movement"?

Though I may be rushing in where angels fear to tread, I would like to spend the remainder of this essay trying to unpack the meanings and significance of these singular prayers. I would propose first that when prayers are practiced, instead of merely spoken, they are more easily understood and reflected upon. Then I will argue, returning to my theme of remembrance, that the obligatory prayers are more efficacious than other Bahá'í prayers because, unlike other prayers, they enlist both body and mind in a discipline of remembrance.

In the obligatory prayers, bodily postures and gestures express and reinforce inner attitudes. For example, a believer's sense of humility in the face of the mystery of God is symbolized in a bow to the floor; a desire to purify oneself spiritually is translated into ritual washings of hands and face; an anticipation of God's help is transformed into expectant gazes and raised hands. To be sure, enacting our beliefs somehow makes them more real: humility, submission, love, praise—all are observed visually, experienced bodily, and processed cognitively in the obligatory prayers.

In a way, all inner dispositions are iconographically displayed in the postures of the obligatory prayers in such a way that they can be critically reflected upon. Observing themselves with hands raised in supplication, believers might question the depth of their dependence on God. Do I need God enough to raise my hands to him and ask for his help? Do I feel inside the love I am expressing outwardly? There is a certain complementarity to thought and action in these prayers: bodily postures can express, reinforce, and even challenge inner attitudes, and vice-versa. Perhaps this is what Shoghi Effendi meant when he pointed out that the movements of the obligatory prayers help believers "fully concentrate when praying and meditating."[33] In these prayers, attitudes and actions, words and deeds, harmonize to become, in 'Abdu'l-Bahá's words, a "beautiful prayer."

The body is not passive in this process. On the contrary, I would argue that the body can actually determine what is learned, felt, or remembered while praying the obligatory prayers. Evidence for this claim comes from several sources. First of all, Bahá'í scriptures themselves repeatedly point out the connections between outer behaviors and inner dispositions. 'Abdu'l-Bahá points out in several passages that the body (or more generally, the material world) can dramatically influence the life of the spirit. "The eye sees; the heart is affected. The ear hears; the spirit is influenced. The heart is at rest; the thoughts become serene, and for all the members of man's body a pleasant condition is realized." In short, the sensations of the body affect the spirit.[34] In another passage that seems to corroborate this point, Shoghi Effendi points out that the "mystic *feeling* which unites man with God" is principally "brought about and maintained by means of meditation and prayer."[35] In other words, outer acts of worship do not just express inner attitudes of devotion—they cultivate these attitudes.

Applying this argument to the obligatory prayers, I would argue that the act of bowing one's forehead to the ground actually creates a sense of humility; that the act of washing one's face and hands actually creates a feeling of inner purity; that raising one's hands to God actually creates a sense of expectation. This may seem an odd or counter-intuitive conclusion, especially for those of us living in cultures that distinguish sharply between mind and matter, and identify spirituality only with the former. Nevertheless, that seems to be the conclusion suggested by the Bahá'í scriptures and, for that matter, by a great deal of corroborating literature in the social sciences beginning with the James-Lange theory of emotions.[36] An important implication of my conclusion here is that people who would like to believe—people who would like to feel a love for God but do not—can pray with the hope that the act of praying itself will bring about belief. Those interested in exploring the question of God or belief in him might experiment with prayer.

In addition to expressing, creating, and sustaining inner dispositions, the body is accomplishing something else in the obligatory prayers—it is remembering. Remembering the words and meanings of the obligatory prayers takes place on a bodily level as physical postures and gestures are associated with certain attitudes and dispositions towards God. As the body sits, as it stands, as it drops to the ground, or raises its hands, it calls to mind the verses and inner dispositions associated with these postures. The body, in other words, becomes a mnemonic device. In the long obligatory prayer for example, the believer stands, gazes to the right and the left "as if awaiting the mercy of his Lord" and invokes God by saying "O Thou Who art the Lord of all names and the Maker of the heavens!" After several more verses, the believer raises both hands and supplicates God with more prescribed verses. Then the believer kneels, bows with head to the ground and recites: "Exalted art Thou above the description of anyone save Thyself . . . "[37] The series continues—a different verse is associated with each posture. When the prayer is repeated, the body and its postures and gestures help cue in memory the appropriate verses and their meanings. In several cultures around the world, novices memorize their own traditions and scriptures in a similar way—that is, by associating them with head or body positions.[38]

Scholars who have studied how peoples and cultures remember their traditions have argued recently that the body itself has an ability to remember and know. Paul Connerton and Tom Kasulis have observed that habitual bodily activities, like typing for instance, remain a kind of knowledge and memory in the body. We remember how to type when we sit at the keypad not because we think about "the place of each letter among the keys," but because our bodies have a "knowledge bred of familiarity in our lived space."[39] In other words, our fingers know where the letters are without us having to "think" about where they are. Many examples could be chosen to illustrate how the body learns and remembers through habitual activity. Playing tennis, playing a musical instrument, driving a car—all involve the body in a kind of embodied knowing and remembering that is made possible by habitual activity. This is also a type of memory that is particularly robust. Every culture, Connerton writes, "will entrust to bodily automatisms the values and categories which they are most anxious to conserve. They will know how well the past can be kept in mind by a habitual memory sedimented in the body."[40] Borrowing Connerton's language, we might say that the "bodily automatisms," or the coordinated postures and verses of the obligatory prayers, are "sedimenting" some of the most important values of the Bahá'í religion in each worshipper's body. This is, to be sure, a powerful type of "remembering."[41]

The "bodily automatisms" of prayer can be just that—mindless rituals. And they can be seen as such by scholars. But they also can be read as those actions that incarnate Bahá'í principles, translating ideas into actions in ways that protect them from the forgetting that invariably comes with the passage of time. Human absorption in the "changes and chances" of the world, as I have suggested, can leave us forgetful of our true origins in, and with, God. Once recalled in prayer and scripture however, knowledge of our kinship to God has the potential to remake us in the present: by rehearing Bahá'í ideals in our mind and enacting them with our bodies, Bahá'í worship practices literally transform us into those ideals. In the end, then, prayer is not about remaking God but remaking—actually, "re-membering"—the human self. Prayer reconstitutes the self as a self-in-God. In the obligatory prayers, as we have seen, this discipline finds its most powerful form, for here body and mind, gesture and word, recreate the whole person in God's image.

Notes

Christopher White has Master's degrees and a Ph.D. from Harvard University where he currently teaches history and religion.

1. 'Abdu'l-Bahá, *Selections from the Writings of 'Abdu'l-Bahá* (Haifa: Bahá'í World Centre, 1978) p. 202; Shoghi Effendi, *Directives from the Guardian* (New Delhi: Bahá'í Publishing Trust, 1973) pp. 86-87.
2. Bahá'u'lláh, *The Kitab-i-Aqdás: The Most Holy Book* (Haifa: Bahá'í World Centre, 1992) p. 73.
3. The Báb, *Selections from the Writings of the Báb* (Haifa: Bahá'í World Centre, 1976) pp. 93-94.
4. See Bahá'u'lláh, *Gleanings from the Writings of Bahá'u'lláh* (Wilmette: Bahá'í Publishing Trust, 1994) p. 185. The passage reads: "Considering what God hath revealed, that 'We are closer to man than his life-vein,' the poet hath, in allusion to this verse, stated that, though the revelation of my Best-Beloved hath so permeated my being that He is closer to me than my life-vein, yet, notwithstanding my certitude of its reality and my recognition of my station, I am still so far removed from Him." For the quranic verse, see Sura 50:16.
5. Bahá'u'lláh, *The Hidden Words* (Wilmette: Bahá'í Publishing Trust, 1990) p. 7.
6. Ibid., pp. 6, 17. Elsewhere in the Bahá'í writings the human capacity to know and love God is associated with the "soul," as seems to be the case in Bahá'u'lláh, *Gleanings,* pp. 158-59: "Know, verily, that the soul is a sign of God, a heavenly gem . . . It is the first among all created things to declare the excellence of its Creator, the first to recognize His glory, to cleave to His truth, and to bow down in adoration before Him." "Soul" and "heart" seem to be used synonymously in the Bahá'í scriptures.
7. This is not a new idea. For centuries, Christian theologians and Muslim mystics (particularly Sufis such as Rumi and Attar) have spoken of an inborn capacity to know God.
8. Bahá'u'lláh, *Gleanings*, p. 4.

9. Bahá'u'lláh, *The Hidden Words*, p. 29. See also Bahá'u'lláh, *Gleanings*, p. 185.
10. Bahá'u'lláh, *Gleanings*, p. 185.
11. Though it is beyond the purview of the current paper, we might also argue that the main purpose of Bahá'í life in general is remembrance. In other words, remembrance can be understood not simply as one activity (e.g., prayer) but as the central activity of collective Bahá'í life, especially as it is institutionalized in, for example, the Mashriqu'l-Adhkár (literally, the dawning-place of the remembrance of God). There are many other ways in which memories of both God and Bahá'í traditions are institutionalized in Bahá'í life (e.g., in texts, statuary, architecture and art).
12. Using an internet search tool called "TrueSeeker" (http://www.ibiblio.org//Bahai/TrueSeeker/), I scanned several of Bahá'u'lláh's writings for the words "remember" and "forget" and their variants ("remembered," "remembering," "remembrance," "remembers," "forgot," "forgotten," "forgetful," "forgetfulness," and "forgets"). The results from my analysis of *Prayers and Meditations* (Wilmette: Bahá'í Publishing Trust, 1938) were as follows: "remember" occurred 16 times; "remembered," 4 times; "remembering," 13 times; "remembrance," 66 times; "remembers," 0 times; "forgot," 0 times; "forgotten," 4 times; "forgetful," 4 times; "forgetfulness," 3 times; "forgets," 0 times. Any irrelevant "hits" were left out of the tallies here (e.g., "forgot" actually appears once in *Prayers and Meditations* but it is not used to describe worship or worship practices. It was therefore left out of the final count.)
13. *Prayers and Meditations*, XV, pp. 29; LXXVII, pp. 126-27.
14. Ibid., XLIV, p. 63; XL, pp. 56-57.
15. Ibid., LXIV, p. 102.
16. Ibid., LXXXV, p. 144; XXXII, p. 39.
17. Ibid., XC, pp. 151-52.
18. Annemarie Schimmel, *Mystical Dimensions of Islam* (Chapel Hill: University of North Carolina Press, 1975) p. 171.
19. Ruzbihan Baqli, quoted in Schimmel, *Mystical*, pp. 167-8. The practice of *dhikr* has some quranic warrants. Sura 33:40 commands believers to "recollect God often." Sura 13:28 confirms that "the recollection of God makes the heart calm." See Schimmel, *Mystical*, pp. 166-90.
20. See Steven Scholl's paper "The Remembrance of God: An invocation technique in Sufism and the Writings of the Báb and Bahá'u'lláh" and rejoinders. Published in *Bahá'í Studies Bulletin*, Vol. 2, no. 3 (1983) pp. 73-104ff.
21. Bahá'u'lláh, *The Hidden Words*, pp. 27-28.
22. Quoted in *Bahá'í World Faith: Selected Writings of Bahá'u'lláh and 'Abdu'l-Bahá* (Wilmette: Bahá'í Publishing Trust, 1976) p. 393.
23. See 'Abdu'l-Bahá, *Selections*, p. 207.
24. Ibid.
25. Bahá'u'lláh, *Prayers and Meditations*, p. 127.
26. Lawrence Sullivan, "Memory Distortion and Anamnesis: A View from the Human Sciences," in Daniel Schacter, et al., eds., *Memory Distortion: How Minds, Brains and Societies Reconstruct the Past* (Cambridge: Harvard University Press, 1997) p. 387.

27. See Augustine, *Confessions* (trans. John Ryan) (New York: Doubleday, 1960) X:8, p. 236 and X:17, p. 246.
28. William C. Chittick, quoted in Lawrence Sullivan, "Memory Distortion and Anamnesis," p. 388.
29. See Paul Connerton, *How Societies Remember* (Cambridge University Press, 1992) *passim*.
30. From a letter written on behalf of Shoghi Effendi, dated 4 January 1936 to an individual believer, qtd. in *The Compilation of Compilations,* Vol. 2 (Maryborough: Bahá'í Publications Australia, 1991) p. 238.
31. Quoted in *Compilation*, Vol. 2, p. 232.
32. Ibid., p. 233.
33. From a letter written on behalf of Shoghi Effendi, dated 5 November 1934 to an individual believer. Quoted in ibid., p. 237.
34. 'Abdu'l-Bahá, *Some Answered Questions*. (Wilmette: Bahá'í Publishing Trust, 1985) pp. 244-7. There are, of course, many ways in which the body affects the spirit in Bahá'í belief and practice. We might cite Bahá'í teachings on cleanliness or on chastity as two suggestive examples.
35. Shoghi Effendi, *Directives,* pp. 86-7. My emphasis.
36. Contemporary advocates of the James-Lange theory contend that bodily activities (smiling, crying, etc.) are often prior to their corresponding emotions. In other words, these thinkers argue that bodily activities cause feelings. For an introduction to this literature, see Robert Zajonc et al., *Emotions, Cognition and Behavior* (New York: Cambridge University Press, 1984). See also William James, *Principles of Psychology* (vol. 2) (New York: Holt, 1890) p. 1066; Robert B. Zajonc, "Feeling and Thinking: Preferences Need no Inferences," *American Psychologist* 35 (1980) pp. 151-75; Robert Zajonc, "The Face as a Primary Instrument of Social Process," in R. Zajonc and S. Moscovici (eds.), *Social Psychology and the Emotions* (Cambridge: Cambridge University Press, in press); and Gerald Clore, *Can Emotions be Nonconscious?* (New York: Oxford University Press, 1994).
37. For the prayers themselves and the instructions that go with them see Bahá'u'lláh, *Prayers and Meditations,* pp. 314-23.
38. See for example Tom Kasulis's excellent collection of essays on bodily practices in Asian religions entitled *Self as Body in Asian Theory and Practice* (Albany: SUNY Press, 1993). The chapter by Frits Staal, "Indian Bodies," (pp. 59-102) is particularly useful.
39. Paul Connerton, *How Societies Remember,* p. 95.
40. Ibid., p. 102. We could also talk about the kind of remembering Connerton describes here as "procedural," that is, as memory of skills and procedures, as opposed to "declarative" (memory of names, dates and other facts). It may be an important corroboration of Connerton that psychologists have found procedural memory more robust than declarative memory in the elderly and in those with amnesia and dementia.
41. We should note that the remembering that goes on in prayer, and the reflection on that process of remembering that the prayers themselves call for, are constitutive of the prayer experience itself. Bahá'í prayers themselves participate in their interpretation (by interpreting prayer, to give one example,

as remembrance) and encourage reflection on prayer as a part of prayer. Using this definition, we might understand this essay and any other reflection on prayer as an act of worship.

Understanding Texts

ILLUMINATED PAGES OF THE QUR'AN

Scripture as Literature

Franklin Lewis

This essay attempts to trace the genres and styles of various parts of the corpus of Bahá'í scripture to antecedent models in Judeo-Christian and Islamic sacred texts, as well as in Persian and Arab literary texts. It argues that knowledge of the specific scriptural or literary models appealed to by certain Bahá'í texts will provide a deeper understanding of the theological import of those texts. Furthermore, because more is known about the literary milieu in which Bahá'u'lláh's texts were revealed, studying the intersection of Bahá'í scripture and its literary background may help illuminate, by way of comparison, the literary influences which gave shape to the form and style of the Hebrew Bible, the Gospels, and the Qur'an.[1]

Blessed Echoes

In the mid-fourteenth century A.D., the Italian poet Petrarch wrote of his courtly love for Laura (from Sonnet No. 47):

> Bendetto sia'l giorno e'l mese et l'anno
> e la stagione e'l tempo et l'ora e'l punto
> e'l bel paese e'l loco ov'io fuit giunto
> da'duo begli occhi che legato m'ànno

Every English-speaking Bahá'í child will find that these lines of Petrarch, once rendered into English, have a remarkably familiar ring:

> Blessed be the day and the month and the year
> and the season and the time and the hour
> and the instant and the beautiful countryside
> and the place where I was struck by the two
> lovely eyes that have bound me.[2]

A Bahá'í reader will hear echoes of an Arabic prayer by Bahá'u'lláh,[3] for Petarch's sonnet shares a parallel rhetorical structure and even some of the imagery of a passage adorning the title page of the common English-language Bahá'í prayer book:[4]

> Blessed is the spot, and the house,
> and the place, and the city,
> and the heart, and the mountain,
> and the refuge, and the cave,
> and the valley, and the land,
> and the sea, and the island,
> and the meadow where mention
> of God hath been made,
> and His praise glorified.

This uncanny resemblance is in all likelihood a mere coincidence, but it highlights the essential poetic or literary quality of the prayers, letters, treatises, and books written by Bahá'u'lláh.

Bahá'ís, of course, believe that Bahá'u'lláh was a Manifestation (*zuhûr*), or major prophet, of God and that the corpus of his writings constitute a revelation (*wahy*) from God. Among the community of his followers, this speech is endowed with numinous power and qualities and therefore enjoys sacred status as scripture. Nevertheless, there is the recognition that the Manifestation must pour divine truth into a particular form, shaped by the vessel of language in which it is contained, which in the case of Bahá'u'lláh's scripture happens to be Arabic and Persian. This essay will attempt to uncover some of the particular literary models which Bahá'u'lláh has chosen as the frame of expression for his revelation of scripture.

Scripture versus Literature

Christians have worried for several centuries about the relationship between pagan literature and scripture and the confluence of both the Jewish and the pagan Hellenistic traditions in the formation of Christian culture. Konrad of Hirsau, who died about 1150 A.D., recounts that a pupil once asked a teacher to prove that it is not harmful to study the pagan Latin and Greek authors and poets, whereupon the teacher replied:

> Would you reject the writings of Moses and the Prophets because in places they borrow words and expressions from pagan writers? Have I not already told you that all that is true that has ever been said by any human beings or all that is correct that has ever been thought has come from Him Who created us?5

In the Islamic context, the doctrine of the inimitability of the Qur'an (*i'jâz al-Qur'ân*) began to take shape in the tenth century A.D., with Arab theologians and rhetoricians holding to the notion that the Qur'an itself was a miracle, either because of its contents or because God prevented Muhammad's contemporaries from composing a stylistically similar work. Indeed, the word *âyat*, or verse of scripture, is the same word as that used for a divine sign or miracle. The Qur'an came to be seen as an uncreated work, the exact words of which were recorded in a heavenly tablet (*lawh mahfûz*), which was so lofty in its phrasing and its content that mere mortals could not imitate it.[6] There is some justification for this view in the Qur'an itself, but it seems clear that Muhammad himself recognized the roots of his rhyming prose style (*saj'*) in the prognostications of sooth-sayers (*kâhin, kuhhân*) and the considerable body of stories about Moses, Abraham, Jesus, and the other Semitic prophets from biblical and Midrashic sources and from Arab folklore. The particular form and expression of the truths of the Qur'an, therefore, is indebted to the literary milieu in which it was revealed, though Muhammad frequently points out that the revelation of the Qur'an is not to be confused with the mere speech of poets, soothsayers, and storytellers.

In the Bahá'í context, we do not find exact parallel to the doctrine of the inimitability of the Qur'an. The Báb, criticized by the Shiite clergy for his occasional failure to conform to the expected norms of

Arabic grammar, replied this way in the first chapter of the second *vâhed* of the Persian Bayân:

> *va agar nokte-giri dar e'râb-e qarâ'at yâ qavâ'ed-e 'arabiye shavad, mardud ast zirâ ke in qavâ'ed az âyât bar dâshte mi-shavad na âyât bar ânhâ jâri mi-shavad*

> And if exception be taken on the basis of vocalization of the text [*e'râb-e qarâ'at* denotes how the short vowels, not written down in Arabic script, are pronounced, which affects issues of conjugation and declension] or the rules of Arabic grammar, it is groundless, for such rules are derived from revealed verses, nor do revealed verses flow forth according to them.[7]

Indeed, Arab grammarians of the eighth to tenth centuries A.D. cited the quranic text as an authority for unusual grammatical formations, as it was by then considered matchlessly eloquent and a touchstone text to exemplify correct Arabic usage. The Báb, therefore, suggests in the above passage that, instead of criticizing his grammar, his readers should look to the status of the Bayán as revelation from God, and, as such, its grammar should not be criticized but emulated. Also in the first chapter of the second *vâhed* of the Persian Bayân, the Báb alludes to the doctrine of the inimitability of the Qur'an:

> *khodâvand Qor'ân râ be-a'lâ 'olovv-e fesâhat nâzel farmud va u râ mo'jeze-ye Rasul Allâh qarâr dâd . . . khodâvand-e 'âlam kalemât-e qor'âniye râ be-sha'ni nâzel farmude ke agar mâ 'alâ al-arz jam' shavand va be-khwâhand âye dar moqâbel-e âyât-e qor'ân biâvarand, nemitavânand*[8]

> The Lord revealed the Qur'an in the utmost perfection of eloquence and established it as a miracle of the Messenger of God . . . the Lord of the World sent down the quranic words in such manner that should all who are on earth gather together in the desire to produce a verse comparable to the verses of the Qur'an, they could not do so.

This test of inimitability or the miraculous quality of revealed language is also applied to the Bayân, citing as proof of its divine origin the fact that a thousand lines (*bayt*) were revealed by the pen of the Báb in the space of five hours, so quickly in fact that the scribe could barely take them down.[9]

The Báb did, indeed, adduce the speed with which he revealed verses as proof of his divine inspiration, and echoed the doctrine of quranic inimitability with respect to his own writings:

> In this Revelation the Lord of the universe hath deigned to bestow His mighty utterances and resplendent signs upon the Point of the Bayán, and hath ordained them as His matchless testimony for all created things. Were all the people that dwell on earth to assemble together, they would be unable to produce a single verse like unto the ones which God hath caused to stream forth from the tongue of the Point of the Bayán. Indeed, if any living creature were to pause to meditate he would undoubtedly realize that these verses are not the work of man, but are solely to be ascribed unto God, the One, the Peerless, Who causeth them to flow forth from the tongue of whomsoever He willeth, and hath not revealed nor will He reveal them save through the Focal Point of God's Primal Will. He it is, through Whose dispensations divine Messengers are raised up and heavenly Books are sent down. Had human beings been able to accomplish this deed surely someone would have brought forth at least one verse during the period of twelve hundred and seventy years which hath elapsed since the revelation of the Qur'án until that of the Bayán. However, all men have proved themselves impotent and have utterly failed to do so, although they endeavored, with their vehement might, to quench the flame of the Word of God.[10]

Though Bahá'u'lláh occasionally echoes this idea, and Shoghi Effendi does make a similar point about the speed with which Bahá'u'lláh revealed his books and tablets—just two days and two nights in the case of the Kitáb-i Íqán—there is no fixed doctrine of Bahá'u'lláh's writings as inimitable. In a letter dated 13 May 1953, Shoghi Effendi, authorized interpreter of Bahá'u'lláh's writings, describes Bahá'u'lláh's teachings as having "matchless potency,"[11] and elsewhere speaks in passing of "His matchless utterance,"[12] but he has also called Tahirih's poems "matchless"[13] and evaluated the Kitáb-i Íqán, as did E. G. Browne before him, in terms of its literary qualities. Shoghi Effendi writes:

> A model of Persian prose, of a style at once original, chaste and vigorous, and remarkably lucid, both cogent in argument and matchless in its irresistible eloquence, this Book, setting forth in outline the Grand Redemptive Scheme of God, occupies a position unequalled by any work in the entire range of Bahá'í literature, except the Kitáb-i-Aqdas, Bahá'u'lláh's Most Holy Book.[14]

In this description, Shoghi Effendi concurs with E. G. Browne's high estimation of the Íqán in his *A Literary History of Persia*. Browne hailed the Íqán as a model representative of the neo-classical "return" movement (*báz-gasht*) in nineteenth-century Persian literature, which aspired to the simplicity and concision of pre-Mongol Persian prose. In contrast to the "flabby, inflated, bombastic style" characterized by much of the intervening period, Browne gives high praise to the Íqán:

> Yet simplicity and directness is to be found in modern as well as in ancient writers of Persian verse and prose; the Íqán ("Assurance") of the Bábís, written by Bahá'u'lláh about A.D. 1859, is as concise and strong in style as the Chahár Maqála, composed some seven centuries earlier.[15]

Scripture as Literature

In the comments that follow, I would like to explore the intersection of literature and scripture a bit further, approaching the writings of Bahá'u'lláh as revealed texts in dialogue with the literary traditions of Iran and the Arab world. There is nothing new in this approach to scripture. For over a century, scholars have attempted to understand the various books of the Hebrew Bible, such as the wisdom literature of Ecclesiastes and Proverbs, or the liturgical literature used at temple services found in the Psalms, in terms of their genres or forms. Form criticism, like many other modern approaches to the Bible, was pioneered by Germans who attempted to identify the genre, or *gattung*, to which specific books of the Bible conform, as well as the real-life context or purpose, *sitz-im-leben*, to which they respond. As John Barton defines it:

> A *Gattung* or genre is a conventional pattern, recognizable by certain formal criteria (style, shape, tone, particular syntactic or even grammatical structures, recurring formulaic patterns), which is used in a particular society in social contexts which are governed by certain formal conventions.[16]

By knowing the genre and social purpose of a particular passage of scripture (was it a personal letter, public sermon, liturgical text, or what?), one might gain insight into the framework of expectations an ancient reader brought to that particular text and thereby better understand what it might originally have meant to that reader.

There are several reasons I propose that we should consider Bahá'u'lláh's revealed works in this light:

- By placing Bahá'u'lláh's works in their historical and literary context, and understanding what generic conventions they follow or break, we can better understand what they meant in their original context and what they might mean for us today.
- Read as a philosophical or spiritual genre of literature, as many secular non-believing people now read the Bible or the Qur'an, several of the works of Bahá'u'lláh are of a literary quality that ought to secure for them a place in the pantheon of nineteenth-century Persian and Arabic literature.
- Because we possess a large body of texts and other documentary evidence about the literary and theological traditions of nineteenth-century Iran, we know much more about the literary matrix from which Bahá'u'lláh's revelatory texts were born than we do about the literary milieu in which the Hebrew Bible, the New Testament, and the Qur'an appeared. By tracing how Bahá'u'lláh's writings have incorporated and reworked the prevailing literary and theological traditions of his day into scripture, we may come to better understand the process of moulding a scriptural tradition from a literary tradition and discover comparative models or data that may illuminate the shaping of the styles of the Bible and the Qur'an.

God's Logos, Man's Lingo

A theological objection was, of course, raised to the method of form criticism in the Judeo-Christian tradition. Whereas literature is a human product, and human authors are obviously influenced by the literary history that proceeds them, God (as speaker of the Qur'an, for example) is unconstrained by such human limitations.[17] However, a theological response to this would be that by choosing to speak in human language (rather than, let's say, by intuition or visual signs) the infinite accepts the constraints and limitations of human readers, and must perforce accommodate itself to human literary and linguistic conventions. If it failed to do so, it could not be understood. Indeed, Bahá'u'lláh, himself, operates on this very assumption, explaining that divine Revelation assumes a form other than its pure state in order that mortal beings may understand. For example, from his Kitáb-i Aqdas:

> *hâdhâ dhikrî 'alâ qadrikum lâ 'alâ qadr Allâh. Yashhadu bi-dhâlika mâ fî 'ilm Allâh law antum ta'rifûn wa yashhadu bi dhâlika lisân Allâh law antum tafqahûn. Tallâh law nakshifu al-hijâb antum tansa'iqûn.*[18]
>
> These words are to your measure, not to God's. To this testifieth that which is enshrined within His knowledge, if ye be of them that comprehend; and to this the tongue of the Almighty doth bear witness, if ye be of those who understand. I swear by God, were We to lift the veil, ye would be dumbfounded.[19]

and again, from the Hidden Words (*kalemât-e maknune*):

> *Kullumâ nazzaltu 'alayka min lisân al-qudrat wa katabtuhu bi-qalam al-quwwat qad nazzalnâhu 'alâ qadrika wa lahnika, lâ 'alâ sha'nî wa lahnî*
>
> All that I have revealed unto thee with the tongue of power, and have written for thee with the pen of might, hath been in accordance with thy capacity and understanding, not with My state and the melody of My voice.[20]

The word *lahn*, which essentially means "tune" or "melody," is translated by Shoghi Effendi, in his capacity as Guardian and authorized interpreter of Bahá'u'lláh's writings, in its second occurrence in this passage as "the melody of My voice" and in the first instance as "understanding." Thus, revelation, in what amounts to a normative statement of Bahá'í doctrine, is seen as a melody or language or accent, as it were, comparable to the language of humankind, not to that of God, and therefore obviously susceptible to the influences of human forms of speech.

Scripture Quoting Scripture

That Bahá'u'lláh was familiar and conversant with the literary history of Persian and Arabic is abundantly clear from even a cursory examination of his writings. He makes references to lines of verse from a number of Persian poets and makes ample and powerful use of the symbols of his literary tradition. Though not formally educated in a *madrase*, Bahá'u'lláh was tutored at home and was familiar with his culture, which was and continues to be heavily influenced by its literary and specifically poetic heritage. Thus, although Bahá'u'lláh states that "we perused not the books which men possess and we acquired not the learning current amongst them," nevertheless, he explicitly tells us in the Lawh-i Hikmat (Tablet of Wisdom):

> *kullumâ aradnâ an nadhkura bayânât al-'ulamâ' wa al-hukamâ' yazharu mâ zahar fî al-'âlam wa mâ fî al-kutub wa al-zubûr fî lawh*^{in} *imâma wajh rabbika, narâ wa naktub . . .*
>
> Whenever we desire to quote the sayings of the learned and of the wise, presently there will appear before the face of Thy Lord in the form of a tablet all that which hath appeared in the world and is revealed in the Holy Books and Scriptures. Thus do We set down in writing that which the eye perceiveth.[21]

Bahá'u'lláh's writings, many of which have yet to be published, are believed to number about 15,000 documents, including prayers, letters, epistles, tablets, and books in Persian and Arabic, all of which are regarded as divinely revealed scripture. For the purposes of this essay (and following the periodization of quranic verses as Meccan or Medinan), Bahá'u'lláh's writings can be broadly divided into two periods: the first from his imprisonment in 1852 through the end of his stay in Baghdad (1863); and the second from the public announcement of his claim to be a Manifestation of God in 1863 to the end of his life in 1892. The latter period includes among other categories, tablets proclaiming to the kings, rulers, and clergy of Europe and Islamdom the advent of his Revelation; the Kitáb-i Aqdas, a book which establishes new laws for the Bahá'í community, abrogating much of the Islamic and Bábí *sharî'a*; and a series of tablets and epistles variously called *lawh, sûra, risâla,* which outline his blueprint for collective international security and world government.

This last category does not have a strong Islamic prototype—indeed, it appeals more to the spirit of the 1815 Congress of Vienna and Immanuel Kant's 1795 tractate *Perpetual Peace: a Philosophical Sketch (Zum ewigen Frieden: Ein philosophischer Entwurf)* than to Islamic tradition. However, it ought to be mentioned in this context that Abu al-Fazl (1551-1602), the vizier of the Moghul emperor Akbar, in his court history *Akbar-nâme* includes the phrases *solh-e koll*, meaning tolerance for all and being at peace with all others, and *mahabbat-e koll*, meaning universal love in which the welfare of all people, irrespective of their religion is fostered, which seem to presage Bahá'u'lláh's vision of the lesser and most great peace (*solh-e asghar, solh-e akbar*).

The Kitáb-i Aqdas, on the other hand, is clearly conceived as being in the genre of previous scriptures—the greater Book of the people of the Book—particularly the Qur'an, which it mirrors stylistically by jumping from one subject to another, sometimes without apparent logical order. Bahá'u'lláh's tablets to the rulers of the world,[22] meanwhile, clearly appeal to the tradition preserved by Ibn Ishâq, the biographer of Muhammad, that the Prophet sent emissaries to the Byzantine emperor Heraclius, the Persian Shah, Khosrow, and various Arab potentates calling them to Islam.[23]

Certain phrases can be seen to have biblical literary precedents, such as Bahá'u'lláh's frequent:

> *bude va hast va khwâhad bud*
>
> as it was, is and ever shall be

which recalls Revelations 14:8:

> Holy, Holy, Holy, Lord God Almighty, which was, and is, and is to come.

or the *Gloria Patri* in the *Book of Common Prayer*:

> Glory be to the Father, and to the Son, and to the Holy Spirit: as it was in the beginning, is now and ever shall be, world without end.

There is likewise the despairing lament of Bahá'u'lláh's Fire Tablet (*qad ihtaraq al-mukhlisûn*), "How long . . ." which also occurs in similar contexts approximately thirty times in the Psalms, (e.g., Psalm 6:4 and Psalm 13). Then whole sentences are sometimes borrowed from the Hebrew or the Arabic translations of the Bible with which Bahá'u'lláh would have been familiar.[24] For example, Psalm 51:12, which in the King James Version reads: "Create in me a clean heart, O God, and renew a right spirit within me," is, of course, simply an older (and to my ear, inferior) translation of the Guardian's rendering of one of Bahá'u'lláh's prayers:[25]

> Create in me a pure heart, O my God, and renew
> a tranquil conscience within me, O my Hope!

Bahá'u'lláh's Writ and Its Literary Matrix

It is not surprising that the motifs and stylistics of scripture would find their way into Bahá'u'lláh's writings; after all, he sees his writings as a new chapter in the book of scripture. Perhaps somewhat less expected, though, are quotations from the works of poets, mystics, and philosophers which punctuate Bahá'u'lláh's writings, in typical epistolary style, especially in the early period of 1853-1863. Unlike Muhammad, revelation seems to have come at will to Bahá'u'lláh; even though his revelations, considered as divinely revealed or sent down (*manzul*), apparently differed from normal speech or thought, some passages speak in the voice of God and others in Bahá'u'lláh's own voice. Nevertheless, all are accorded the status of revelation, even those texts dating to the period before Bahá'u'lláh's public claim to be a Manifestation.

The earliest text in Bahá'u'lláh's corpus seems to be a nineteen-line Persian poem in the Sufi tradition entitled *Rashh-e 'amâ* (Sprinklings from the Cloud of Unknowing) dating to 1269/1852-53, which contains the refrain (*radif*) "it pours from us" (*-e mâ mi-rizad*), as in the opening line:

> *rashh-e 'amâ az jazbe-ye mâ mi-rizad*
>
> From our rapture the sprinkles of the cloud of unknowing trickle down[26]

Persian poets prior to Bahá'u'lláh, from the Safavid period onward, had used this refrain, as in the last line of the following poem by Sâ'eb (1607-1675):

mi-shavad da'vi-ye khun ruz-e qiâmat Sâ'eb
rang-e har gol ke ze nazzâre-ye mâ mi-rizad

There will be a bloody fight on the day of Judgment, Sâ'eb,
over the color of every rose that fades under our gaze[27]

A 217-line poem in Arabic, complete with auto-commentary bearing the Persian title *Qaside-ye varqâ'iye* (The Dove's Ode) was written between 1270-72/1854-56 for a certain Shaykh Ismâ'îl, the head of the Khalidiya branch of the Naqshbandi Sufis, who had made Bahá'u'lláh's acquaintance in the mountains of Iraqi Kurdistan,[28] and, being impressed with his piety and knowledge, had requested him to write a *qasîda* in imitation of the famous *Tâ'îyat al-kubrâ*, or Magnificent Ode rhyming in "Ti," by Ibn al-Fârid (576-632/1181-1235), composed 600 years earlier.[29] In such poems, Bahá'u'lláh incorporates Bábí theology and a measured Sufi vocabulary which steers away from the monism or pantheism of both *wahdat al-shuhûd* and *wahdat al-wujûd* ("oneness of Being and Manifestation") varieties without making a contentious doctrinal issue of it.[30]

Throughout their ministries, Bahá'u'lláh, 'Abdu'l-Bahá, and also Shoghi Effendi wrote a great number of personal confessional prayers (*monâjât*), a genre of Persian prose canonized by the eleventh-century Sufi of Herat, 'Abd Allâh Ansâri (1006-1088 A.D.). In some Bahá'í *monâjât* (also called *do'â*, as opposed to obligatory prayers, or *namâz*), the echoes of quotations or near-quotations from earlier Islamic prayers or poems can occasionally be heard. For example, in the prayer-like tablet of 'Abdu'l-Bahá beginning "*Ay jân feshân-e yâr-e bi-neshân*,"[31] he quotes a line of verse from the famous thirteenth-century poet of Shiraz, Sa'di:

'âqelân-e khushe-chin az serr-e Layli ghâfel-and
in karâmat nist joz Majnun-e kherman suz râ[32]

The learned
  who but glean the fields of love
 are ignorant

of Layli's secret
this bounty
only Majnun
who scorches his whole harvest
can know

Of course, this quote conjures up a whole range of associated images from the cycle of stories about the star-crossed lovers, Layli and Majnun, just as a single sentence from Juliet to Romeo—"Swear not by the moon, th'inconstant moon"—let's say, would conjure up the important scenes of Shakespeare's play for an English audience.

In the early period Bahá'u'lláh also revealed a series of esoteric commentaries (*tafsir*) on various verses or suras of the Qur'an and the New Testament, usually written in response to questions or requests submitted to him. The most notable of these is the Kitáb-i Íqán, which expounds Bahá'u'lláh's doctrine of progressive revelation by focussing on the passage in the Qur'an (33:40) on the "Seal of the Prophets" (*khâtam al-nabiyîn*), as well as the passage in Matthew (24:29-31) about the Son of Man coming in the Clouds of Glory. Although works in the Qur'an commentary genre usually set out to cover the entire Qur'an verse-by-verse, there are a few works, such as Ibn 'Arabî's thirteenth-century work, *Fusûs al-hikam* (Bezels of Wisdom),[33] and some of Mullâ Sadrâ's treatises (b. Shiraz?, d. Basra 1050/1640), which treat specific themes in the Qur'an or single verses,[34] as does the Kitáb-i Íqán.

Likewise, in the *Lawh-e Ra'is*, Bahá'u'lláh describes a puppet show he viewed in his youth, in which all the pomp and glory of the material world and all the important personages were laid to rest in a box by the puppeteer at the end of the show. The conclusions he draws from this event may be shaped somewhat by the *Oshtor-nâme*, traditionally attributed to the famous Farid al-Din 'Attâr (d. 618/1221),[35] who describes a Turkish puppet player folding all the puppets into the box of *tawhid*, or Divine unity, after the performance.

Also from the *Lawh-e Ra'is* is this quotation from the poet Sanâ'i (d. 525/1131):

Hakim Sanâ'i 'alayhe al-rahmat gofte:
pand girid ay siâhi-tân gerefte jâ-ye pand
pand girid ay sepidi-tân damide bar 'edhâr

> The sage Sanâ'i has said:
> Take counsel, all you more blackened than counselled!
> Take counsel, O you whose beards begin to whiten!

According to the modern edition of his collected poems (*divân*), the second hemistich of this poem is somewhat incorrectly quoted in the Seven Valleys (*'ozr ârid* "seek forgiveness" is given rather than *pand girid* "take counsel," though it has little change on the overall import of the verse).[36] Saná'i was received as a mystic and homiletic poet by the later literary tradition, though he also wrote much profane poetry as well.[37] The Mevlevi tradition understood Sanâ'i, along with 'Attâr, to be the poetic and spiritual predecessors of Jalál al-Din Rumi, and as such, quoting Sanâ'i situates one's remarks in the Persian gnostic tradition. This is the third line of a very famous poem, and Bahá'u'lláh's quotation of it would probably call to the mind of an educated nineteenth-century reader the previous lines of the poem, as well:

> *ay khodâvandân-e mâl al-e'tebâr al-e'tebâr*
> *ay khodâ-khwânân-e qâl al-e'tezâr al-e'tezâr*
> *pish az ân k-in jân-e 'ozr âvar foru mi-rad ze notq*
> *pish az ân k-in chashm-e 'ebrat bin foru mânad ze kâr*
> *pand girid . . .*

> O lords of wealth, take heed, take heed!
> O you who call on God in pretense, repent, repent!
> Before your forgiveness-seeking soul falls forever silent
> before your lesson-learning eye closes forever shut
> take counsel . . .

Perhaps the most interesting work of Bahá'u'lláh, at least insofar as genre studies are concerned, is his Hidden Words (*Kalemât-e maknune*), a work of rhymed prose composed in 1274/1858 while Bahá'u'lláh was in Baghdad. Though conceived as an organic unity, *Kalemât-e maknune* consists of brief ethical and mystical counsels: 71 in Arabic and 83 in Persian. This book was originally known by the Bábís among whom it circulated in manuscript form as the *Sahife-ye Fâtemiye* (The Book of Fatima), thus identifying it with the Twelver Shí'í tradition of the *moshaf Fâteme* (scroll of Fatima), a series of inspiring thoughts supposedly whispered into the ear of Fatima by an angel to console her upon the death of her father—the Prophet

Muhammad. The scroll of Fatima was believed to be handed down by the Imams from generation to generation along with the weapons of the Prophet. Of course, we do not now possess any such text, if it ever did exist, so that we have here a curious case of intertextuality with a non-textual text, or more precisely, the apocryphal tradition of a text. Hence the name—Hidden Words.[38]

The Arabic introduction to the *Kalemât-e maknune* alludes to this tradition and to the revelations that Bahá'u'lláh had received:

> *hâdhâ mâ nuzzila min jabarût al-'izzat bi lisân al-qudrat wa al-quwwat 'alâ al-nabiyyîn min qablu wa innâ akhadhnâ jawâhirahu wa aqmas-nâhu qamîs al-ikhtisâr fadl*[an] *'alâ al-ahbâr*

> This is that which hath descended [*nuzzila*, also "hath been sent down"] from the realm of glory, uttered by the tongue of power and might and revealed unto the prophets of old. We have taken the inner essence thereof and clothed it in the garment of brevity as a token of grace unto the righteous. (trans. by Shoghi Effendi)

Although the Hidden Words can be seen in the broader context of wisdom literature (*hekam*, *andarz*) and the homiletic tradition, especially the counsels of 'Alî as related in the *Nahj al-balâgha*, it is specifically, though not explicitly, to the *Hadîth qudsî*, or sacred hadith, that the Hidden Words appeal. Generally held by Muslims to be the direct word of God, though not necessarily miraculous in nature as is always maintained for the verses of the Qur'an, the *hadîth qudsî* were a favorite source of allusion for Sufis and Persian poets. They are often prefaced by addresses such as *yâ 'ibâdî* (O my servant), *yâ ibn Âdam* (O son of Adam), etc. In the *Kalemât-e maknune*, we find these addresses, and others similar to them: *yâ ibn al-insân*, "O son of Man" (an appellation of Christ in the Bible); *yâ ibn al-rûh*, "O son of Spirit;" *yâ ibn al-wujûd*, "O son of existence." In addition to thus echoing the addresses of the *hadîth qudsî*, the Hidden Words also reflect their themes and counsels. Take, for example, the following Arabic passage:

> *Yâ ibn al-insân: kuntu fî qidam dhâtî wa azaliyyat kaynûnatî 'araftu hubbî fîka khalaqtuka wa alqaytu 'alayka mithâlî wa azhartu laka jamâlî*

> O Son of Man! Veiled in My immemorial being in the ancient eternity of My essence, I knew My love for Thee, therefore I created thee, have engraved on thee Mine image and revealed to thee My beauty. (trans. by Shoghi Effendi)

This passage ought to bring to mind the famous *hadîth qudsî*:

> *kuntu kanz*^{an} *makhfiy*^{an} *fa ahbabtu an 'urafa fa-khalaqtu al-khalq likay u'rafa*
>
> I was a hidden treasure and desired to be known, hence I created the creation in order to be known.

There are numerous other parallels of this sort. For example, another of Bahá'u'lláh's Hidden Words alludes to the same *hadîth*, though with the love of God for man, rather than the love of God for God foregrounded (on which, see 'Abdu'l-Bahá, *Some Answered Questions*):

> *yâ ibn al-insân, ahbabtu khalqaka fa-khalaqtuka fa-ahbibnî kay adhkuraka wa fî rûh al-hayât uthabbitaka*
>
> O Son of Man! I loved thy creation, hence I created thee. Wherefore do thou love Me, that I may name thy name and fill thy soul with the spirit of life.

Compare also the following *hadîth qudsî:*

> *rasûl Allâh qâla: qâla Allâh: anfiq yâ ibn Âdam unfiq 'alayka*
>
> The Messenger of God said: "God has said, 'O Son of Adam! Spend upon (my creatures) that I may spend upon thee.' "

and the following Hidden Word:

> *unfiq mâlî 'alâ fuqarâ'î li tunfaqa fî al-samâ' min kunûz 'izz*^{in} *lâ tafnâ wa khazâ'in majd*^{in} *lâ tablâ wa-lâkin wa 'umrî, infâqu al-rûh ajmal law tushâhidu bi 'aynî*
>
> Bestow my wealth upon my poor, that in heaven thou mayest draw from stores of unfading splendor and treasures of imperishable glory. But by My life! To offer up thy soul is a more glorious thing couldst thou but see with Mine eye. (trans. by Shoghi Effendi)

There are parallels between the Hidden Words and the Qur'an, as well:

> *wa idhâ adhaqnâ al-nâs rahmatan farihû bihâ wa in tusibhum sayy-i'atun bimâ qaddamat aydihim idhâ hum yaqnatûn (Q30:36)*
>
> When we make men to taste of a blessing they rejoice at it, but if evil befalls them because of what their own hands have wrought, then they despair.
>
> *yâ ibn al-bashar in asâbatka ni'mat*^{un} *la tafrah bihâ wa in tamassaka dhillat*^{un} *la tahzan minhâ lianna kiltayhimâ tazûlâni fî hîn*^{in} *wa tabîdâni fî waqt*^{in} *(HW, Arabic #52)*
>
> O Son of Man! Should prosperity befall thee, rejoice not, and should abasement come upon thee, grieve not, for both shall pass away and be no more. (trans. by Shoghi Effendi)

And finally, consider this *hadîth qudsî*:

> *yâ 'ibâdî innî harramtu al-zulma 'alâ nafsî wa ja'altuhu baynakum muharram*^{an} *fa lâ tazâlamû*
>
> O My Servants! I have forbidden oppression to Myself and have made it unlawful to you, therefore be not an oppressor one to another . . .

in light of this Persian Hidden Word (#64):

> *ay zâlemân-e arz! az zolm dast-e khod râ kutâh namâ'id ke qasam yâd nemude-am az zolm-e ahadi nagozaram va in 'ahdi-st ke dar lowh-e mahfuz mahtum dâshtam va be khâtem-e 'ezz makhtum*
>
> O Oppressors on Earth! Withdraw your hands from tyranny, for I have pledged Myself not to forgive any man's injustice. This is My covenant which I have irrevocably decreed in the preserved tablet and sealed it with my seal of glory.

The Persian Hidden Words are even more intriguing than the Arabic from a literary point of view, in that they tend to be less proverbial and more esoteric, more firmly rooted in the later tradition of rhymed prose (*saj'*), and frequently allude to well-known motifs and episodes from Persian poetry. Although perhaps the greater portion of his writings are in Arabic, it is primarily from the Persian literary tradition, as opposed to the religious literature of Arabic, that Bahá'u'lláh's writings draw their motifs and models (with some exceptions, such as the *Lawh-i sultán*). His early Persian prose works should be read in the light of the Sufi literary tradition, particularly as found (or at least as popularly received) in the major classical poets: 'Attâr, Sa'di, Rumi, and Hâfez, scattered lines of whose verse are quoted here and there in Bahá'u'lláh's epistolary works, especially *Haft vâdi* (Seven Valleys). There is surprisingly little stylistic influence from Bábí texts, though a good deal of terminology and doctrine come from those sources. Similarities with the philosophical and theological prose tradition, particularly the illuminationist school, which tended to blend literary and philosophical prose, can also be found.

It should be further remembered that Persian poets and prose writers in the nineteenth century had rejected the ornateness of the Indian style (*sabk-e hendi*) and had called for a return (*bâz gasht*) to the models of the 11th-13th centuries. Bahá'u'lláh's prose language in the Persian Hidden Words suggests the influence of Sa'di's *Golestân* and Ansâri's *Monâjât*; undoubtedly additional examples and parallels can be isolated. The themes and motifs, on the other hand, were those that had saturated later Persian literature, and could be evoked by elliptical allusions that would resonate with and perhaps call to the reader's mind an elaborate series of associations, as in the first Persian Hidden Word, which reads almost like a catalogue of classical motifs:

ay sâhebân-e hush
va gush
avval sorush-e dust in ast
ay bolbol-e ma'navi
joz dar golbon-e ma'âni jây ma-gozin
va ay hodhod-e solaymân-e 'eshq
joz dar sabâ-ye jânân vatan ma-gir
va ay 'anqâ-ye baqâ
joz dar qâf-e vafâ mahall ma-pazir

in ast makân-e to
agar be lâ-makân be par-e jân bar pari
va âhang-e maqâm-e khod râyegân namâ'i

All Ye people that have minds to know and ears to hear: The first call of the Beloved is this: O Mystic nightingale! Abide not but in the rose-garden of the spirit. O Messenger of the Solomon of love! Seek thou no shelter except in the Sheba of the well-beloved, and O immortal phoenix! Dwell not save on the mount of faithfulness. Therein is thy habitation, if on the wings of the soul thou soarest to the realm of the infinite and seekest to attain thy goal. (trans. by Shoghi Effendi)

In the following Persian Hidden Word, the gnomic tradition (*andarz*) in Persian literature, which stretches back at least into Sasanian and probably into Parthian times, is clearly evident. This example, like most of the Persian Hidden Words, echoes with the aphoristic rhymed prose of Sa'di's *Golestân*:

Ay dust dar rowze-ye qalb joz gol-e 'eshq makâr
va az zayl-e bolbol-e hobb o showq dast madâr
mosâhebat-e abrâr râ ghanimat dân
va az morâfeqat-e ashrâr
dast o del har do bar dâr

O friend! in the garden of thy heart plant naught but the rose of love, and from the nightingale of affection and desire, loosen not they hold. Treasure the companionship of the righteous and eschew all fellowship with the ungodly. (trans. by Shoghi Effendi)

The following (and final) example subtly alludes to the legends about the Prophet Muhammad's ascent into heaven (*me'râj*):

ay pesar-e hobb
az to tâ rafraf-e emtenâ'-e qorb
va sedre-ye ertefâ'-e 'eshq
qadam-i fâsele
qadam-e avval bar dâr
va qadam-e digar bar
'âlam-e qedam gozâr
va dar sorâdeq-e khold vâred show
pas beshnow
ânche az qalam-e 'ezz nozul yâft

Here I am using my own translation to emphasize certain points of the *me'râj* legend:

O Son of Love!
you are but one step away from the *rafraf*
that will take you to the impenetrable heights of nearness
and the lote tree of the boundary of love
Take the first step
and with the second
step into the world of pre-existence
and the pavilion of eternity

Then listen
to what has been revealed by the Pen of Might

Here the reader is being told that s/he, too, can aspire in a personal spiritual journey to repeat Muhammad's ascent to heaven (*me'râj*) on the *rafraf*, which can mean pillows or cushions, but since the Arabic root *R-F-F* has the connotation of flapping wings, these cushions are like flying carpets. Most versions of the legend have Muhammad riding on a mythical beast, *Burâq*, a kind of winged donkey (an iconographic association with the Messiah riding into Jerusalem on an untamed ass) provided by the angel of Revelation, Gabriel. The *rafraf* will take us beyond the *sidrat al-muntahâ*, the lote tree beyond which there is no passing. During his *me'râj*, Muhammad came within two bows' lengths of this tree and, as stated in a passage of the Qur'an (53:1-18), gazed upon it with unswerving eyes (*mâ zâgha al-basar*) only to see that it was shrouded in mystery (*idh yaghshâ al-sidrata má yaghshâ*, literally: when the lote tree was covered by what covered it). These verses of the Qur'an have been greatly elaborated in non-canonical materials called the stories of the prophets (*qisas al-anbiyâ*), similar to the Jewish haggadah, in order to round out the story. In the Sufi tradition, the light (*nûr*) of Muhammad's worship is what covered the tree.

Although Muhammad was unable on his *me'râj* (ascent to heaven) to advance beyond the sacred precincts of the *sidrat al-muntahâ*, Bahá'u'lláh tells us that we—the children of love (*'eshq*, a term used technically by Sufis since the second/ninth century to mean the mystic love of God, though exoterically it continues to mean romantic human love, as well)—can take two steps beyond this, into the pre-eternal realm, where God's covenant was made with the soul, and into the eternal pavilion, where, according to Sufi interpretation, man will actually see God, a blessing that was denied to Moses on Sinai. This, of course, is a metaphoric journey that takes place in the believer's heart, the same journey that Shams al-Din of Tabriz urged Jalâl al-Din Rumi to take in the thirteenth century:

> To follow Mohammad is this: He went on the me'ráj, you, likewise, must go in his footsteps. Strive to attain [this] abode in your heart.[39]

Though Bahá'u'lláh invokes the Sufis' mythopoesis of the beatific vision of God in eternal paradise, God is ineffable, and cannot be seen or heard, as we know from numerous other tablets of Bahá'u'lláh. The human point of contact with the divine is through the revealed text, that which is revealed by the Pen of Might, and it is through what it has revealed that we make our internal ascent unto God. Scripture, then, which as we have seen flows in and through the medium of human language and literature, is man's vehicle (*rafraf*) to God. Having been transported by it to the proximity of the divine, however, we must take our own steps to reach the sanctum sanctorum.

As Bahá'u'lláh states elsewhere, human beings could not bear the direct knowledge of the divine transcendence, so God reveals only a relative truth, that which can be understood in the form of human language. This is all that we require to make that extra two-step leap into the pre-eternal and infinite realm. As the epilogue to the last Persian Hidden Word states:

> I bear witness, O Friends! that the favor is complete, the argument fulfilled, the proof manifest and the evidence established. Let it now be seen what your endeavors in the path of detachment will reveal. In this wise hath the divine favor been fully vouchsafed unto you and unto them that are in heaven and on earth.

Bahá'u'lláh was not, of course, the first to employ this *me'râj* trope and its associated imagery. Though many modern post-secular Iranian readers would have to consciously excavate the *rafraf* passage to discover its leitmotif, the trope was a favorite of many pre-modern poets and was so ingrained in the Persian poetic consciousness that it would have been immediately obvious to an initiated reader. Saná'i alludes to the same trope in this line from his *Sayr al-'ebâd elâ al-*

ma'âd (The worshippers' journey to the promised hereafter) with which Bahá'u'lláh's just-quoted Hidden Word seems to resonate:

> *su-ye shahr-e qedam qadam bar dâr*
> *khâne-ye ostokhwân be-sag bogzâr*
> Take a step toward the city of pre-existence
> Leave this house of bones to the dogs

Elsewhere, in his *Hadiqat al-haqiqat* (The Walled Garden of Truth), Sanâ'i says: *az to tá dust nist rah besyâr* (from you to the Friend there is but a little way to go).

Literate Versus Literal Readings of Scripture

Despite these and numerous other examples, Western Bahá'ís steeped in a devotional approach to Bahá'u'lláh's texts in translation may insist that knowledge of their literary context, while interesting, does not particularly elucidate their functional import—the pragmatic implications of Bahá'u'lláh's statements and their significance for Bahá'í law, ethics, and daily praxis. It would, however, be a great mistake to assume that only esoteric and symbolic allusions are lurking in the literary sediment. Juan Cole has shown in his article "Problems of Chronology in Bahá'u'lláh's 'Tablet of Wisdom' "[40] that echoes of previous works may sometimes give us clues about the nature of what is being said. We can sometimes conclude, on the basis of traceable allusions to previous works (historical works in the above case), that what is being said is metaphorical, historically or mythically bound, or perhaps truthful in a cultural context without necessarily being factual in a scientific sense.

This can also be true in "legal" texts, as the following example from the Kitáb-i Aqdas illustrates, where, I think, it is necessary to know the quranic parallels in order to understand the full intent of Bahá'u'lláh's law. In the Aqdas (verse 107), we find:

> *qad hurrimat 'alaykum azwâja abâ'ikum*
>
> it is forbidden you to marry your father's wives

The Questions and Answers section indicates that the matter of marriage between relatives is left to the House of Justice. This, of course, presents no particular problem, until we ask if it is not strange that Bahá'u'lláh should specifically forbid marriage to one's stepmother(s), while apparently neglecting to forbid marriage to one's own mother or sister or daughter?

This dilemma can be easily solved if we assume that Bahá'u'lláh had in mind the quranic laws about marrying one's relatives, found in Sura 4 (*Sûrat al-nisâ'*). Recall that the Qur'an appears to allow the espousal of four wives simultaneously. However, specifically excluded from matrimonial possibility are the wives one's father has married, i.e., one's stepmother(s), like the text of the Aqdas. The Qur'an, however, then launches into a much longer list in the next verse that includes mothers, daughters, sisters, father's sisters, mother's sisters, brother's daughters, sister's daughters, wet-nurses, foster-sisters, wives' mothers, stepdaughters, daughters-in-law, and two sisters. Indeed, if we compare the passages, we find that the Qur'an verse begins with the same wording employed in the Aqdas (*hurrimat 'alaykum*). This, then, is an instance where quotation from a previous work apparently intends for us to summon up similar semiotically proximate passages which are not explicitly quoted. With one word, "wives," Bahá'u'lláh summons up the entire list of the Qur'an, given in two longish verses. Hence the meaning and content of the previous text, in this case the Qur'an, bleeds somewhat into the meaning and intent of Bahá'u'lláh's text, and we must be cognizant of the provenance of the quote in order to recover the full context of meaning.

Indeed, many readers have expressed difficulty in understanding why the Kitáb-i Aqdas jumps from one subject to the next without any obvious logical connection. The principle of organization animating the style of the Kitáb-i Aqdas can be seen in the literary model of the Qur'an. Indeed, a secretary writing on behalf of Shoghi Effendi singled out this non-linear structure as distinctively quranic and characteristic of divine revelation in general for a western Bahá'í apparently confounded by the style:

> All Divine Revelation seems to have been thrown out in flashes. The Prophets never composed treatises. That is why in the Qur'án and our own Writings different subjects are so often included in one Tablet. That is why it is "Revelation."[41]

While it is true that the Aqdas was revealed piecemeal, Bahá'u'lláh (unlike Muhammad, who did not himself collect the Qur'an in written form) could have organized it logically, section by section, point by point, much as the treatises and manuals on Islamic law (*fiqh*) were organized. But the language of God does not flow according to human language, as we have seen in the beginning. To follow such a logical plan of organization would have evoked associations of the genre of systematic law books, the class of clerics and knowledge acquired by years of academic study. Bahá'u'lláh, who insists that he has not studied law and theology, appeals instead to the structure of the Qur'an with its juxtapositions, pericopes, and disjunctions, as is appropriate to the claim that God has revealed the book.

Scholars have already focused a great deal of attention on the literary criticism of the Hebrew Bible. The various approaches of source criticism, form criticism and redaction criticism have taught us a great deal. More recently Robert Alter and Meir Sternberg have devoted attention to the narrative and poetic art of the Hebrew Bible, while Frank Kermode and others have done the same for the New Testament. Such approaches will undoubtedly prove quite useful in deepening our understanding of Bahá'u'lláh's writings and how meaning is internally produced in his texts. A prerequisite to this avenue of inquiry is a general understanding of the sources, forms and genres to which his texts appeal. A similar process, as applied to the Hebrew Bible, has been disparagingly described by Edmund Leach as "unscrambling the omelette."[42] We might call this task sifting scripture, not in the culinary sense, but in the sense of an excavation, a kind of literary archaeology, that seeks to recover parts of the past lying just below the surface layers of the text and help us situate the meaning of those scriptural artifacts in their literary context. In this respect, we might also consider the etymology of the word "text," which denotes weaving of different strands into a patterned whole. Scripture, of course, is experienced by the body of believers as having a sacred texture, the fabric of which, though woven of past and present, human and divine, knits together the hearts of the faithful in a new communion.

NOTES

FRANKLIN LEWIS is Associate Professor of Persian Language and Literature at Emory University in Atlanta.

1. The basic ideas presented here were first set forth in a paper for a course at the University of Chicago on Bahá'ú'lláh's writings taught by my mentor and friend, Professor Heshmat Moayyad. That paper was presented at a Bahá'í history conference in 1985 and a substantially modified version of it was then delivered at the conference of the American Oriental Society in Chicago in 1987. A further version of the paper was delivered at the Háj Mehdi Arjomand conference on scripture in Wilmette in 1994, and subsequently circulated on the Internet and made available on Jonah Winters' web site for Bahá'í academics. The present form of the argument, though not purged of all its oral features, supersedes all previous versions.
2. *Petrarch's Lyric Poems*, trans and ed. by Robert M. Durling (Cambridge: Harvard University Press, 1976) pp. 138-39.
3. Variously transliterated as "Baha'Allah" in modern scholarly convention and as "Bahá'u'lláh" according to the official Bahá'í convention.
4. Translated by Shoghi Effendi in *Advent of Divine Justice* (Wilmette: Bahá'í Publishing Trust, 1971) p. 70. This book was first published in 1939, and has many times been reprinted or reissued. In more recent editions the passage appears at pp. 83-84. The passage is included in most English prayer books, e.g., *Bahá'í Prayers: A Selection of Prayers Revealed by Bahá'u'lláh, the Báb, and 'Abdu'l-Bahá* (Wilmette: Bahá'í Publishing Trust, 1985), and is frequently sung by Bahá'í children.

   The Persian translation of *Advent of Divine Justice*, *Zohur-e 'Adl-e Elâhi*, 2nd ed., (Iranian Bahá'í Publishing Trust, 133 B.E./1976-77) p. 171, includes the original prayer, which is in Arabic, but the source is not specified.
5. Anders Piltz, *The World of Medieval Learning*, trans. David Jones (Totowa, NJ: Barnes and Noble Books, 1981) p. 34, citing the following: R. B. C. Huygens, ed., "Dialogus super Auctores," *Collection Lanonus*, Vol. 17 (1955) pp. 52-53.
6. See for example, al-Rummânî (d. 384/994), *al-Nukât fi I'jâz al-Qur'ân*; al-Khaṭṭâbî (d. 386/996), *al-Bayân I'jâz al-Qur'ân*; and al-Bâqillânî (d. 403/1013), *I'jâz al-Qur'ân*.
7. E. G. Browne, "The Bábís of Persia. II: Their Literature and Doctrines," *Journal of the Royal Asiatic Society*, Vol. 21 (1889) p. 918 n1. See the reprint in Moojan Momen, ed., *Selections from the Writings of E. G. Browne* (Oxford: George Ronald, 1987) p. 224 n1. The translation is my own, as I believe Browne has imperfectly understood the import of the word *bar dâshte mishavad*: to be lifted, taken from; Browne renders: "these rules are removed from [revealed] verses," but it does not here mean that revealed verses are exempted from grammatical rules, but rather that the proper rules of Arabic are deduced by the classical Arab grammarians from the revealed verses of the Qur'an (as well as pre-Islamic poetry). Therefore, the rules of

grammar are "taken from" the example of scripture rather than scripture flowing forth according to the rules of grammar.

8. *Bayân-e Fârsi*, n.p., n.d. (This edition was published by Azalis in Iran). Provisional translation by the author.
9. See Momen, ed. *Selections from the Writings of E. G. Browne*, pp. 325-26.
10. From the Persian *Bayán*, II, 1 in *Selections from the Writings of the Báb*, trans. Habib Taherzadeh et al., (Haifa: Bahá'í World Centre, 1976) pp. 104-105.
11. ". . . placing their whole trust in the matchless potency of Bahá'u'lláh's teachings, in the all-conquering power of His might and the infallibility of His glorious and oft-repeated promises . . ." Shoghi Effendi, *Citadel of Faith: Messages to America, 1947-1957* (Wilmette: Bahá'í Publishing Trust, 1965) p. 120.
12. "To emperors, kings, princes and potentates, to rulers, governments, clergy and peoples, whether of the East or of the West, whether Christian, Jew, Muslim, or Zoroastrian, He addressed, for well-nigh fifty years, and in the most tragic circumstances, these priceless pearls of knowledge and wisdom that lay hid within the ocean of His matchless utterance." Shoghi Effendi, *The Promised Day is Come* (Wilmette: Bahá'í Publishing Trust, 1941) p. 6.
13. "Many are those whose conduct has been ennobled by her inspiring example, who have committed to memory her matchless odes . . ." Shoghi Effendi, *God Passes By* (Wilmette: Bahá'í Publishing Trust, 1944 [1974]) pp. 76-77.
14. Shoghi Effendi, *God Passes By*, pp. 138-139.
15. *A Literary History of Persia*, v. 2 (New York: Charles Scribner's Sons, 1906) p. 89. Browne's dating of the text is slightly early; the actual date of composition appears to have been 1278/1861-62 as per the English translation of the Íqán (p. 226), though Fâzel-e Mâzandarâni in *Asrâr al-âsâr* (124 BE/1967) Vol. 1, pp. 267-68, argues for the date 1279 A.H.
16. John Barton, *Reading the Old Testament: Method in Biblical Study* (Philadelphia: Westminster Press, 1984) p. 32.
17. Not all religious communities would conceive their scriptures in these terms, nor is any given religious tradition unified in its concept of scripture. For a good synopsis of Jewish, Muslim, and Christian attitudes toward scripture, see F. E. Peters, *Judaism, Christianity and Islam: The Classical Texts and Their Interpretation* (Princeton University Press, 1990). Cf., also W. Graham, *Beyond the Written Word: Oral Aspects of Scripture in the History of Religion* (Cambridge University Press, 1987).
18. *Kitáb-i-Aqdas* [Arabic text] (Haifa: Bahá'í World Centre, 1995) pp. 167-68.
19. Bahá'u'lláh, *The Kitáb-i-Aqdas, the Most Holy Book* (Haifa: Bahá'í World Centre, 1992) K176, p. 83.
20. Bahá'u'lláh, *The Hidden Words*, trans. Shoghi Effendi (Hofheim-Langenhain, Germany: Bahá'í Verlag, 1983) Arabic #67 (Arabic and English text).
21. *Tablets of Bahá'u'lláh, revealed after the Kitáb-i-Aqdas*, trans. Habib Taherzadeh, et al. (Haifa: Bahá'í World Centre, 1978) pp. 148-49. For the

original Arabic, see *Majmu'e-i az alvâh-e Jamâl-e Aqdas-e Abhâ (ke ba'd az Ketâb-e Aqdas nâzel shode)* (Langenhain, Germany: Lajne-ye nashr-e âsâr-e amri be-zabân-e Fârsi, 137 B.E./1980) p. 89.

22. Collected in English translation in *The Proclamation of Bahá'u'lláh to the kings and leaders of the world* (Haifa: Bahá'í World Centre, 1972).
23. A. Guillaume, *The Life of Muhammad: A Translation of Ibn Ishaq's Sirat Rasul Allah* (Karachi: Oxford University Press, 1967) pp. 652-58.
24. For an analysis of the theological role Bahá'u'lláh's quotations from the Gospels play in his teachings, see Juan Ricardo Cole, "Behold the Man: Bahá'u'lláh on the Life of Jesus," *Journal of the American Academy of Religion*, Vol. 65, no. 1 (1997) pp. 47-71.
25. Bahá'u'lláh, *Prayers and Meditations*, trans. Shoghi Effendi (Wilmette: Bahá'í Publishing Trust, 1938) CLV, pp. 248-9.
26. See for the text and an excellent annotated translation, Stephen Lambden's "An Early Poem of Mírzá Husayn 'Alí Bahá'u'lláh," *Bahá'í Studies Bulletin* Vol. 3, no. 2 (1984) pp. 4ff.
27. *Kolliyât-e Sâ'eb*, ed. Adibi Tehrâni (Tehran, 1362/1983) p. 393.
28. See Juan R. Cole, "Bahá'u'lláh and the Naqshbandí Sufis in Iraq, 1854-1856," in Juan Cole and Moojan Momen, eds. *From Iran East and West* (Los Angeles: Kalimát Press, 1984) pp. 1-28.
29. Compare the translation of Ibn al-Fárid offered by Reynold Nicholson, *Studies in Islamic Mysticism* (Cambridge University Press, 1921) pp. 199-266, to the translation and exchange over Bahá'u'lláh's poem in the *Bahá'í Studies Bulletin*, Vol. 2, nos. 2-4 (1983-84). For further information on Ibn al-Fárid, see Th. Emil Homerin, *From Arab Poet to Muslim Saint* (Columbia: University of South Carolina, 1994).
30. These doctrines are mentioned by name in Bahá'u'lláh's *Haft vâdi* in *Âsâr-e qalam-e a'lâ*, Vol. 3, (Tehran?: Mo'assese-ye melli-ye matbu'ât-e amri, 121 B.E./1964) p. 133. In the seventh and final valley of Absolute Poverty and True Nothingness (*faqr-e haqiqi va fanâ-ye asli*) the seeker passes beyond the belief in these two views of reality. For the English, see *The Seven Valleys and the Four Valleys*, trans. Marzieh Gail and Ali-Kuli Khan (Wilmette: Bahá'í Publishing Trust, 1945 [revised edition, 1975]) p. 39.
3.1 I do not recall seeing the text of this tablet in a printed work, but it circulates hand-to-hand among Iranian Bahá'ís in personal lectionaries, copied down from friends and/or in Bahá'í classes.
32. *Ghazaliyât-e Sa'di*, v. 2 of *Kolliyât-e Sa'di*, ed. Mohammad-'Ali Foroughi, introduction by 'Abbâs Eqbâl (Eqbâl, 1363/1984) p. 10.
33. Ibn al-'Arabî (560-638/1165-1240). For an English translation, see *Ibn Al'Arabi: The Bezels of Wisdom*, trans. R.W. J. Austin (New York: Paulist Press, 1980) and also, *The Wisdom of the Prophets*, trans from Arabic to French by Titus Burckhardt and from French to English by Angela Culme-Seymour (Aldsworth, Gloucestershire: Beshara Publications, 1975).
34. See Fazlur Rahman, *The Philosophy of Mullâ Sadrâ* (Albany: State University of New York Press, 1975) esp. pp. 16-20.
35. It has been shown by Sa'id Nafisi, however, that this work is not by the

famous 'Attâr, but probably by an 'Attâr of Tun living in the 15th century; see Nafisi, *Jostoju dar ahvâl o âsâr-e Farid al-Din 'Attâr-e Nayshâburi* (Tehran, 1320/1941) pp. 145ff.

36. *Divân-e Abu al-Majd Majdud ebn Âdam Hakim Sanâ'i-ye Ghaznavi*, ed. M.T. Modarres-e Razavi, 2nd ed. (Ketâbkhâne-ye Sanâ'i, 1362/1983) p. 182.
37. See Franklin D. Lewis, "Reading, Writing and Recitation: Sanâ'i and the Origins of the Persian Ghazal," Ph.D. Dissertation, University of Chicago, 1995.
38. Note that Fayz-e Kâshâni (1006-1090/1597-1679), two centuries earlier, had written a book by the title *Kalemât-e maknune*, but it is more a philosophical work than a collection of spiritual and ethical aphorisms.
39. From the collected discourses of Shams, only recently published in Iran: *Maqâlât-e Shams-e Tabrizi*, ed. Mohammad-'Ali Movahhed (Tehran: Enteshârât-e Khwârazmi, 1369/1990) p. 647.
40. *World Order*, Vol. 13, no.3 (1979) pp. 24-39.
41. In a letter dated 8 January 1949 written to an English Bahá'í by a secretary of the Guardian published in *The Unfolding Destiny of the British Bahá'í Community* (London: Bahá'í Publishing Trust, 1981) p. 454.
42. Edmund Leach and D. Alan Aycock, eds. *Structuralist Interpretations of Biblical Myth* (Cambridge University Press, 1983) p. 3. Leach is actually referring to the modern scholarly endeavor of unscrambling those parts of scripture that are historically true or factual from those that are factually untrue. This approach he condemns for obscuring the religious truth that the texts convey and that was formerly understood.

MUSLIM YOUTH
gather in Tehran to hear Ayatollah Khamenei denounce reformism.

Fundamentalism and Liberalism

Moojan Momen

This essay describes features of "fundamentalism" and "liberalism" in the religious world. It suggests that these different outlooks arise largely from psychological, rather than sociological, origins. Each represents a particular cognitive style, a general way of looking at the world, and a mode of organizing knowledge. This essay also looks at some of the resources in the Bahá'í Faith for dealing with the tensions that can arise within the Bahá'í community as a result of these different mind-sets.

The upsurge of fundamentalism that has occurred in many different religions and countries of the world has gained a great deal of attention in recent years. Disagreements between fundamentalists and liberals appear to affect almost every religious community to one extent or another. This paper explores a number of questions related to this phenomenon. Are the various social movements popularly called fundamentalism in different cultural contexts all truly different expressions of the same social phenomenon? What are the features distinguishing fundamentalism from its putative counterpart, liberalism? Can we distinguish any underlying basis for the fundamentalism/liberalism dichotomy?

Some may prefer to use the term "traditionalist" or "conservative" rather than "fundamentalist." I have preferred not to use "traditionalist" because this would seem to exclude those fundamentalists, such as most Protestant groups, who tend to be radical and opposed to tradition. I am aware of the counter-argument that the term "fundamentalist" has historically been closely identified with radical Protestantism and may therefore seem to some to be inappropriate in a more general context. Overall, it seems to me that the term "fundamentalist" is now, in popular terms, being used in a more general way about other religions and is therefore the more suitable word.[1]

Although the word fundamentalism dates from the publication of a series of radical Protestant pamphlets, *The Fundamentals*, in the United States from 1910 to 1915, the phenomenon has a long history in religion. It is a mistake to see fundamentalism as a reaction to modernity and thus limit its occurrence to modern times (although it must be admitted that modernity has brought fundamentalism very much to the fore). Nor indeed should fundamentalism be limited to Christianity or even to the Western religions.[2] As fundamentalism and liberalism are defined in this paper, the split can be seen to have been operating at various times in the histories of different religions. In the Islamic world, for example, we can see elements of it in the Ash'ari-Mu'tazili disputes in the 'Abbasid Empire in the ninth century; in the dispute between the philosopher-mystics and the orthodox jurists in Safavid Iran during the sixteenth and seventeenth centuries; in the opposition to Sufism and "religious laxity" by such persons as Ibn Taymiyya (d. 1328) and Ibn 'Abdu'l-Wahhab (d. 1787); as well as in the upheavals of the present-day Islamic world.[3]

The original definitions of fundamentalism made by writers such as Niebuhr included what has since become the stereotype of the popular view of fundamentalists: that they take the words of their holy scripture literally and are opposed to science. This is a view that dates back to the time when Christian fundamentalists were trying to fight the implications of Darwinian evolutionary theory.[4] However, as with all stereotypes, it has become less and less valid as the years have passed. Fundamentalists have changed and adapted since that time. They no longer oppose science, and indeed they take great pride in the extent that they can advance scientific proof for their positions. Nor are they strictly bound to a literal interpretation of the Bible.

I will here try to present the main features of fundamentalism and liberalism and where they differ. Of course, in order to show up the differences, it has been necessary to depict the extremes of the two positions. I may characterize the differences as follows:

Scriptures

Fundamentalists look to the scriptures of their religion as absolute and unchanging truth. The first concern of the fundamentalist is to establish that the scripture is "the word of God." Therefore, it is impossible that there be any error in it. All laws and commandments in these texts are to be applied inflexibly and to the letter. Even religions that have no concept of a scripture revealed by God—Theravada Buddhism, for example—may nevertheless have a similar attitude towards their scriptures.[5] The liberal looks to the holy scripture of religion more as a source of guidance for how to lead one's life. As such, the liberal accepts that the meaning, the "truth," of the scriptures may change as the circumstances of the individual and society change. It is a relative, rather than an absolute, truth.

However, the usual idea of the fundamentalist's literal understanding of scripture requires some degree of elaboration. Where the text is clearly meant to be symbolic, in the parables of Christ for example, even the most extreme fundamentalist does not, of course, believe that these parables actually occurred physically. In addition, where there are inconsistencies in the text, the more sophisticated fundamentalist (the fundamentalist scholar, for example) is willing to allow for some latitude in interpretation. But the important point is that the fundamentalist always regards the scripture as referring to real existent situations and facts. The main criterion for scriptural truth is correspondence with empirical reality. For example, even if heaven and hell are acknowledged not to be physical places above and below the earth, these two words nevertheless do refer to existent realities. Barr has pointed out that the importance of preserving the first principle, the inerrancy of the text, will often compel the fundamentalist to relax the second principle and allow some degree of non-literal interpretation.[6] The liberal, on the other hand, is prepared to see other types of truth—typological, metaphorical, or mythological—in scripture. The truth lies in the significance of the statement rather than its correspondence with any external actuality.[7]

The principal concern of the fundamentalist appears to be to extract an exact meaning from the text of the scriptures. The millennialists of the mid-nineteenth century were certain that their calculations pointed to the return of Christ in 1843 or 1844. When the "Great Disappointment" occurred and there was no literal fulfilment of their expectations, the group that became the Seventh-Day Adventists resolved the problem by formulating an explanation that the prophecy had been fulfilled: on that date, Christ had entered the Most Holy of the heavenly sanctuary and he had a work to perform there before coming to earth. This is a clearly non-literal explanation of a prophecy that most other Christian denominations expect to occur literally and on earth. The Seventh-Day Adventists are nevertheless a fundamentalist denomination.[8] Their interpretation of the "Great Disappointment" has the ability to give an exact meaning to the scripture when a literal meaning has been ruled out in their history. Another instructive example relates to the question of Noah's flood. Some Christian fundamentalist scholars are willing to accept that this may have been a local flood in Mesopotamia rather than a world flood (which the literal text would imply), as this would be less problematical scientifically. Nevertheless, the story of the flood does, for these scholars, refer to an actual physical event—any non-physical interpretation is ruled out.

Much modern Christian fundamentalist literature is taken up with detailed explanations of how the events of the Bible can be explained scientifically. Scientific explanations are desirable as they are considered to provide a guarantee of certainty and exactness of interpretation. The liberal, however, is willing to allow that the texts of the books are open to more than one interpretation. External factors in society may influence the way that the scriptures are interpreted. Allegorical and symbolic interpretations may be used particularly of passages that appear to contradict human reason. Traditional interpretations may be examined for whatever useful insights they may present, but they have no binding force on the present.

The liberal is much more willing to acknowledge that scripture is a historical document. This often means that it has been written down by fallible men, sometimes many years after the events portrayed.

Therefore, almost certainly errors and myth-making have crept in; almost certainly, theological ideas current at the time of writing have been read back into the past. If the fundamentalist does accept the historical nature of the scriptures, he will insist that they were divinely protected from the intrusion of alteration or error. Certainly no external factors, such as the social conditions at the time that the scripture was written down, can be allowed to influence the understanding of the texts. Another characteristic fundamentalist attitude is that the whole of the scripture stands or falls together. This view maintains that since scripture is the word of God, and therefore infallible, the inerrancy of every single sentence of the scripture must be maintained. Otherwise, the slightest error in even the smallest part casts doubt on the whole. The liberal will, on the other hand, be much more willing to accept that parts of the scripture are more "true"—in the sense of being more likely to have actually occurred physically—than other parts.

Another way of expressing the difference between fundamentalists and liberals would be to say that for fundamentalists the meaning of the scripture is inherent in the text and can be apprehended directly without interpretation; while for the liberal, the scripture is something that must be applied to one's life; that is to say, it must be interpreted in accordance with the context in which it is being applied.[9]

Religious Traditions

The traditions of the religion are looked at differently by different types of fundamentalists. In this paper, I propose to describe two types, although other commentators have identified additional sub-groups.[10] The first group of fundamentalists are conservative and traditionalist. They regard tradition as an element in religion that is as authoritative as the scriptures themselves. In Christianity, there is very little in the Bible to act as a basis for most of the Church structure and ritual, and therefore the major source of authority for this is tradition.[11] In Islam, the concept of the *sunna*, the deeds and words of Muhammad as the perfect example for all Muslims to follow, and the doctrine of *ijm'a*, the concept that whatever the whole of the Muslim world agrees upon as a consensus view must be correct, act as powerful forces for maintaining traditional attitudes and positions. If any of the religion's structures or doctrines seems to be in conflict with society then it is society that must change to conform with what is perceived to be the divine. These fundamentalists are very concerned with building up bodies of doctrine and dogmatic statements as well as elaborating the holy law and its provisions. This enables the true believer to be sorted out from the waverer and the potential heretic. Doctrines and dogmas must, like scripture, be understood literally, while the holy law must be followed to the letter.

The second group of fundamentalists are of the evangelical, radical, revivalist type. These regard the traditions of the religion as the main obstacle to a return to the "pure" original religion that they consider can be reconstructed from the texts of the scripture. They would like to see all traditional structures swept aside in favor of the scriptures themselves.

Radical and traditionalist fundamentalists only differ in the boundary of what they consider to be unalterable and inerrant—the radicals place the boundary around just the scriptures while the traditionalists extend this to the traditions of the religion also. Whether fundamentalists are of one type or the other appears to depend on the basic tendency of their religious background. Thus, for example, a religious background that stresses tradition seems to produce fundamentalists mainly of the traditionalist kind. In the Christian world, Roman Catholicism holds that the traditions of the Church are of equal authority to the scripture[12] and the fundamentalists among the Catholics tend to be traditionalist. At the extreme of the fundamentalist wing among the Catholics we find the followers of ultra-traditionalist Archbishop Marcel Lefebvre.[13] Radical fundamentalists in the Christian world are to be found among the Protestant sects, Protestantism being a movement that arose as a reaction to the traditionalism of Catholicism. In the Muslim world, most fundamentalists are traditionalists since Islam is a religion in which tradition plays an important part, but there are a few modern radical groups—for example, the followers of Rashad Khalifa[14] and of 'Ali Shari'ati in Iran.[15]

Mutual Recriminations

Fundamentalists tend to blame liberals for allowing into the religion dubious ideas and doctrines which have no basis in the religion itself but are accommodations to the secular world, the intrusion of secular views, or ideas from other religions. In the context of the modern world, a good example is the liberation theology which originated in Latin America and which fundamentalists regard as being no more than a back-door method for introducing Marxism into Christianity. Similarly, fundamentalists tend to blame liberalism for a moral laxity in society in general.

A more basic criticism levelled by fundamentalists at liberals concerns the arbitrary nature of those parts of the scriptures that liberals regard as being the religious core, and therefore to be preserved, and those parts that are culturally determined, and therefore can be dispensed with or interpreted liberally. From a fundamentalist viewpoint it appears that the line dividing the two is not defined by any discernible logical rules but rather by whatever happens to be the current social fashion. In one decade, feminism is to the fore and so the liberals dispense with those parts of the scripture which seem to give a low status to women; the next, championing gay rights is fashionable and so the liberals jettison that part of the scripture too. Are fashion and current secular sensibilities to be the arbiters of the stand-point of faith? If so will the inevitable result not be to jettison everything eventually?[16]

Liberals consider that the harsh, intolerant attitudes of the fundamentalists are both contrary to the true spirit of religion and doing religion a great deal of harm in the modern world. The liberal tends to see the traditions and structures of the religion in relation to society and is always asking the question: does the religious tradition and structure serve the needs of society? If any part of religious structure or doctrine is not relevant to society, then it is necessary to see how it can be adapted in order to become relevant. The traditions, doctrines, and dogmas of the religion, as well as the holy law, are all guidelines for action that can be interpreted according to circumstances.

Attitude Towards Diversity Within Religion

The fundamentalist is intolerant of wide divergences of religious expression within his or her own religion. All divergence from the main orthodox tradition is suspect. There is an ever-present prospect of heresy insidiously creeping in under various, seemingly innocent, guises. The religion must be protected from it at all costs. The history of religion points to numerous episodes in which much suffering and bloodshed has been caused by those wishing to impose a narrow interpretation of their religion on their fellow believers. In Christianity, this was seen in the past in the Inquisition and the numerous bloody suppressions of heresies. It also operates in the present.[17] In Islam, there have been periodic persecutions of marginal sects as well as such groups as Sufis.[18]

The liberal will tolerate the existence within the community of a wide variety of viewpoints. As long as a viewpoint does not explicitly deny the veracity of the prophet/founder or the holy scripture, it can usually be accommodated within the community of believers. Even if a viewpoint is considered too extreme to be acceptable, the preferred method for trying to counter it will be argument and persuasion rather than compulsion.

Attitude Towards Religious Pluralism

The fundamentalist sees other religions as being the result of error. Since they are in open competition with the true religion, the usual response is to regard them as the work of the devil, to be strongly opposed, and even persecuted if necessary. The only possible exception to this is those religions towards which the prophet/founder himself showed respect—these must, by definition, be religions that preceded the prophet/founder. Thus, for example fundamentalist Christians will tolerate Judaism but reject Islam; fundamentalist Muslims will tolerate Judaism and Christianity but reject the Bahá'í Faith. But even this toleration wears thin at times and merges into persecution—as witnessed by past persecutions of Jews by Christians, and Jews and Christians by Muslims. A related phenomenon in modern times is the linking of a xenophobic fundamentalism to a strident nationalism in many parts of the world. This can be seen in Arya Samaj Hinduism in India, in some forms of Nichiren Shoshu Buddhism in Japan,[19] among Sinhalese Buddhist supporters of the Sri Lankan Freedom Party,[20] in the Gush Emunim movement in Israel,[21] and in the Moral Majority in fundamentalist Christianity in the USA.[22]

The fundamentalist's conviction of possessing the truth leads to a strong tendency to try to correct the errors of the unbelievers. Thus, the inter-religious activity of the fundamentalist is typically evangelism and missionary work. The inter-religious activity of the liberal, on the other hand, tends towards ecumenicism and inter-faith dialogue. The fundamentalist has no time for such activities. Since his or her own religion already possesses the absolute truth, there is no point in looking elsewhere for it. The liberal will look to other religions as alternative views of religious truth, though many liberals will give their own religion some form of priority. An example is the Catholic theologian Rahner's concept that truly religious persons of other religions are "anonymous Christians."[23] Other liberals are willing to go even further and regard other religions as being of equal validity to their own —but, perhaps, more suited to their cultures.[24] A liberal society, such as Muslim Spain in the medieval period, allowed the efflorescence of intellectual and artistic excellence from whatever quarter, Christian, Jewish, or Muslim.

Social and Political Differences

With regard to social and political differences, we are treading on the most difficult ground in our enquiry. This is because there appears to have been some degree of change in the modern period, compared to the characteristic features of these groups in former times. Historically, there does not appear to have been any characteristic political stance from either fundamentalists or liberals. If anything, both parties often tended to political quietism. Socially, the majority of fundamentalists have tended to be isolated either by forming separate communities, such as the Hutterites in North America, or by minimizing contact with the rest of the society through associating as much as possible only with fellow fundamentalists (fundamentalist trade and vocational associations, clubs, colleges, holiday centres, etc.). Personal asceticism and rejection of wealth characterized many fundamentalists, while liberal views were often found among the wealthy. Recently, much of this has greatly changed. Both sides have taken on characteristic political attitudes and fundamentalists have left their social isolation and entered social and political life in every part of the world.

During the modern period, fundamentalists have tended to be found at the right of the political spectrum,[25] encouraging individual self-reliance, and stressing such social teachings of religion as justice. Some fundamentalist groups have even reversed the previous trend by tending to adopt a positive, encouraging attitude towards the accumulation of wealth. These groups have become actively involved in politics, advocating capitalism and a laissez-faire social philosophy while raising communism to an almost mythological level of evil. The best-known example of this is the religious right (also known as the "Moral Majority" movement) in the USA, which contributed to Ronald Reagan's electoral success.[26] An important social and political feature of fundamentalism is the tendency to promote a traditional role for women in society, that is to say, confinement to home and children rather than coming out to work and taking a political role. This tendency to try to control women applies as much to Christian fundamentalism in the USA, where the religious right campaigned against the Equal Rights for Women Amendment, as it does in the Islamic and Jewish worlds.[27]

Liberals, on the other hand, have politically tended to the left in modern times, due to their concern with social issues. Some groups have even engaged in Christian-Marxist dialogue. They tend to stress such religious teachings as showing love towards one's fellow human beings. They have also reversed their previous tendency and are now inclined towards asceticism and have a negative attitude towards the accumulation of wealth. They support the emancipation of women.

The extreme wing of fundamentalism holds the view that existing political structures, because they are products of man's thinking and efforts rather than divine revelation, should be overthrown in favor of a political structure based on the holy scripture. Khomeini advocated such a program and the Iranian Revolution of 1979 was intended to inaugurate such a theocracy.[28] It should not be thought, however, that it is only within Islam that such positions are being advocated. In Christianity, there are groups such as the Christian Reconstructionists in the United States which, under the leadership of Rousas J. Rushdoomy, advocate an overthrow of democratic institutions in order to establish a theocracy under biblical law. In Israel and India, there are several extreme Jewish and Hindu religious parties that advocate a similar position.

Bruce has pointed out that the social manifestations of fundamental-ism and liberalism are, to a large extent, a consequence of their doctrinal or ideological positions. The fundamentalist rejection of all doctrinal positions outside their own leads to highly demarcated, tightly knit, highly committed, socially isolated communities. Liberals, on the other hand, regard the beliefs of the rest of the world sympathetically and are socially much more integrated. The great diversity of beliefs amongst them, however, hinders the formation of coherent groups and also reduces the possibility of a high degree of commitment.[29]

Towards a Definition of Fundamentalism

Put succinctly, we may characterise the fundamentalist as having turned inwards to the center of the religion—the scripture, doctrines, and traditions—and seeking to protect these from the intrusions of the modern, secular world; while the liberal has turned outwards, seeking to break down the barriers between the religious world and the secular world. For the fundamentalist, the secular world must adapt to and come under the control of the religious world, while the liberal considers it the job of the religious world to adapt to and become relevant in the secular world. For the fundamentalist, religion is addressed to the individual and individual salvation comes first; social salvation and ordering may then result from an aggregation of individual salvations. Liberals, on the other hand, are primarily concerned with society as a whole. Religion is for social salvation; individual salvation is best achieved within an enlightened society. To strive for individual salvation when society itself is not saved is egotistical and reprehensible.

The differences described above between fundamentalists and liberals have purposely been wide-ranging because the same phenomenon reappears in slightly different ways among different religions. None of these differences is sufficient by itself to identify an individual as a fundamentalist or a liberal. With Hinduism and Buddhism, for example, the inerrancy of scripture is not an important issue. On the other hand, almost all Muslims believe in the inerrancy of the Qur'an, but this does not make them all fundamentalists. To differentiate between fundamentalists and liberals in the Hindu, Buddhist, and Muslim worlds, one must go to the sphere of social relations and examine attitudes toward modernity and religious diversity. This may also account for the fact that, in the nineteenth century, when an uncritical acceptance of the inerrancy of the Bible was much more in the mainstream of Christianity (i.e., a similar situation to Islam today), it was possible for individuals to hold to Biblical inerrancy while at the same time advocating liberal social principles.[30] It would appear that our ideas about fundamentalism and liberalism should be sufficiently flexible to allow for such individuals not to be classed as fundamentalists.

Thus the arguments presented in this paper appear to be moving towards a position wherein fundamentalism and liberalism are defined not in any absolute terms, but in terms that are relative to the particular situation of the individual in relation to religion and time. In other words, fundamentalism and liberalism must be identified through a pattern that changes from one religion to another (partly as a result of the different emphases within each religion) and also changes with time. It would seem therefore that a satisfactory definition of fundamentalism or liberalism at the social level can only be achieved on a multi-factorial basis.

Fundamentalism and Modernity

Although I have thus far given examples of the way that liberalism and fundamentalism have manifested themselves in the past, it should be borne in mind that, for three reasons, the contrast between the two has been emphasized and brought into stark relief only in modern times.[31] First, in most of the world until the present century, and in the West until the Age of Enlightenment, the religious and secular worlds were not sharply defined and separated. Religious and metaphysical assumptions and ethical values pervaded all aspects of society: family life, social mores and customs, intellectual life, and politics. Therefore, there was not much opportunity for the secular world to challenge the religious. Second, we can postulate that the complexities of modern life and the mass of problems that face humankind (the nuclear threat, drug/alcohol problems, environmental threats, the North-South divide, etc. which are brought to the immediate attention of all through modern means of communications) have induced great uncertainty and anxiety. One response to the fear induced by this state is to retreat into the greater certainty offered by fundamentalism. It presents a retreat from the confused maelstrom of modernity. Third, until the nineteenth century, the religious world was not so acutely challenged by genuine competition from other religions. At that time, the colonial powers took Christianity to every part of the world, while during the present century, we have seen an increasing flow in the opposite direction, both as a result of migration and of missionary activity by Hindus, Buddhists, Muslims, etc.

Therefore previously, the fundamentalist was rarely challenged with intrusions into the religious world, while the liberal had only occasional opportunities for seeking to adapt the religious world to new external circumstances. Thus, it has been the phenomenon of secularization and religious pluralism in the modern world that has brought the liberal/fundamentalist split to the fore of religious life. In country after country, the arrival of modernity resulted in a traditionalist fundamentalist backlash. In the United States, the challenge laid down by modern science, and the theory of evolution in particular, was one of the most important factors leading to the rise of fundamentalism. In Iran, in the early years of the twentieth century, the liberal reforms advocated by the Constitutionalists were opposed by the fundamentalist traditionalist ulama led by Shaykh Fadlu'llah Nuri.[32]

It is perhaps in India that we find the best example of this pattern. Under attack from the Christianity of the colonial power, as well as from the challenge of Western science, a number of liberal reform movements arose among India's Hindus in the nineteenth century—the Brahmo Samaj founded by Rammohan Roy in 1828, and the very similar Prartharma Samaj. These movements adopted many of the ideas of the Christian West into a Hindu framework. This development produced two types of reaction among Hindus corresponding to the two types of fundamentalism described above. The radical fundamentalists, such as Dayananda Saraswasti, who founded the Arya Samaj in 1875, felt that Hinduism could best be revitalized by returning to its Vedic roots. Thus they opposed the inclusivist social reform movements that accommodated Christian Western ideas and rejected what they considered to be the accretions of ritual and tradition (such as idol worship) that had been added to "pure" Vedic Hinduism. Secondly, there were traditionalist fundamentalists who rejected both the inclusivism of social reform movements and the radicalism of the Arya Samaj and wanted to maintain Hinduism as it was, with all of its rituals, traditions, and social structures, including the caste system. They formed themselves into numerous groups (such as the Sanatana Dharma Sabha) which came under an umbrella organization, the Bharata Dharma Mahamandala in 1902.[33]

Social and Intellectual Basis

Although little research has been done on the psychological and social bases of the fundamentalist/liberal dichotomy, those that have observed these categories are agreed that we must go beyond the old view that fundamentalism represents an anti-scientific backlash of the old rural, agriculturally based communities against the urban, scientific culture. In the next few paragraphs, I shall review the evidence that, first, fundamentalism is not necessarily anti-scientific and, second, that sociological observations tend to discount any significant social differences between fundamentalists and liberals.

Fundamentalist writers often go to great lengths to show that their positions are in accordance with science. However, critics would maintain that this is a veneer of pseudo-science applied in order to increase the plausibility of the fundamentalist worldview[34] and that fundamentalists remain inherently opposed to the inductive approach of the scientific method.[35] Among many fundamentalists there remains a strong advocacy of anti-evolutionary (anti-Darwinian) positions under the name of creationism. However even this position bows to science, in that it claims to use scientific method to prove its case. Indeed, religious critics of fundamentalism argue that by striving to adapt the Bible stories so that they conform to science, the fundamentalist is in fact effectively adopting a materialistic stance and placing science above God's word.[36] But whatever the strengths or weaknesses of fundamentalist science, it remains true that fundamentalists no longer see themselves as intellectually opposed to science. Their argument, as it has been reformulated in recent decades at least, is with historical and literary criticism.

Even outside the Christian West, where fundamentalism is often centered on a reaction to the intrusion of modernity into traditional societies, the fundamentalists are not against science and technology itself. They are quite happy to utilize these. Ayatu'llah Khomeini's success in overthrowing the Shah, for example, owed a great deal to the skill of his supporters in utilizing such modern inventions as the telephone and the cassette recorder to disseminate the Ayatu'llah's speeches. What they are against are the alien values and morals (and in particular the skeptical and critical approaches to religion) being imported along with science and technology.

We may also state that there is no justification for the commonly held view that the fundamentalist is against logic and rationality. On the contrary, the fundamentalist mentality is much predisposed to using very precise logical argumentation. Shi'i Islam is an interesting example to consider further in this respect. Both the theology (*kalam*) and the jurisprudence of Shi'i Islam are built on foundations of rationalism and logic. From the ninth century onwards, Shi'i scholars have prided themselves on being able to derive their doctrine, as well as their legal judgments, from logic as well as from the traditions. Indeed, the study of logic forms an important part of the academic curriculum at the religious colleges of Qum and Najaf.[37]

Also to be questioned is the view of fundamentalism as mainly a phenomenon of poor rural areas. In fact fundamentalists and liberals are likely to come from similar social and educational backgrounds. Many modern fundamentalists appear to arise from educated middle class backgrounds—precisely the same background from which the majority of liberals come. This has been asserted for British fundamentalist groups,[38] and for Americans.[39] Similar conclusions have also been drawn about the Muslim world whether in Egypt, Iran, or West Africa.[40]

It is as yet premature to dismiss social factors entirely, but the evidence certainly does not support a blanket association of fundamentalism with any particular social category or factor. These findings, if confirmed by further research, point to the likelihood that the fundamentalist/liberal difference comes not so much from social differences as from differences in psychology.

Psychological Basis

In psychological terms, we may characterize fundamentalism and liberalism as two different ways of thinking, two cognitive styles. Cognitive style refers to the individual's characteristic and consistent manner of organizing and categorizing perceptions and concepts. It is a value-free term in that the variety of cognitive styles are not judged to be good or bad in themselves, although any particular style may be more or less favorable in a given situation or for the purpose of achieving a given goal.[41]

The fundamentalist mentality is characteristically one that sees things in terms of black-and-white, in terms of clear-cut boundaries which determine what is and what is not acceptable belief, who is and who is not in the community. Any person, situation or object belongs either within the orbit of the "saved" or is outside it; there are no intermediate stations. No matter how good a life a person may lead, if that person is not among the "saved," then he or she must be among the "damned." The lines between good and evil are clearly drawn and there are no intermediate positions. The liberal is more inclined to allow for "grey areas," intermediate situations. Although a person may not be a believer, if his actions are good, then he cannot be totally bad. In pursuing this line of thought, we are gradually coming to the point at which it is possible to see that the fundamentalist/liberal split is not something that affects religion alone, but rather is one facet of a much larger psycho-social phenomenon.[42]

Another way of describing this would be to say that one of the underlying differences between fundamentalists and liberals is that the former are driven by a desire for certainty. Hofstadter has called this the "one-hundred per cent mentality." Such a person will "tolerate no ambiguities, no equivocations, no reservations, and no criticism."[43] For the fundamentalist, certainty is only to be found in objectivity. The indecisive world of the liberal who is willing to see some truth in all opinions, the uncertain field of historical and literary criticism where different opinions abound, are all tainted by personal opinion, and therefore by subjectivity. This is deeply unsatisfactory to the fundamentalist psyche. The only way of achieving objective truth is to adopt a standard that lies outside of the human subjectivity. While a liberal Christian would be happy to accept just a statement of belief in Christ from someone, this is not sufficient for a fundamentalist. It is too liable to the whims of subjectivity. It might include all sorts of doctrinally objectionable positions. Acceptance of the Bible as inerrant, however, is considered by fundamentalists to constitute objectivity, for one is not forming a personal view of the Bible but rather accepting the Bible's own view of itself. This, the fundamentalist considers, gives one a standard of absolute truth,[44] and hence objectivity, and hence certainty.

This desire for certainty probably accounts for the enthusiastic adoption of scientific (or, as their critics would maintain, pseudo-scientific) approaches by fundamentalists. Scientific method acts, for the modern mind, as a guarantor of the correctness of one's conclusions. It also accounts for the fact that fundamentalists are often very keen on building up elaborate logical arguments. The mathematical certainty of logic appeals to such minds. The fundamentalist favors absolutes, while the liberal favors relativistic styles of thinking.

One cognitive style that has been described appears to be of particular interest with regard to the fundamentalism/liberalism dichotomy. It is called "field-dependence versus field-independence." This relates to the way that an individual relates a figure in the perceptual field to its background.[45] Field-dependent persons tend to see the figure only in relation to its background, while field-independent persons tend to isolate the figure and extract it from its background. There seems to be some provisional similarity here between field-dependence and liberalism (in that liberals tend to see religion only in terms of its social background) and between field-independence and fundamentalism (in that fundamentalists tend to see religion as an absolute, isolated from its social background).

There are also some similarities between what psychologists call the convergent style of thinking and fundamentalism, while divergent thinking corresponds with liberalism. Convergent thinking focuses down from the general to the particular, dissecting and analyzing. It prizes rational, deductive thought and aims towards certainty. It tends to be found among certain types of scientists and engineers in particular. Interestingly, we find that when scientists (especially from the physical sciences) and engineers become religious, they often tend towards fundamentalist religion.[46] Divergent thought, on the other hand, goes from the particular to the general, integrating the particulars into a general picture. It prizes inductive, intuitive thinking and aims towards inclusivity rather than certainty. It tends to predominate among artists and social scientists. These two modes of thinking have, in experimental psychology, been tentatively linked to brain structure and function.[47]

Although fundamentalism can be defined in terms of a particular cognitive style, there is a problem: Which phenomenon causes which? Does a particular cognitive style cause a person to be attracted to the fundamentalist worldview or does the ideology of fundamentalism and the pressures of a fundamentalist community induce a particular cognitive style? This is probably a question of the chicken-and-egg variety that has no answer.

Fundamentalism, Liberalism, and the Bahá'í Faith

What has all this to do with the Bahá'í Faith? It must be clear from the above that both fundamentalism and liberalism are wide-spread phenomena. They are part of peoples' constitutional make-up. While a cognitive style may not be as fixed a thing as the color of one's eyes, if it changes, it only does so very slowly. Therefore, if the Bahá'í Faith is to be truly a universal religion, it must be able to incorporate people of all types; not just all types of races and cultures but also all types of cognitive styles. The Bahá'í community has to be wide enough in its outreach and flexible enough in its workings to enable it to contain both types of persons without fragmenting into schisms and conflict. It cannot, however, be denied that the presence of fundamentalists and liberals does cause a certain amount of tension within the Bahá'í community. There have been numerous episodes and situations known to the author of this article, and no doubt to any other person who has been a Bahá'í for any length of time, where this tension has caused problems and even damage.

Historically, it could be said that the situation in the West in the time of 'Abdu'l-Bahá tended to favor the liberals. The cultic milieu out of which many Bahá'ís came was a tradition in which a very liberal interpretation of religion was inherent. However, there was also a fundamentalist tension present, possibly as a result of those who came into the Bahá'í community from a millennialist background—because they considered that Bahá'u'lláh had fulfilled the prophecies of the Bible. During Shoghi Effendi's time the balance swung in favor of the fundamentalists. Shoghi Effendi's concentration in the early years of his ministry on building up the Bahá'í administration would have tended to favor the tidy administrative mind of the fundamentalist. The concentration on missionary expansion in the later years of Shoghi Effendi's ministry would also have favored those with a fundamentalist stance—fundamentalists wish to convert others to their view since they know that it is the correct view and there can be no other truth. In more recent times, we may discern the beginnings of a new balance. The recent emphasis from the Universal House of Justice on qualitative goals, social and economic development, and dialogue with other religions and organisations is likely to bring people of a more liberal stance to the fore in the community.

Within the Bahá'í community, there are several factors that alleviate potential tensions between those of a fundamentalist bent and those with leanings towards liberalism and that encourage dialogue between them. As the Bahá'í Faith is a young religion, it addresses many of the features of the modern world which have caused so much pain and discord in other religions. Its scriptures already deal with most current issues in relevant ways. Since there are scriptural endorsements of such matters as the equality of men and women and the abolition of extremes of wealth and poverty, these matters cause few problems of principle—whatever problems they may cause are with regard to their implementation. The rigid desire to follow the text of the scripture forces those in the Bahá'í community who tend towards fundamentalism to adopt what would in other religions be considered a liberal position on these questions. Thus many of these issues, which cause much heart-searching and a fundamentalist/liberal spilt in other religions, are the subject of clear pronouncements in the scriptures around which both fundamentalists and liberals can unite.

Second, the main mechanism of public discourse and decision-making in the community is consultation. Bahá'u'lláh has exhorted his community to "take counsel together in all matters."[48] The process is regarded as a spiritual reponsibility, and it is a duty incumbent upon all to ensure that virtues such as fairness, integrity, forbearance, respect, and courtesy are brought to bear upon the process.[49] To succeed completely in establishing consultation on such grounds is of course difficult, but to strive towards it is incumbent upon the participants.

Third, the Bahá'í Faith has no real dogma. There are a number of statements regarding Bahá'u'lláh, his station and relation to previous prophets, as well as the concept of the Covenant, which may be regarded as dogmatic positions—but these are in fact matters of establishing authority rather than establishing theological doctrine. And whatever dogma one may consider exists today in the Bahá'í Faith, it is unlikely to increase, as there are no mechanisms for establishing any new dogma. Bahá'ís are, and they remain Bahá'ís, not so much because they share the theological positions of other Bahá'ís, but because of their common vision of the direction that humanity is taking.

A fourth factor in the Bahá'í Faith that helps in the dialogue between liberals and fundamentalists is the overriding command to unity in the Bahá'í teachings. This imperative is higher than all other considerations. Thus Shoghi Effendi, referring to a dispute that occurred in Bahá'u'lláh's lifetime that was typical of the sort of disagreement that occurs between fundamentalists and liberals, related: "During the days of Bahá'u'lláh some of the prominent teachers of the Cause in Persia were divided as to the station of Bahá'u'lláh and at last wrote to Him for arbitration. In answer Bahá'u'lláh said that if they were united both sides were right and if they were divided both were wrong."[50] In summary then, being united is considered a higher truth in the Bahá'í Faith than being right. This has obvious implications for a dialogue between liberals and fundamentalists. Whatever sincere disagreement there may be between the two sides, there should be an overriding concern to maintain unity. This unity does not mean uniformity. In other words, individuals are entitled to hold different views, but these should not become the basis of the creation of parties and platforms within the community. Indeed, the formation of such factions is expressly forbidden and can result in administrative sanctions against individuals trying to carry out any such program.

Closely connected to this teaching of unity in the Bahá'í Faith is the concept of the Covenant. This concept means that the primary focus of loyalty and unity in the Bahá'í Faith is not towards any set of doctrines or dogmas—and these are, of course, the usual focus of disagreement between fundamentalists and liberals. A Bahá'í is free to hold whatever opinion she or he pleases: "At the very root of the Cause lies the principle of the undoubted right of the individual to self-expression, his freedom to declare his conscience and set forth his views."[51] The source of unity in the Bahá'í Faith is a focus on and loyalty towards the designated center of the Faith—at the present time this means the Universal House of Justice, which is an elected body. That body was created by Bahá'u'lláh to administer the affairs of the Bahá'í Faith and to make rulings in any areas of law that are not covered in the writings of Bahá'u'lláh. It is not a body that makes definitive rulings on theological and doctrinal matters. This means that Bahá'ís are not asked to subscribe to a creed as a precondition of membership, but rather to express their loyalty to a body, which administers the Bahá'í community. They express their loyalty by submitting to the decisions of the Universal House of Justice, which are usually of an administrative and functional nature rather than doctrinal or interpretative. This is a matter that again does not divide fundamentalists and liberals: the fundamentalist because the provisions of the Covenant are unequivocally laid down in the scripture; the liberals because they can see that only through united action can the liberal social agenda of the Bahá'í Faith be realized.

The net effect of these factors is to give both liberals and fundamentalists a large degree of freedom to hold whatever views they wish and to voice their opinions. If they disagree with a decision of their local or national administrative bodies, they are free to appeal this ultimately to the highest level, the Universal House of Justice. If the decision of the Universal House of Justice goes against them, they may, if they wish, continue to hold the opinion. What they may not do, under the terms of the principle of unity and the doctrine of the Covenant, is to try actively to create a party for their opinion. In this way, the Bahá'í Faith tries to maintain a wide range of opinions and personalities within the community. Both liberal and fundamentalist views can coexist within the community, both groups being united in their overriding aim, the effort to promote the Bahá'í message of peace and unity.

NOTES

MOOJAN MOMEN has recently published *The Phenomenon of Religion* (Oneworld, 1999) and *Islam and the Bahá'í Faith* (George Ronald, 2000). Much of the material presented in this paper is published in *The Phenomenon of Religion.*

1. W. Shepard, "'Fundamentalism' Christian and Islamic", *Religion*, Vol. 17 (1987) pp. 355-78; and "Islam and Ideology: Towards a Typology", *International Journal of Middle East Studies*, Vol. 19 (1987) pp. 307-36, suggests the term "rejectionist neo-traditionalist." One feels, however, that whatever advantage such a term may have is more than counter-balanced by its unwieldiness.
2. For a survey of fundamentalism across the world in Eastern as well as Western religions, see Lionel Caplan, ed., *Studies in Religious Fundamentalism* (London: MacMillan, 1987) and Marty and Applebly, *Fundamentalisms Observed* (Chicago: Chicago University Press, 1991).
3. For accounts of these, see G. Makdisi, "Remarks on Traditionalism in Islamic Religious History" and Osman Amin "Some aspects of Religious Reform in the Muslim Middle East" in C. Leiden, ed., *The Conflict of Traditionalism and Modernism in the Muslim Middle East* (Austin: Texas University Press, 1966); M. Momen, *Introduction to Shi'i Islam* (New Haven: Yale University Press, 1985) pp. 115-16. See also, E. Sandeen, *The Roots of Fundamentalism* (Chicago University Press, 1970). Sandeen has shown how the fundamentalist movement in the early twentieth century grew out of, and represents the continuation of the concerns of, the millenarianism of the nineteenth century.
4. It particularly relates to the "Monkey Trial" in Dayton, Tennessee in which J. T. Scopes, a teacher, was prosecuted for teaching the theory of evolution. The definition seems to have been first formally advanced by H. Richard Niebuhr in "Fundamentalism," *Encyclopaedia of the Social Sciences* (London: MacMillan, 1931) pp. 526-27.
5. King, *A Thousand Lives Away* (Oxford: Bruno Cassirer, 1964) pp. 53-57.

6. Barr, *Fundamentalism* (London: SCM Press, 1977) pp. 40-50.
7. Barr, *Fundamentalism*, pp. 49-50; Bruce, *Firm in the Faith* (Aldershot: Gover, 1984) pp. 3-4.
8. At least traditionally they have been, although there is now a marked movement back to the center ground of Christianity.
9. Bruce, *Firm in the Faith*, pp. 186-93
10. I have here sub-divided fundamentalists into two groups, traditionalists and radicals, while keeping liberals as one group. Other writers have created even more sub-divisions. See for example Shepard ("Islam and Ideology: Towards a Typology") who has developed a typology for Islam with eight sub-divisions. See also Smart's classification in *Religion and the Western Mind* (Basingstoke: MacMillan, 1987) pp. 52-53.
11. Although, of course, many Protestant Churches, especially the Calvinists, tried to base the whole of their church structure and ritual on the Bible.
12. This has been the official Catholic position since the Council of Trent (1563). The Orthodox Church also has a high regard for its traditions.
13. Lefebvre advocated a return to the traditional forms of the Catholic Church and in particular the Latin Mass. He claimed to have had several million followers and sympathizers among Roman Catholics, especially in France.
14. Rashad Khalifa put the Qur'an into a computer and discovered that the entire book revolves around the number nineteen and its multiples. He regarded this a proof of the miraculous nature of the book and asserted that Islam should be based on the Qur'an alone with a downgrading of the traditions. This has been strongly advocated by proponents of his ideas in countries as far apart as the USA, Egypt, and Malaysia.
15. Shari'ati, during the period just prior to the 1979 Revolution in Iran, advocated a return to Islam. By this he did not intend the traditionalist Islam of the ulama but rather a radical reinterpretation which he considered to be the original Shi'i Islam.
16. See S. Akhtar, "The Virtues of Fundamentalism," *Scottish Journal of Religious Studies*, Vol. 10 (1989) pp. 41-49; P. Berger, *The Heretical Imperative* (London: Collins, 1980) pp. 116, 118.
17. See also Barr, *Fundamentalism*, pp. 316-17, for a reference to the manner in which fundamentalist coerciveness operates today in the Christian world.
18. See, for example the activities of Mulla Muhammad Baqir Majlisi in seventeenth-century Iran (Momen, *Introduction to Shi'i Islam*, pp. 114-17).
19. See G. B. Sansom, *Japan* (London: Barrie and Jenkins, 1976) pp. 334-35; Takakusu, *Essentials of Buddhist Philosophy* (Honolulu: University of Hawaii, 3d ed, 1965) pp. 178-81.
20. Donald Taylor, "Incipient Fundamentalism: Religion and Politics among Sri Lankan Hindus in Britain" in *Studies in Religious Fundamentalism* (ed. L. Caplan) pp. 146-150.
21. See Lustick, "Israel's Dangerous Minority," *Foreign Policy*, Vol. 68 (1987) pp. 118-39.
22. Erling Jorstad, *The New Christian Right 1981-1986: Prospects for the Post-Reagan Era* (Lewiston: Edward Mellen Press, 1987); Bruce, "The Moral Majority: The Politics of Fundamentalism in Secular Society" in Caplan,

Studies in Religious Fundamentalism, pp. 177-94; idem, *Firm in the Faith*, pp. 171-73.

23. See Rahner, "Observations on the problem of the 'Anonymous Christian,' " *Theological Investigations*, Vol.14 (New York: Seabury, 1976) pp. 280-94.
24. See for example Hick, *God Has Many Names* (London: MacMillan, 1980) and *Problems of Religious Pluralism* (London: MacMillan, 1985).
25. During the nineteenth century, however, a fundamentalist position was not incompatible with social reformism. See Bruce, *Firm in the Faith*, pp. 12-13, 147. But see below for a possible reason for this.
26. Bruce, "The Moral Majority."
27. See Caplan, *Studies in Religious Fundamentalism*, pp. 18-19; Bruce, *Firm in the Faith*, p. 155.
28. It should be noted that, in practice, Khomeini had to retreat from the theoretical positions advocated in his writings, and Iran still possesses many of the political institutions derived from the Western political systems that Khomeini so despised.
29. Bruce, *Firm in the Faith*, pp. 78-89.
30. See note above.
31. For further discussion of this point, see Berger, *Heretical Imperative*, Ch. 1; Berger, Berger and Kellner, *The Homeless Mind* (Harmondsworth: Penguin, 1974) pp. 75-77, 140-42, 165-67.
32. See Lahidji, "Constitutionalism and Clerical Authority" in Said A. Arjomand, ed., *Authority and Political Culture in Shi'ism* (Albany: State University of New York Press, 1988) pp. 133-58. Bayat, *Iran's First Revolution: Shi'ism and the Constitutional Revolution of 1905-9* (New York: Oxford University Press, 1991) pp. 6, 57, 134-35, 174-76, 206-207.
33. Charles Heimsath, *Indian Nationalism and Hindu Social Reform* (Princeton University Press, 1964) pp. 317-21. J. N. Farquhar, *Modern Religious Movements in India* (London: MacMillan, 1929) pp. 316-23.
34. Because science has become such an overwhelmingly important guarantor of plausibility, everyone wants to think of themselves as being in line with it. On this factor of science and the plausibility of the religious worldview, see P. Berger, *Heretical Imperative*, pp. 17-22, 105.
35. It may also be said that although fundamentalists are not against the traditional Newtonian view of science, there are much more substantial grounds for a conflict between modern relativistic science and fundamentalist thought. But this issue has hardly yet been tackled by fundamentalist writers.
36. Barr, *Fundamentalism*, p. 93-96; Bruce, *Firm in the Faith*, p. 128.
37. Momen, *Introduction to Shi'i Islam*, pp. 79-80, 159-60, 185-87, 201.
38. Barr, *Fundamentalism*, p. 91, and Walker, "Fundamentalism and Modernity: The Restoration Movement in Britain" in L. Caplan, ed., *Studies in Religious Fundamentalism*, pp. 203-204.
39. Sandeen, *Roots of Fundamentalism*, pp. xi-xii and Ch. 6-10 *passim* but see in particular pp. 152, 163-64, 250-69; Marsden, *Fundamentalism*, pp. 199-205.
40. E. Davis has surveyed the membership of the Muslim Brotherhood, a fundamentalist Muslim group in Egypt, over a period of fifty years and found that

the typical active member was an urban, middle-class, well-educated professional man—much the same group that liberals come from; Davis, "Ideology, Social Class and Islamic Radicalism in Modern Egypt" in S. A. Arjomand, ed., *From Nationalism to Revolutionary Islam*, (Albany: State University of New York Press, 1984) pp. 141-45 and tables. See also Amselle, "A Case of Fundamentalism in West Africa" in Caplan, *Studies in Religious Fundamentalism*, pp. 81-82. For further evidence of the middle class background of Muslim fundamentalists, see the survey in Munson, *Islam and Revolution in the Middle East* (New Haven: Yale University Press, 1988) pp. 95-98.

41. See N.A. Haynie, "Cognitive Learning Styles," *Encyclopedia of Psychology* Vol. 1, pp. 236-38. H. A. Witkin, "Psychological Differentiation and Forms of Pathology," *Journal of Abnormal Psychology*, Vol. 70 (1965) pp. 317-36. Idem, "A Cognitive-style Approach to Cross-Cultural Research," *International Journal of Psychology*, Vol. 2 (1967) pp. 233-50.
42. It is easy to see how any point of view, such as communism or nationalism, that is strongly held by a group of people can become the basis for the development of such a mentality. Barr, for example, hints at parallels between fundamentalism and the Cultural Revolution in China, *Fundamentalism*, p. 327. The Tappers point to similarities between fundamentalism and secular nationalism in Turkey, "Fundamentalism in a Turkish Town."
43. R. Hofstadter, *Anti-intellectualism in American Life* (London: Jonathan Cape, 1964) pp. 118-19.
44. Barr, *Fundamentalism*, pp. 312-13.
45. H. A. Witkin, "Psychological Differentiation and Forms of Pathology."
46. Barr, *Fundamentalism*, pp. 90, 349 n.1. Bruce, *Firm in the Faith*, p. 128. Davis found a disproportionately large number of engineers among the leadership of the fundamentalist Muslim Brotherhood. See note above.
47. The classical work on the split-brain was done by Sperry and his associates at the California Institute of Technology. See R. W. Sperry, "Cerebral Organisation and Behaviour," *Science*, Vol. 133 (1961) pp. 1749-57; M. Gazzaniga, et al., "Some Functional Effects of Sectioning the Cerebral Commissures in Man," *Proceedings of the National Academy of Science*, Vol. 48 (1962) pp. 1765-69. On the functions of the two halves of the brain see R.D. Nebes, "Hemispheric Specialization in Commisurotomized Man", *Psychological Bulletin*, Vol. 81 (1974) pp. 1-14. A useful summary can be found in Robert Ornstein, "The Two Sides of the Brain" in Richard Woods, *Understanding Mysticism* (London: Althone Press, 1981) pp. 270-85.
48. Bahá'u'lláh, *The Kitáb-i-Aqdas* (Haifa: Bahá'í World Centre, 1992) Notes, p. 190.
49. On consultation in the Bahá'í community, see John Kolstoe, *Consultation: A Universal Lamp of Guidance* (Oxford: George Ronald, 1985).
50. From a letter written on behalf of Shoghi Effendi in *Lights of Guidance* (New Delhi: Bahá'í Publishing Trust, 2nd ed., 1988) no. 1350, p . 405.
51. Shoghi Effendi, *Bahá'í Administration* (Wilmette: Bahá'í Publishing Trust, 1928 [1968]) p. 63.

"HUMPTY DUMPTY SAT ON A WALL
Humpty Dumpty had a great fall . . ."

The End of History?

Sholeh A. Quinn

This essay presents an accessible overview of historical methodology. Its purpose is to make non-academic audiences familiar with the kinds of questions historians ask and how they go about answering them. These ideas are illustrated with examples from a variety of texts, including a nursery rhyme, a Bábí chronicle, and a Bahá'í prayer.

A recently published compilation prepared by the Research Department of the Universal House of Justice states that Bahá'í scholarship is an endeavor for everyone. The introductory letter to that compilation from the Universal House of Justice states:

> This scholarly endeavor should be characterized by the welcome it offers to all who wish to be involved in it, each in his or her own way, by mutual encouragement and cooperation among its participants, and by the respect accorded to distinguished accomplishment and outstanding achievement.[2]

Since this call reaches out to every Bahá'í to be involved in scholarly activity, we can assume that every Bahá'í will not be involved in the same way. Indeed, the diversity of the Bahá'í community, and the wide range of professions, vocations and areas of expertise that are represented preclude and discourage such uniformity of thought and approach. The present paper will (1) introduce and locate one particular academic discipline, history, within the context of Bahá'í scholarship, and vice versa; (2) present a brief introduction on historical methodologies as practiced in the history profession; and (3) explain the limitations of these methodologies. It will conclude with a discussion of what sorts of contributions professional historians and other academics can make to Bahá'í scholarship.

Professional History and Bahá'í Scholarship

There are countless ways one can envision engaging in the sort of "scholarly activity" mentioned in the letter cited above. For some, it might mean reading scholarly books and articles on Bábí and Bahá'í studies.[3] Others might enroll in evening courses offered at a local community college or university. For still others, it could mean conducting classes of a scholarly nature in our local communities: deepenings on the Kitáb-i Aqdas, for instance, or on Islamic history. For yet others, it might mean delving even deeper into one's own area of expertise. Some Bahá'ís are professional scholars and members of the academy —that is, they make their living by engaging in scholarly activities, teaching courses, conducting research, and presenting that research within professional academic settings, usually colleges, universities, or research institutes. Some Bahá'ís, for instance, are professional economists, others are sociologists, engineers, specialists in literature and languages, or historians. Within this group of professional scholars, a few Bahá'ís, along with other scholars who are not Bahá'ís, have chosen as their area of specialization the study of the Bahá'í religion.

These individuals study the Bahá'í religion from the perspective of their specific academic disciple, whether it be history, sociology, political science, or literature. However, whether one is a professional academic, a part-time researcher, or a thinking person interested in the life of the mind, the letter quoted above indicates that everyone in the Bahá'í community, with all its tremendous diversity and variety of perspectives and backgrounds, is welcome to do what he or she can to engage in "scholarly endeavor."[4]

Let us now examine the scholarly endeavors of one area of learning: history. The field of history is vast. It incorporates a wide diversity of people using a variety of approaches. Nearly everyone is familiar with history in one form or another—for some, the mere mention of the word causes grimacing and brings back unpleasant memories of an agonizing process of memorizing names, dates, and places. Others love history, although their professional training may be in the sciences or other areas not at all related to history. People from a variety of walks of life, for example, read historical works of various types, watch televized historical documentaries, and otherwise engage in historically related activities. For some people, history becomes important when they learn about the roots of their own family, whether through joining genealogical societies or recording the stories heard from grandparents or other elderly individuals. Other individuals spend much of their lives deeply studying historical eras in which they are interested. In the United States, for example, history related to the Civil War and, more generally, military history are popular fields.

In the same way that a field like astronomy encompasses both amateurs (people genuinely interested in and often engaged in the study of the stars, but whose profession is something else) and professionals (those who make a living as astronomers), history also has amateur and professional domains. Professional historians make their living by studying the past. They find employment in a number of places: historical societies, museums, local archives, colleges, and universities. Those who make a profession of history, therefore, are only a subset of all those who consider themselves historians, are interested in history, or view themselves as "historically minded." Similarly, those professional historians who study the Bahá'í religion as their special field of research form a subset of all those individuals, professional or amateur, scientist or humanist, and many others, engaged in Bahá'í scholarship.

In today's society, history often seems to be at the center of numerous controversies. Current debates over historical issues—such as the publicity generated by certain historical exhibitions at museums, like the Enola Gay exhibit at the Smithsonian museum in 1998, or the debates on multiculturalism—show that far from being a marginalized, obscure endeavor, history is in fact a powerful force. People from all backgrounds and walks of life have deep concerns about that power, not only in relation, for example, to whose history is taught in schools, but to how it is taught as well.[5] Therefore, unlike certain other professions, where debates involving non-professionals or amateurs might be less passionate, history is seen as something to which everybody may feel the right of access.

Historical Methodology

The fact that history is so accessible, and so many people are involved in historical enterprises of various sorts, tends sometimes to make one lose sight of the fact that the professional side of the discipline exists. And like its fellow academic disciplines in the arts and the sciences, it is subject to its own methodologies, its own rules, and its own approaches. For instance, the approach taken by a professional historian can in fact differ—although it does not necessarily have to—from that taken by a non-professional historian, in the same way that someone who has a general interest in cooking may undertake the preparation of food differently than a highly trained professional chef. The lack of understanding of how professional historians "do history," as opposed to more popular approaches, has led to some of the controversies and debates mentioned above, and perhaps to tensions within the Bahá'í community as well. Far from exhibiting unique features, the debates over history on various Bahá'í and Bahá'í-related internet forums mirror the larger context in which they are carried out. On some of these internet discussion groups, for instance, professional Bahá'í scientists have engaged in debates about historical methodology with both non-professional and professional Bahá'í historians, all claiming the right of access to history. Those debates, however, did not often address what it is that professional historians actually do. In order to contribute to a greater understanding of historical methodology as it is practiced in the academy, a brief introduction is provided below.

Historians work primarily, though not exclusively, with written texts in order to understand the past. We may define historical methodology as the process by which historians read and interpret those written texts, sometimes called "sources" or "historical sources." This process goes by many names, some of which include "source criticism," "critical analysis," "textual analysis," or "historical criticism." It is extremely important to keep in mind two points: (1) an historian may use any written text for his analysis, and (2) any text that an historian may use for his analysis can be used by different individuals in different ways, and for different purposes, which go well beyond the limits of "historical methodology."

Let us take the following well-known text as an example:

> Humpty Dumpty sat on a wall
> Humpty Dumpty had a great fall
> All the king's horses and all the king's men
> Cannot put Humpty Dumpty together again.[6]

Most of us are familiar with this verse as a nursery rhyme which parents will sing or recite to their children. In this case, it is the recitation of the text which serves the function of entertaining the child. The parent is not particularly interested in any historical or literary questions that the rhyme raises.

A professional literary critic will look at the nursery rhyme as a literary text. Unlike the parent who sings or recites the text, the literary specialist will "interrogate" the text, ask it specific questions in order better to understand its literary nature. Some possible questions might include: What is the rhyme metre of the verse? What are the literary allusions being made? How is this rhyme related to other texts, which collectively form the literary genre known as "nursery rhymes"? Here, as a result of interrogating the text in a specific way, the text reveals certain answers that would be of interest to those who study literature.

A professional historian will ask a different set of questions, which will cause the text to yield a different set of answers. In standard accepted historical methodology, the questions asked of a particular text, if one is going to use that text for historical purposes, remain constant regardless of which text is being read, whether it be a nursery rhyme, a medieval legend, or a Bábí chronicle. These basic questions include the following: What is the text? Who wrote it? When was it written? Where was it written? Why was it written, and under what circumstances? For whom was it written? By answering these questions, one learns about the greater "historical context" in which the text was produced.

"Doing history"—writing about the past—therefore, requires one to ask and answer the specific questions listed above (and many others) of any given text. By applying these questions to the Humpty Dumpty nursery rhyme, we learn the following: this text originated in fifteenth-century England as a popular political protest allegory, in which Humpty Dumpty refers to King Richard III; "sat on the wall" means "attacked a Welshman," who in this case was Henry Tudor, grandson of Queen Catherine, widow of King Henry II of England. Humpty Dumpty's great fall refers to Richard III's defeat at a battle in Leicestershire, where despite his large army of 23,000 men ("all the king's men"), he still suffered defeat ("cannot put Humpty Dumpty together again").[7]

In the example of this nursery rhyme, the parent, the literary critic, and the historian each use the Humpty Dumpty text for different purposes. In each separate reading, the text performs very different functions. It helps entertain a child, it reveals something about the literary nature of nursery rhymes, and it provides information about fifteenth-century British history and popular political thought. None of these functions of the text need to be in conflict with the other. The historian, who studies the political implications of the Humpty Dumpty nursery rhyme, is not threatening the legitimacy or validity of the same text to the parent, who enjoys entertaining the child by reciting the rhyme.

Another important consideration for historians who seek to understand the past is deciding which text to rely on. If a number of written texts describe the same events, and no two writers are exactly the same, then no two texts will be exactly the same. But this raises the question: Which version should one read, and which version should one believe? By asking the five historical questions listed above, we can better evaluate any given text. Generally, historians favor the accounts written closer to the time of the events they describe over those written later. Likewise, accounts written by eyewitnesses are favored over those who have received their information second hand. These criteria, however, must be weighed in light of the personal biases of the author; and since all human beings are subjective creatures, there is no such thing as a perfectly "objective" text. It is best, therefore, to read all available accounts of the same historical event.

Turning now to another example that illustrates this issue, we find the following passage in a nineteenth-century historical account:

> Mírzá Aḥmad-i-Qazvíní, the martyr, who on several occasions had heard Mullá Husayn recount to the early believers the story of his moving and historic interview with the Báb, related to me the following: "I have heard Mullá Husayn repeatedly and graphically describe the circumstances of that remarkable interview . . . 'We soon found ourselves standing at the gate of a house of modest appearance. He knocked at the door, which was soon opened by an Ethiopian servant. "Enter therein in peace, secure," [Q 15:46] were His words as He crossed the threshold and motioned me to follow Him. His invitation, uttered with power and majesty, penetrated my soul . . . Might not my visit to this house, I thought to myself, enable me to draw nearer to the Object of my quest?' "[8]

Here again is a text for which we may envision numerous uses. Certainly, many Bahá'ís can remember participating in celebrations of the anniversary of the Báb's announcement of his prophethood, and will recognize this as a passage from Nabíl's Narrative, also known as *The Dawn-Breakers*. One of the important functions of this text has been to encourage and inspire the Bahá'ís in the West, who—as they are taken back to Shiraz, and they imagine that historic meeting between Mullá Husayn and the Báb—are partaking of the fruits of Shoghi Effendi's tremendous effort when he translated and interpreted this chronicle.[9] In this scenario, Bahá'ís would probably most often use this text for inspirational purposes, to convey the spirit of that day of declaration to their fellow believers.

The non-professional historian, or the historically minded individual, might use this text to different ends: to obtain a better understanding of Bábí history, as many Bahá'ís are interested in the Bábí roots of their own faith. Since not everyone is able to read Persian or Arabic, Bahá'ís are indebted to Shoghi Effendi for producing this English translation and interpretation, for it helps bring to life the historical figures of the past: Shaykh Ahmad and Sayyid Kázim, the Letters of the Living, the Báb himself. A non-professional historian might use *The Dawn-Breakers* as a basis from which to write a popular account of Bábí history, more accessible to the general public, or to lead a local community deepening class.

The professional historian will use the same text in very specific ways in order to learn and analyze the past. As in the nursery-rhyme example, the uses of the text differ, as do the questions posed of the text and the answers it gives. Note that the historian will ask the exact same questions of Nabíl's text that she asked of the nursery rhyme. Again, she wants to know: When was this text written? By whom? What was the author's background? The answers to these general questions give rise to more specific questions, which might include the following: The author, Nabíl, claims to have heard the story from Mírzá Ahmad Qazvíní, who heard it from Mullá Husayn. When did Mírzá Ahmad-i Qazvíní tell the story to Nabíl? Did Mírzá Ahmad Qazvíní tell the same story to anyone else? Did Mullá Husayn tell anyone else, and do we have other versions of the same episode? If so, how do they differ from Nabíl's? Furthermore, if they do differ, whose account do we "privilege," and how do we account for the differences in the various versions?

Thus, historians analyze any number of texts in a uniform way in order to understand the past, and they present their analysis in a manner that conforms to certain standard rules, sometimes known as "scholarly apparatus." For instance, one important aspect of this scholarly apparatus is that professional historians must cite their sources by means of a footnote or endnote reference, so that the reader may check the original "text" in order to evaluate the historian's analysis. By providing examples and citations from their sources, historians provide evidence to back up, or "prove" their conclusions. Entire undergraduate and graduate seminar courses at universities are devoted to teaching students how to ask questions, how to weigh evidence, how to read and interpret texts, and how to present one's findings or conclusions. It is important to note that the questions and methods can become detailed and complex, as students and scholars delve deeper and deeper into their topic.

Professional historians in academia specialize in various areas or "fields" of history, which are the subjects that they teach and/or research. These fields include areas such as "European history," "world history," "social history," "women's history," and "East Asian history." Within these broad areas are subfields and more specifically designated areas of specialization. These fields of history require different sorts of special skills. Historians like to read sources in the languages in which they were written, so that less will get lost in the translation; thus specialities require language skills. For instance, historians of China need to be able to read their sources in the original Chinese, economic historians need to have some knowledge of economics, and so forth. In the case of professional historians studying early Bábí and Bahá'í history, the field requires advanced training in (1) historical methodology, (2) Islamics, and (3) the Persian and Arabic languages.[10]

History, then, as it is practiced in the academy, is a sort of "craft." Like gardeners who must learn the various methods of tending a garden and know how to use specific tools and materials in order to perform their tasks, so too must historians learn to use the tools of their craft, which include the skills mentioned above. Learning to master the profession and perfect one's use of the "tools" requires time, training, and commitment. Since the tools of the trade are the same regardless of what period of history one studies, the approaches used in the professional study of Bahá'í history are no different from the approaches used in the professional study of any other period or area of history, for example, early Christianity, medieval India, or modern Canada.

Limitations of the Discipline

Having outlined the sorts of questions historians ask and the methods they use to answer them, a few words must be said about the limits of the discipline. We often hear what historians do; we do not often hear what historians cannot or should not do. For professional historians, the kinds of questions that can be asked of a text are limited. Returning to the garden analogy, the number of tools in our garden shed are not infinite. They can only fix certain kinds of problems. In the case of gardening, a gardener's tools, no matter how sophisticated, cannot prevent a winter storm from freezing the plants. Nor can these tools help the gardener explain why the storm occurred in the first place, or predict when the next one is due. To require the gardener to answer such questions is making the gardener go beyond the limits of what his discipline (gardening) can tell him. Similarly, historians can only explain certain aspects of events, and answer certain questions in certain ways, due to the limitations of the discipline. It is for this reason that sometimes people read the scholarship of professional Bahá'í historians and claim that they have a problematic identity: "being Bahá'ís but writing like non-Bahá'ís." Such perceptions are a result of not having sufficient knowledge of what history *cannot* do.

I have already established that historians ask certain types of questions of a particular text: they ask questions that the text is able to answer within the limits of the discipline. Like the gardener whose hoes, weeders, and bags of fertilizer are unable to predict winter storms, there are certain questions that history cannot answer.

One final example aptly illustrates this point:

> O Aḥmad! Forget not my bounties while I am absent. Remember My days during thy days, and My distress and banishment in this remote prison. And be thou so steadfast in My love that thy heart shall not waver, even if the swords of the enemies rain blows upon thee and all the heavens and the earth arise against thee.[11]

This is from one of the best known writings of Bahá'u'lláh, the Tablet of Ahmad. Bahá'ís frequently recite this passage to gain spiritual strength and comfort from its words, which according to Shoghi Effendi have "special potency and significance." For most believers, this work's primary use is for prayer and meditation.

As in the example of the nursery rhyme, however, an historian—believer or not—can also use this text, and do so for an entirely different purpose. This does not take away its "spiritual" function or invalidate its use as a prayer or a devotion. The questions an historian would ask of this text, in order better to understand the past, should by now sound familiar. Who is the author? When did the author write it? For whom? Why? Specific questions could include the following: Who is Ahmad? Why is he distressed? Where is the remote prison? How long was the author in that prison? Who, specifically, are the enemies whose swords may rain down upon Ahmad?

The first of the general questions—who is the author and what is his background—is one of the first that historians routinely ask. In this case, the text is from the writings of Bahá'u'lláh. The historian writing for academic audiences would answer the first question with something like the following: "The author of this Tablet is Mírzá Husayn 'Alí, who took the title Bahá'u'lláh (Glory of God). He was a nineteenth-century Persian who claimed to be a Manifestation of God." The professional historian, whether Bahá'í or not, cannot justifiably state the following: "The author of this Tablet is Bahá'u'lláh, who is the Manifestation of God for this day." The reason has to do with the limitations of the discipline. An historian could very well believe that Bahá'u'lláh is a Manifestation of God, or not; but the fact that this is a text-based discipline means that the historian cannot use textual evidence to back up the second statement. The gardener may very well believe that the storm will return the next day, but his gardening tools do not, cannot, and should not be used to prove his opinion. Historians can only reach certain kinds of conclusions based on textual evidence. Bahá'ís may appear to be "writing as non-Bahá'ís," but in fact they are writing as historians, restricted by the tools of their trade, able to analyze only certain problems and say things in certain ways.

What Can Professional Historians Contribute?

Why is it so important for us to understand what professional academics do? In 1989, the Universal House of Justice wrote:

> Newly enrolled professionals and other experts provide a great resource for the development of Bahá'í scholarship. It is hoped that, as they attain a deeper grasp of the Teachings and their significance, they will be able to assist Bahá'í communities in correlating the beliefs of the Faith with the current thoughts and problems of the world.[12]

What are some of the "current thoughts" in the world, which the Universal House of Justice has asked Bahá'í scholars to correlate with the beliefs of the Faith? In academia, these include newer fields of study that have attracted the attention of scholars in a number of both traditional and new disciplines, including history. The Bahá'í writings and texts all have a great deal to offer in these areas. As these "professionals and other experts" try to correlate "the beliefs of the Faith with the current thoughts and problems of the world," it is no coincidence that some of the most fervently debated issues in some segments of the Bahá'í community reflect this current thought.

For example, current thought in the newer fields of gender studies, feminist studies, and women's history (which includes discussions about feminist approaches to texts) cannot help but lead to discussions about women serving on the Universal House of Justice. "Current thought" on hermeneutics and how one may interpret and analyze a text "correlates" with questions related to theories of the interpretation of Bahá'í texts, which incidentally have included a discussion on the relative advantages and disadvantages of "compilations," and even the relationship between science and religion. "Current thought" on the history of nationalism and religion raises issues of the relationship between church and state in Bahá'í patterns of future government.* "Current thought" on post-colonialism and subaltern studies, with their emphasis on studying how some groups (such as the nineteenth-century European colonial powers) have traditionally categorized other groups (such the colonized peoples of the Middle East) in order to maintain power over them, has led to "correlated" discussions about attitudes within the Bahá'í community towards the "Other"—whether that Other is a person of color, a woman, an historian, a homosexual, a Persian, a "scholar," etc. As time passes, the issues that form "current thought" will of course change. Bahá'ís in academia should be able to engage in a meaningful discussion of whatever the current discourse of the time may be.

Conclusion

This essay has suggested that there are not only many ways to read a text, but that any given text can be read, analyzed, and used for a number of different purposes. For professional history, any given text yields only certain kinds of information which can be presented only in certain ways. As individuals, we have the freedom to ask any and all questions of any text. As professional historians, there are only certain questions that our discipline allows us to ask and answer. Instead of creating false dichotomies between professional historians, popular

*See, for example, the article by Sen McGlinn, "Theocratic Assumptions in Bahá'í Literature" in this volume, pp. 39-80.

historians, and Bahá'í scholars, multiple approaches to the text, like the many approaches to Bahá'í scholarship, should co-exist. Given the broad call by the Universal House of Justice to all Bahá'ís to develop Bahá'í scholarship and to welcome all who wish to be involved in it, that welcome should include professional academic historians, who along with other academics, form just one small subgroup of all people engaged in Bahá'í scholarship.

Notes

Sholeh Quinn is Associate Professor of History at Ohio University.

1. This paper was originally a talk presented at Bosch Bahá'í school in 1997 to a non-academic audience. It was written specifically for a Bahá'í audience with no background at all in history or historical methodologies. In my view, it is important that academics continue to communicate something about their various methodologies to Bahá'ís without any university background.
2. From a letter on behalf of the Universal House of Justice, dated 10 February 1995, published as the introduction to the "Compilation on Scholarship," *Bahá'í Studies Review*, Vol. 5, no. 1 (1995) pp. 105.
3. See, for example, *From Iran East & West*, eds. Juan R. Cole and Moojan Momen (Los Angeles: Kalimát Press, 1984); H. M. Balyuzi, *Eminent Bahá'ís in the Time of Bahá'u'lláh* (Oxford: George Ronald, 1985); *Studies in Honor of the Late Hasan M. Husayn Balyuzi*, Moojan Momen, ed., (Los Angeles: Kalimát Press, 1988); Abbas Amanat, *Resurrection and Renewal* (Ithaca: Cornell University Press, 1989); Denis MacEoin, *The Sources for Early Bábí Doctrine and History: A Survey* (Leiden: E. J. Brill, 1992); Juan R. I. Cole, *Modernity and the Millennium* (New York: Columbia University Press, 1998); and various articles in the *Bahá'í Studies Bulletin*, ed. by Stephen N. Lambden.
4. 'Abdu'l-Bahá explains why developing one's intellect may be so compelling to some: "All blessings are divine in origin, but none can be compared with this power of intellectual investigation and research, which is an eternal gift producing fruits of unending delight. Man is ever partaking of these fruits. All other blessings are temporary; this is an everlasting possession" ('Abdu'l-Bahá, *Foundations of World Unity* [Wilmette: Bahá'í Publishing Trust, 1945] p. 61).
5. For example, some of these debates took place following the publication of Alan Bloom, *The Closing of the American Mind* (New York: Simon and Schuster, 1987).
6. *The Illustrated Treasury of Children's Literature*, ed. Margaret E. Martignoni (New York: Grosset and Dunlap, 1955) p. 29, and reprinted in many other places.

7. See Albert Mason, *The Nursery Rhyme: Remnant of Popular Political Protest* (Kansas: Coronado Press, 1968) pp. 67-81.
8. Nabíl Zarandí, *The Dawn-Breakers: Nabíl's Narrative of the Early Days of the Bahá'í Revelation*, ed. and trans. Shoghi Effendi (Wilmette: Bahá'í Publishing Trust, 1938 [1970] pp. 52-54).
9. I use the word "interpret" here based on Rúhíyyih Khánum Rabbaní's statement: "Although ostensibly a translation from the original Persian Shoghi Effendi may be said to have re-created it in English, his translation being comparable to Fitzgerald's rendering of Omar Khayyam's *Rubaiyat* which gave to the world a poem in a foreign language that in many ways far exceeded the merits of the original." (Rúhíyyih Rabbaní, *The Priceless Pearl* [London: Bahá'í Publishing Trust, 1969] p. 215.) Those who care to read both English and Persian might find it an interesting exercise to compare Fitzgerald's translations with Khayyam's original, and see just how much Fitzgerald changed the original Persian quatrains. One of the primary reasons why Shoghi Effendi translated this work was to inspire the Bahá'ís in the West. In a cable to the United States in 1931, the Guardian urged the study of this translation for he felt it an "essential preliminary to [the] renewed intensive Teaching Campaign necessitated by [the] completion [of the] Mashriqu'l-Adhkár" (ibid., p. 217). See also *Priceless Pearl,* pp. 214-18, for a general summary of the history of this translation.
10. A sample question faced by historians could be the following: "Official Qajar historical writing is a continuation of earlier traditions of Safavid, Afsharid, and Zand historical writing, where imitative historiographical methods are utilized. Did Nabíl utilize the same imitative methods, and if so, which earlier texts was he imitating?" (The Persian original of Nabíl must be consulted in order to answer this particular question.)
11. Bahá'u'lláh, Tablet of Ahmad, reprinted in *Bahá'í Prayers: A Selection of Prayers Revealed by Bahá'u'lláh, the Báb, and 'Abdu'l-Bahá* (Wilmette: Bahá'í Publishing Trust, 1985) and many other places.
12. From a letter written on behalf of the Universal House of Justice, dated 18 April 1989, cited in "Compilation on scholarship," no. 41.

Applying the Teachings

A NATIVE AMERICAN DEPICTION OF
(l. to r.) Deganawida, Hiawatha, and Thadodaho at the founding of the Iroquois Confederacy.

Bahá'í Universalism and Native Prophets

Christopher Buck

Academic and popular attention has revived interest in native spirituality. This essay explores the possibility of accepting prophets from indigenous cultures into Bahá'í doctrine, reflecting a development that has already taken place in popular Bahá'í belief in North America. A hitherto under-studied Persian text of 'Abdu'l-Bahá establishes this principle in such a way that its explicit enunciation is now possible. The prophetic credentials of Iroquois culture hero and statesman Deganawida are critically examined as a test case. The legend of Deganawida has a kernel of historicity overlaid by hagiography, with admitted Christian influence. Nonetheless, if the Bahá'í principle of "progressive revelation" can assimilate the Amerindian spiritual legacy as distinct from and developmentally asynchronous with Irano-Semitic and Sino-Indic religious histories, then it might be possible to accord Deganawida a theoretical status within Bahá'í prophetology, and affirm Bahá'u'lláh's unifying role in world history, as oral cultures take their place alongside the more familiar "literate" traditions.

> Thereupon Tekanawita [Deganawida[1]] stood up in the center of the gathering place, and then he said: "First I will answer what it means to say, 'Now it is arriving, the Good Message.' This, indeed, is what it

> means: When it stops the slaughter of your own people who live here on earth, then everywhere peace will come about, by day and also by night, and it will come about that as one travels around, everyone will be related.
>
> Now again [?], secondly I say: " 'Now it is arriving, the Power,' and this means that the different nations, all of the nations, will become just a single one, and the Great Law will come into being, so that all now will be related to each other, and there will come to be just a single family, and in the future, in days to come, this family will continue on.
>
> Now in turn, the other, my third saying: " 'Now it is arriving, the Peace,' and this means that everyone will become related, men and also women, and also the young people and the children, and when all are relatives, every nation, then there will be peace. Then there will be truthfulness, and they will uphold hope and charity, so that it is peace that will unite all of the people, indeed, it will be as though they have but one mind, and they are a single person with only one body and one head and one life, which means that there will be unity. When they are functioning, the Good Message and also the Power and the Peace, these will be the principal things everybody will live by; these will be the great values among the people." (Deganawida, Iroquois prophet, circa 1450 C.E.)[2]

The United Nations declared 1993 the International Year of Indigenous People. This reflects a widespread renewed interest, popular and academic, in native spirituality. In Canada, such concern with "First Nations"[3] has had an ecumenical impact as well. A strong native presence in the membership of the Canadian Bahá'í community is reflected in the fact that native Canadians represent the most significant influx of new converts to the Bahá'í Faith in Canada, particularly in the Peigan Reserve in southern Alberta. In 1993, the Bahá'í national convention held in Regina focused "on the unique culture, heritage and destiny of Canada's Native peoples."[4] The "destiny" referred to here is the Bahá'í-inspired vision of Amerindian awakening and its anticipated impact on the historic path to world peace. In 1993, the National Spiritual Assembly of the Bahá'ís of Canada, whose chairperson was a native Canadian woman, made a formal submission to the Royal Commission on Aboriginal Peoples.[5]

In its advocacy on native issues,[6] previous representations had been made by that national assembly in 1960[7] and in 1968,[8] the outcome of a history of productive relations with native Canadians. Canadian Bahá'í interaction with native peoples is characterized not only by respect and advocacy, but also by ecumenism. Integration of sacred ceremonies (sweet grass and peace pipe ceremonies, blanket dances, and powwows) into Bahá'í conferences, especially in western Canada, has enriched Canadian Bahá'í experience in a pluralistic (rather than a syncretistic) way.

Reflected in its representations to the Canadian Parliament and in proclamation pamphlets, the relation of the Bahá'í Faith to native Canadians has been a dual one: one of advocacy and one of teaching. Bahá'ís would like to see native Canadians embrace their religion but, at the same time, preserve native cultural identities. The purpose of the present study is to examine the implications of such rapprochement for Bahá'í doctrine.

The "Official" and "Popular" Paradox

A classic paradox in the academic study of religion arises from the formal comparison of "official" and "folk" (or "popular") forms of religion. Ideally, the two should mirror one another. In reality, they often do not. This paper will explore one such paradox: indigenization of sectors of Canadian Bahá'í community life, supported at the policy level but not fully integrated at the doctrinal level.

Rise in the indigenization of Canadian Bahá'í conferences reflects a current trend among missions today in integrating elements of native spirituality with dominant forms of the Canadian religious culture. From a Bahá'í perspective, the major warrant for a religion's spiritual authenticity is the attestation of a bona fide "Manifestation of God" in any given tradition. Acknowledgment of messengers of God among native Canadians would appear to be a specifically Bahá'í innovation, despite the parallel indigenization of Christian worship. Towards this end, the concept of messengers of God to native Canadians has been introduced in the form of localized proclamation pamphlets, officially approved by the National Spiritual Assembly of the Bahá'ís of Canada but never officially adopted as a public teaching for the non-native population. By accepting native traditions as richly spiritual and valid, and through an "indigenization" of Bahá'u'lláh at the missionary level, Bahá'ís have in effect created a body of opinion that may lie outside of the formal teachings of the Bahá'í Faith. No Manifestation of

God from among native peoples has been explicitly recognized in Bahá'í doctrine. Official Bahá'í doctrine, which is at its heart universalist, has yet to establish a formal position with respect to indigenous prophets. This raises the question of the place of native spirituality in Bahá'í prophetology.

Cross-cultural Messianism and Bahá'í Universalism

> She [White Buffalo Calf Woman] has returned. Not in the same form that she came in the first time but really in the teachings of Bahá'u'lláh. (Counsellor Jacqueline Left Hand Bull Delahunt, 1995)[9]

Bahá'í teachers have often appealed to native prophecies to establish the claims of Bahá'u'lláh. This process creates an eschatological bridge between native worldview and Bahá'í universalism, in a linkage between native wisdom teacher and Bahá'í prophet, between vision and fulfilment. As prophecies tend to be teleological, it is natural that Bahá'í recourse to prophecy is primarily one of missionary ingenuity. Neither believer nor teacher, as a rule, ever question prophecy. To do so is religiously imprudent, as the force of the proof text resides in its authority.

Not unlike popular Mormon identification of Jesus Christ with the ancient Toltec culture hero Quetzalcoátl, the figure of Bahá'u'lláh is becoming progressively indigenized in the Americas. Taking the figure of Quetzalcoátl as a prime example of this Bahá'í teaching technique,[10] Bahá'ís have appealed to prophecies surrounding the return of the Toltec civilizer, and to the "mantic history" of the "Books" of the Yucatec Mayan "Chilam Balam" priests as well.[11] The mystique of such a tradition possibly resides in the fact that it is literate[12] (the Mayans had an extraordinary interest in prophecy) and "historical" (calendrical, chronological, cyclical).

In 1975, in the ancient capital of the Peruvian Inca empire, the golden city of Cuzco, Bahá'ís attending an all-Quechua Bahá'í conference (Quechua is the surviving language of the ancient Inca empire, now the second official language of Peru) were photographed beside a sign, which read: "Bahá'u'lláh is the return of Viracocha."[13] Eschatologically, Bahá'u'lláh has become the Inca culture hero Viracocha *redivivus*.[14] The existence of prophecies envisioning the return of Quetzalcoátl and Viracocha predisposed Bahá'í pioneers and converts to identify Bahá'u'lláh with both of these culture heroes, Toltec and Inca.[15] The phenomenon of Quechua converts identifying Viracocha with Bahá'u'lláh might in part be explained by a belief among present-day Incas that the head of the Inca deity Ri actually exists and is reconstituting itself in the Andean underworld, its head growing a body toward its feet. When the body of Ri is restored, the Inca will return.[16]

The number of localized indigenous messianic connections with the eschatological persona of Bahá'u'lláh will continue to grow, but the process has yet to witness official recognition of native spirituality as a feature of Bahá'í doctrine.

Native Teaching and Bahá'í Folk Beliefs

A full-color picture of native Bahá'ís performing at a major Bahá'í event in Montreal is featured prominently on page eight of a publication of the Bahá'í International Community.[17] On page ten of this magazine, it is stated: "Bahá'ís the world over come from all religious backgrounds: Buddhist, Christian, Hindu, Jain, Jewish, Muslim, Sikh, Zoroastrian, *animist*, and non-religious." (Emphasis added) The use of the term "animist" here is politically incorrect.[18] For the same reason, I have avoided using other terms, such as "primitive" and "primal," in this essay.[19]

Further on, page 37 of the same publication states: "People from all of the major religious backgrounds have found that the promises and expectations of their own beliefs are fulfilled in the Bahá'í Faith. *Bahá'ís from Native American, African and other indigenous backgrounds, similarly, find in the Bahá'í teachings fulfilment of prophetic visions.*" (Emphasis added). Here, reference to prophetic visions would logically require the instrumentality of prophets (major or minor) or, if not, then seers or sages. Prophecies and visions are acknowledged far more easily than are prophets and seers, even though the former require the instrumentality of the latter. Thus, on page 34, under the header "Divine Messengers," the Bahá'í International Community states: "Bahá'ís believe that throughout history the Creator has revealed Himself to humanity through a series of Divine messengers. These messengers include: Abraham, Krishna, Moses, Zoroaster, Buddha, Jesus, Muhammad, The Báb, Bahá'u'lláh."

Absent from this list are native prophets and seers, because they are not attested in Bahá'í scriptures, except in principle. The problem of attestation notwithstanding, we get a much different picture when it comes to native teaching work. There are some significant reasons for this.

Throughout Bahá'í history, Bahá'í missionaries ("pioneers") have done more than anyone else to universalize the Bahá'í Faith, both demographically and doctrinally. In 1916-17, 'Abdu'l-Bahá lent considerable impetus to this missionary diversification in his *Tablets of the Divine Plan*, which were addressed to four countries: the United States, Canada, Newfoundland, and Greenland.[20] In fulfilling 'Abdu'l-Bahá's vision of systematic missionary work to be prosecuted throughout the Americas, Bahá'í pioneers dedicated their lives to promoting the Bahá'í gospel of unity. Evidence of such dedication is not lacking: what appears to be a local Mohawk tribute to Bahá'í pioneers, James and Melba Loft, was published in *Tekawennake*.[21]

In the Bahá'í mission field, it was necessary to relate Bahá'í teachings and truth-claims to indigenous traditions. Native-oriented Bahá'í teaching pamphlets were published for that purpose. It is important to note that these pamphlets typically expressed genuine Bahá'í solidarity with elements of native spirituality, which included recognition of some of the great spiritual teachers revered in native traditions. Such pamphlets—some in typescript, others handwritten—were thus on the cutting edge of Bahá'í universalism. In the pamphlet review process, Bahá'í policy has supported the teaching initiatives of Bahá'í pioneers, but official Bahá'í doctrine has not formally assimilated some of the sweeping universalisms published by Bahá'í pioneers or by other authors of teaching materials.

Despite generic concessions to the existence of native messengers of God in principle, in practice there is an explicit Bahá'í stricture against adding actual names of Manifestations of God who are not attested to in the Abrahamic tradition, most notably in the Qur'an. While the Qur'an would appear to have very little to do with indigenous traditions in the New World, and has no binding authority on

Bahá'í doctrine or praxis generally, the Qur'an is seen as a universal scripture, thereby acting as a prophetological constraint on any such authority claims. This has not altogether deterred Bahá'ís from expressing personal interest in the authenticity of culture heroes as possible messengers of God. There are, for example, chapters on the Iroquois prophet Deganawida in two Bahá'í-authored books: *Warriors of the Rainbow* and *Voices of Earth and Sky*.[22]

The Problem of "Adding Names"

Universalism may have its limits.[23] Bahá'í salvation history accounts for the appearance of the great world religions as each having been founded by a "Manifestation of God." A Bahá'í list of the founders of the major religions may be marked by incompleteness. In response to a believer who raised this issue, Shoghi Effendi explained: "Regarding your question: the only reason there is not more mention of the Asiatic Prophets is because their names seem to be lost in the mists of ancient history. Buddha and Zoroaster are mentioned in our scriptures—both non-Jewish or non-Semitic Prophets. We are taught that there have always been Manifestations of God, but we do not have any record of their names."[24] This answer satisfies the problem of inclusivity in cases where all historical traces have vanished. But what of living oral traditions, if and when such narrative events preserve and prolong the memory of a culture hero who is likely to have been a real historical figure in pre-Columbian times? A legend might, after all, have a historical kernel, a basis in history.

While historicity is a necessary warrant of authenticity, it is not a sufficient warrant for determining prophetic credentials. Shoghi Effendi stated why: "Regarding your questions: we cannot possibly add names of people we (or anyone else) think might be Lesser Prophets to those found in the Qur'an, the Bible and our own Scriptures. For only these can we consider authentic Books."[25]

Note that this pronouncement, in principle, does not exclude other religious traditions from recognition. Take the case of Buddhism, for instance. Nowhere in Bahá'u'lláh's writings is Buddhism ever mentioned. In explaining Bahá'u'lláh's silence, Shoghi Effendi reasoned:

"As there were no followers of the Báb or Bahá'u'lláh derived from the religions of the Far East in Their days, this may be the reason that They did not address any Tablets directly to these people."[26] Nor is there any mention in Bahá'u'lláh's writings of the Buddha by name, for the very same reason. Yet Bahá'u'lláh's designated successor and interpreter, 'Abdu'l-Bahá, assimilated both Krishna[27] and Buddha into Bahá'u'lláh's prophetic scheme, which is referred to as "progressive revelation." While 'Abdu'l-Bahá certainly had the authority to add to the number of Manifestations of God attested to in the writings of Bahá'u'lláh, individual Bahá'ís have neither the authority nor the license to do so. In this respect, the Bahá'í canon of named Manifestations of God is, for all intents and purposes, closed.

How is it possible, therefore, for senior Bahá'í officials to add to this list anyway?[28] In the epigraph at the beginning of this paper, former Universal House of Justice member David Ruhe was quoted as saying: "*To the warring tribes 700-800 years ago there came an astonishing Prophet of Peace—Deganawidah.*"[29] This statement was made as the opening remark of the Hasan M. Balyuzi Memorial Lecture, presented at the 18th Annual Conference of the Association for Bahá'í Studies at Harvard University, 1994.

A similar statement was cited above made by Counsellor Jacqueline Left Hand Bull—herself a Lakota Indian—in 1995, when, in a widely televised interview, she declared her personal belief that: "*She* [White Buffalo Calf Woman] *has returned. Not in the same form that she came in the first time but really in the teachings of Bahá'u'lláh.*"[30]

In both these cases, the spirit of Bahá'í universalism has moved beyond the boundaries of formal doctrine. How should we understand this? Since more is known about Deganawida than about White Buffalo Calf Woman, it should prove useful at this juncture to examine the Deganawida legacy, to try to see why it presents itself to not a few Bahá'ís as evidence of an authentic native messenger of God—a conviction that illustrates the paradox of official and popular Bahá'í beliefs.

"The Peacemaker" as a Test Case

In 1993, in my first contact with Native Canadians at an interfaith event held in Mississauga, Ontario, the name of Deganawida was spoken of, with reverence, in the same breath and spirit as the name of Jesus Christ. This spirit of profound reverence made a deep impression on me, and I resolved to find out more about this native Canadian culture hero. In the course of my subsequent reading, I came across this generous assessment of the legacy of Deganawida and the Iroquois, spoken by Richard Pilant in his address to the Institute of Iroquoian Studies in 1960:

> The Six Nations in Canada constitute the most complete survival we have today of one of the highest cultures of one of the races of mankind —the Indian. Unlike the Mayas and the Incas to the South, the Long House People developed a democratic system of self-government. They alone among the Indian nations made a major political contribution in their form of Government which can be maintained to have furnished a prototype for the United States and the United Nations. Socially the Six Nations met the sociologist's test of higher cultures by having given a preferred status to women.[31]

This assessment, though somewhat out of place in an academic setting, shows the kind of recognition Deganawida can enjoy even in learned societies. This may be due in part to the importance of the Iroqouis Great League of Peace (as a cultural and ritual institution) and the subsequent Iroquois Confederacy[32] (as a political and diplomatic entity), and its presumed influence on the framing of the American system of government.[33] (The problem of Iroquois influence will be discussed later in this paper.) The task of disentangling fact from fancy in the Deganawida cycle, though, is even more problematic. But systematic attempts have been made. It should be pointed out that the Deganawida cycle is sacred to the Iroquois nations, and that "the Peacemaker" himself is revered to this day as a messenger from the Creator.

The Deganawida Cycle

Deganawida is a name said to mean, "*Two water currents flowing together*."[34] If tradition warrants, some time between 1400 A.D. [35] and 1600 A.D. (possibly in the year 1451 A.D. when the Iroquois witnessed an eclipse of the sun), Deganawida,[36] the "Heavenly Messenger,"[37] is said to have established the Great League of Peace among the warring Five Nations of the Iroquois (from east to west: the Mohawk, Oneida, Onondaga, Cayuga, and Seneca). The League's origins and purposes are explained in the central Iroquois myth, the Deganawida epic.[38] The nature of this warfare was a cultural pattern known as the "mourning war," essentially a system of blood feuds.

Huron by birth and Mohawk by adoption, Deganawida was a prophet, statesman, and law giver who co-founded with Hiawatha the Iroquois "League of People of the Longhouse," also known as the "Great League of Peace." This League, in actual practice, was vested in a council of fifty peace chiefs, or *sachems* (a term used to distinguish these from other chiefs). Each successor to a League chief was chosen by a "clan mother" presiding over the lineage in which the title was held. The governing council required unanimous consent to render each of its decisions.[39] The symbol of the League was the White Tree of Peace, over which hovered an ever-vigilant eagle.

The historicity of the League of Five Nations is not in dispute, nor is the existence and role of Deganawida himself in the formation of the original Iroquois confederacy. The traditional legend, which survives in several versions, has variations that pose no serious challenge to the unity of the narrative. Mythic elements, of course, give the legend its charm and symbolic depth, which in and of themselves are no less valuable. Christian influence, however, cannot be ruled out. For this reason, the version known as the Code of Dekanahwideh together with the Tradition of the Origin of the Five Nations' League, "Prepared by the committee of chiefs appointed by the Six Nations' Council of Grand River, Canada, and adopted by Council of Chiefs, July 3, 1900," is prefaced with this concession:

> With reference to the origin or birth, character and doings of Dekanawideh [sic] as herein chronicled, it will be observed that they present an analogy or similarity to Hebrew biblical story and teachings.

> This is portrayed strongly in the narration of the birth of Dekanawideh and also in extraordinary powers which he is attributed to have possessed. There is little doubt that some of this influence was brought about as a result of the labours and teachings of the Jesuit fathers among them.[40]

The "extraordinary powers" which Deganawida is said to have possessed need not be of Christian provenance, however, as this is a common feature of aboriginal narratives and of folklore generally.

In the epitome of the Deganawida legend given below, no attempt is made to note variants:[41]

In ancient times, Tarenyawagon ("The Holder of the Heavens") saved the Five Nations from onslaught of the Stone Giants. He conquered monsters and put the world in order. He gave laws for men to follow, taught the art of war, and provided for good fishing. Over time, the five tribes had a disagreement, and went their separate ways. Among the ancestors a child was born to a Huron virgin near the Bay of Quinte near Kingston, Ontario. This child was an incarnation of Tarenyawagon, entrusted with a great mission of peace. His first task was to cure the Iroquois of cannibalism.

Deganawida set out on his mission in a canoe carved from white stone. He crossed Lake Ontario. On the far shore he found hunters whose village had been razed. They told of warmongering, the slaughter of innocents, and of cannibalism. Deganawida then visited Djigonsasa, the Mother of Nations, who fed warriors traveling through. He told her to cease supporting the war parties, and then imparted to the Mother of Nations his gospel of Righteousness, Peace, and Power, symbolized by the Longhouse and the Great Law:

> I carry the Mind of the Master of Life, and my message will bring an end to the wars between east and west. The word that I bring is that all peoples shall love one another and live together in peace. This message has three parts: Righteousness and Health and Power—*Gaiihwiyo, Skenno, Gashedenza*. And each part has two branches.
>
> Righteousness means justice practiced between men and between nations; it means also a desire to see justice prevail.
>
> Health means soundness of mind and body; it also means peace, for that is what comes when minds are sane and bodies cared for.

> Power means authority, the authority of law and custom, backed by such force as is necessary to make justice prevail; it also means religion, for justice enforced is the will of the Holder of the Heavens and has His sanction.
>
> It will take the form of the Longhouse, in which there are many fires, one for each family, yet all live as one household under one Chief Mother. Hereabouts are Five Nations, each with its own Council Fire, yet they shall live together as one household in peace. They shall be the Kanonsiónni, the Longhouse. They shall have one mind and live under one law. Thinking shall replace killing, and there shall be one Commonwealth.[42]

She was the first to embrace Deganawida's message and, in so doing, gave clan mothers priority over men.

Deganawida came to one cannibal's lodge. Deganawida climbed to the roof and lay chest-down by the smokehole. After the cannibal's grisly stew was brewed, as the cannibal was about to eat from a bowl made of bark, he suddenly beheld in it the face of Deganawida. The cannibal thought he saw himself looking up from the depths of the pot. Then Deganawida met the cannibal as he threw away the body. They ate venison together, then buried the corpse. To the cannibal Deganawida explained his message, adding that the Ruler had ordained that antlers be worn as a sign of authority. The cannibal accepted. Thereupon Deganawida named the cannibal, Hiawatha.

Deganawida went next to the Mohawks to preach his message. To the "Flint Nation" Deganawida proclaimed: "The Great Creator from whom we are all descended sent me to establish the Great Peace among you. No longer shall you kill one another and nations shall cease warring upon each other. Such things are entirely evil and he, your Maker, forbids it."[43]

Though persuaded by his message, the Mohawks demanded proof of Deganawida's power to establish such a peace. The prophet obliged, answering: "I am able to demonstrate my power for I am the messenger of the Creator and he truly has given me my choice in the manner of my death."[44] Trial by ordeal was in order, one of his own choosing. He scaled a tree and, after it was felled over a precipice, he emerged unscathed. He then wed the chief's favorite daughter and became a chief himself. The chief accepted Deganawida's message.

Hiawatha tried to convert the cannibal despot Atotarho, his half-brother. Atotarho was a wizard, chief of the Onondagas, with snakes for hair, twisted in body and mind. The wizard frustrated all of Hiawatha's attempts to establish peace. Then, according to one version, Osinoh the Witch transformed herself into an owl and killed each one of Hiawatha's daughters. Hiawatha was distraught, with no one who could comfort him in his grief. Mourning, Hiawatha forsook the Onondagas.

As he wandered, Hiawatha came upon a lake or cluster of lakes, filled with ducks. He startled them, and as they took flight, they took all the lake water with them. Gathering the shells from the lake bottom and stringing them into beads, Hiawatha invented wampum and spoke of its use for consoling those who mourn.[45]

In a cornfield outside a Mohawk village, Hiawatha found a hut where he made a fire and proceeded to make wampum. To messengers from the village, Hiawatha taught protocol in the ritualized use of wampum. The village chief promised Hiawatha a seat of honor at council where they could consult over food, but the promises were broken. Hiawatha again went wandering.

Hiawatha then chanced upon Deganawida, who went about consoling Hiawatha with eight of the thirteen strings of wampum fashioned by Hiawatha. Wampum proved an effective medicine for those who mourn, as Hiawatha's grief was dispelled. Deganawida sent scouts in the form of crows, bear, or deer to find Atotarho's column of smoke. In the meantime, Deganawida and Hiawatha successively won the allegiance of the Oneidas, Cayugas, and Senecas. With the two having the power of unity, Deganawida led the Nations to Atotarho, in order to transform him, singing the Peace Hymn along the way.

As the procession reached Onandaga, Deganawida exorcized Atotarho of his evil spirits. The two Iroquois prophets got Atotarho to agree to be the firekeeper, the principal chief with veto power, and Onandoga as the capital of the Five Nation's territory. After enlisting the Onondaga chief's support, Deganawida planted the Great Tree of Peace in what is now Syracuse, New York. Tradition relates that Deganawida uttered these words as he established the confederacy:

> I am Dekanawidah, and with the Five Nations' Confederate Lords I plant the Tree of the Great Peace.
>
> I name the tree the Tree of the Great Long Leaves. Under the shade

> of this Tree of the Great Peace we spread the soft white feathery down of the globe thistle as seats for you, Adodarhoh, and your cousin Lords.
>
> Roots have spread out from the Tree of the Great Peace, one to the north, one to the east, one to the south and one to the west. The name of these roots is The Great White Roots and their nature is Peace and Strength.
>
> We place at the top of the Tree of the Long Leaves an Eagle who is able to see afar. If he sees in the distance any evil approaching or any danger threatening he will at once warn the people of the Confederacy.[46]

The Iroquois prophet cast weapons of war beneath the Four White Roots of the Tree and so founded the Five Nations Confederacy. This comprised some fifty League chiefs, each invested with a crown of antlers, the wing of a seagull to brush dust away from the council fire pit, and a pole to rid the area of all creeping creatures. Symbolizing the League was the Longhouse with its five fire pits under one roof, wampum belts depicting the Five Nations, Onondaga being a great tree or heart at its center. A meal of beaver tail, with no sharp utensils in the common dish; five arrows bundled together to make them strong; the council fire and pillar of smoke that reached the sky; five stalks of corn emerging from one stalk fed by four roots: all of these symbolized the power of the League.

The League then established its foreign policy, with laws regulating admission into the League. Delegations were sent out to the Ojibways, Cherokees, and other tribes to offer them the Great Peace. The League reserved the right to wage just war against any opposing nation that refused to accept the "Great Peace." The final symbol of the League was the Condolence ceremony, a re-enactment of the rite as performed by Deganawida for Hiawatha, and by both for the exorcism of Atotarho. The Condolence ceremony, with its thirteen wampum strings of Requickening, would serve to swerve the mourner from vengeful grief resulting in never-ending bloo d feuds. Having fulfilled his mission, Deganawida departed, promising to come again in a time of crisis. Deganawida's very name was considered sacred, and for this reason, he is often simply referred to as "the Peacemaker."[47]

Typical of myths narrating the exploits of other culture heroes, Deganawida "travels magically, overcomes a whole series of trials, and battles monsters. The myth of origin, like the legend, tells that the hero's task is to structure the world and society. It is in this sense that myths are the reflection of society."[48]

The historicity of Deganawida, though never in doubt, presents all the problems of the so-called quest for the historical Jesus. Overlooked by Vecsey in his critical treatment of the Deganawida cycle—but in complete accord with his findings—is Seldon's dissertation on Deganawida. After examining differing published versions, along with versions collected by the author himself (documented in English during visits to several Iroquois reserves and reservations including Tyendinaga, Six Nations, and St. Regis), Seldon found that the legend of Deganawida was transformed over time into myth. Furthermore, the roles of Deganawida and Hiawatha altered through time as a function of various social and psychological pressures on the Iroquois.[49] Of the extant versions of the Deganawida cycle, Gibson's narrative is, according to Vecsey, "perhaps definitive."[50]

Mad Bear's Prophecy of Deganawida's Return

Since there is at least one tradition of Deganawida's return, it is probably only a matter of time before Bahá'í pioneers to Iroquois peoples proclaim Bahá'u'lláh to be the return of Deganawida. Let us then examine one tradition foretelling the return of Deganawida.

> Mad Bear (Wallace Anderson), was an Iroquois nationalist, a Tuscarora by birth. In August, 1959, author Edmund Wilson had an interview with Mad Bear . . . [who] proceeded to relate a prophecy ascribed to Deganawida, which was presumably a source of encouragement whenever his collective hopes for his people flagged. He had heard this prophecy from the head clan mother of the Senecas, who resided on the Tuscarora reserve, and "from a number of other sources," which Mad Bear did not disclose.[51]
>
> Vecsey confirms that the prophecy of Deganawida's return is sufficiently attested in Iroquoian tradition to be considered an essential, though not prominent, feature in the Deganawida cycle.[52] The Six Nations' version has the prophet condition his return on times of crisis: "If at any time through the negligence and carelessness of the lords, they fail to carry out the principles of the Good Tidings of Peace and Power and the rules and regulations of the confederacy and the people are reduced to poverty and great suffering, I will return."[53] In 1990, a trade book, *Native American Prophecies*, popularised Deganawida's prophecy as transmitted by Mad Bear.[54]

So ends the Deganawida cycle, but not its enduring legacy. I now take up the Iroquois influence hypothesis, as this informs popular appreciation of Deganawida.

The Iroquois-Influence Hypothesis

Until recently, Hollywood has tended to focus on American Indian war societies. But, according to native peoples, an ancient peacemaking tradition has existed among the First Nations since the dawn of North American aboriginal history. A recent study argues that one of the most compelling bodies of evidence for the existence of a peace movement among indigenous societies during the American Revolution is preserved in the Morgan Papers, a collection of largely unpublished documents relating to the first American Indian peace treaty in 1776.[55] Historical arguments have also been advanced which hypothesize Iroquois influence on Benjamin Franklin, one of the founding fathers of American democracy.[56] In 1751, Benjamin Franklin, in a letter to James Parker, his New York City printing partner, made the comparison explicit:

> It would be a very strange Thing, if six Nations of ignorant Savages should be capable of forming a Scheme for such a Union, and be able to execute it in such a Manner, as that it has subsisted Ages, and appears indissoluble; and yet a like Union should be impracticable for ten or a Dozen Colonies, to whom it is more necessary, and must be more advantageous; and who cannot be supposed to want an equal Understanding of their Interest.[57]

Iroquoisist Elisabeth Tooker has taken to task such a view of history, calling it a "myth."[58] Despite the negative verdict of recent scholarship, the power and prestige of the Iroquois Confederacy was sufficient to impress Benjamin Franklin as a model for comparison. Lack of evidence to substantiate direct influence on American government need not diminish recognition of the Iroquois model, which owes its existence, at least traditionally, to Deganawida.

Scholarship can be relied upon to provide correctives. But, as in the case of Tooker's critique, debunking myth is not always the same as demythologizing myth. Debunking totally discredits the myth, whereas demythologizing salvages from the myth its historical kernel and, if that is lacking, whatever truth might still be gleaned from the intent of the myth. Resolving this controversy exceeds the scope of this paper. No amount of scepticism, however, is likely to dissuade native views on such matters.[59]

The notion of what I shall term *semiticentrism* is crucial here. As formulated and as currently understood, Bahá'í prophetology—in its essential features—differs little from standard Islamic prophetology. It is universal in respect of literate, but not oral, cultures. In other words, religions that lack either an Abrahamic or Indo-Aryan ethnic endowment are unlikely to achieve parity with those religions that are already accepted within the Bahá'í tradition.

The Islamic Legacy: Sabianism As a Procrustean Category

Mírzá Abu'l-Fadl tried to adumbrate forms of indigenous religions (especially African) under the rubric "Sabian"—although Abu'l-Fadl's writings appear to be devoid of reference to New World traditions. Problems of category become apparent in his definition of the Sabians as a reference to "all non-Judaic and non-Indic religions of antiquity."[60] This may be true insofar as the learned apologist was concerned, but his own explanation fails to include, at least in specific terms, the religious traditions of the indigenous, pre-Columbian New World.

The term "Sabian," as I have previously shown, reflects an essentially Islamic view of the history of religions, which entailed an obvious lack of consensus, and indeed confusion, in the use of the term which Bahá'í terminology stood to inherit.[61] Furthermore, Mírzá Abu'l-Fadl's usage of the term was broader than that which Shoghi Effendi was to adopt a few decades later:

> As to the religion of the Sabæans, very little is known about the origins of this religion, though we Bahá'ís are certain of one thing, that the founder of it has been a divinely-sent Messenger of God. The country where Sabæanism became widespread and flourished was Chaldea, and Abraham is considered as having been a follower of that Faith.[62]

The Bahá'í Faith has therefore inherited from Islam an unresolved problem in the use of the term "Sabian." For Bahá'u'lláh, it referred to the religion of John the Baptist.[63] Shoghi Effendi used the term in line with its more common Islamic meaning, however.

Nine is Not Enough

Bahá'ís have traditionally spoken of nine existing world religions: (1) Sabianism; (2) Hinduism; (3) Zoroastrianism; (4) Buddhism; (5) Judaism; (6) Christianity; (7) Islam; (8) the Bábí religion; and (9) the Bahá'í Faith.[64] Shoghi Effendi was quick to recognize the intellectual objections that could be raised to such a fixed and closed canon. Therefore, he counselled Bahá'ís not to lay too much stress on this list.[65] On the evidence of current publications, this foresighted doctrinal flexibility was destined to avoid the pitfalls of a nine-religion exclusivism.[66] The question remains as to how Bahá'í doctrine will adapt to the sociological fact of religious traditions not specified, yet anticipated in principle and accommodated in practice as the result of conversions from increasingly diverse populations.

Bahá'í universalism is circumscribed by the limited possibility of the attestation of prophets by name. In principle, Bahá'í doctrine acknowledges that messengers of God were sent to all peoples at one time or other, and that the names of more than a few of them are lost. Analytically, the Bahá'í list of nine explicitly recognized prophets represents only two families of religions: the Irano-Semitic (Sabianism, Zoroastrianism, Judaism, Christianity, Islam, Babism, and the Bahá'í religion) and Sino-Indic traditions (Hindu tradition, Buddhism, and, to a lesser degree in Bahá'í texts, Confucianism). Native spirituality belongs to neither.

Authority and Attestation: The Constraints of Science on Religion

Authoritative Bahá'í pronouncements do place constraints on what Bahá'ís can integrate into their undisputed, canonical list of divine messengers. However, doctrine is theoretically open to refinement provided other Bahá'í principles are considered.

As a general rule, Shoghi Effendi left questions of history open to historians. In a letter written on his behalf to an individual believer, the Guardian stated: "There are no dates in our teachings regarding the actual dates of the Prophets of the Adamic Cycle; so we cannot give any. Tentatively we can accept what historians may consider accurate." (25 November 1950) On the basis of these statements, the Research Department in a memorandum to the Universal House of Justice concluded: "Because the Writings of the Faith contain no exact information regarding dates of Dispensations prior to that of Muhammad, Bahá'ís can accept the conclusions of scholars, bearing in mind that there is often disagreement among the scholars themselves on such matters."[67]

Synchronic and Diachronic Models of Progressive Revelation

If Mírzá Abu'l-Fadl has acknowledged the existence of two separate and unrelated streams of religious tradition—two relative solitudes, religions of the New World represent neither stream. To suggest that native Amerindian religions are somehow lost tribes of Sabians is, of course, absurd—and reductionist in the extreme. The Research Department of the Universal House of Justice broached this problem when in 1988, it drew attention to the following statement from one of the well-known tablets of 'Abdu'l-Bahá: *"In cycles gone by, though harmony was established, yet, owing to the absence of means, the unity of all mankind could not have been achieved. Continents remained widely divided, nay even among the peoples of one and the same continent association and interchange of thought were well-nigh impossible. Consequently, intercourse, understanding and unity amongst all the peoples and kindreds of the earth were unattainable . . . "*[68] This idea trades on the observation that societies on separate continents functioned as distinct social worlds with independent religious traditions.

This, in turn, invites formal consideration of non-Irano/Semitic and non-Sino/Indic religious traditions along with their respective founders in those traditions which ascribe their origins to such founders. On the basis of other texts in addition to the one just cited, the Research Department, on behalf of the Universal House of Justice, concluded: "In light of everything above, it would appear possible that

Manifestations of God have lived simultaneously in different areas of the globe . . . "[69] This statement is important in that it theoretically allows for formal recognition, at least in principle, of religious traditions outside the Irano-Semitic family.

A more enlightened doctrinal modification might be possible on the basis of a history of civilizations, in which human societies might be seen as undergoing asymmetrical developments. In their respective courses of social evolution, spiritual traditions may be seen as endemic, distinct, and independent of each other, except perhaps for certain universal features (phenomenological, not essentialist). Being virtually cut off from the East prior to Columbus (subsequent to any prehistoric migrations), religious history in the Americas evolved independently of Jesus and Muhammad, such that revelations from God to the Americas were not mediated through Asia. Too narrow a Bahá'í conception of progressive revelation would require that, in theory and assuming a prior date for Zoroaster, a Zoroastrian would be obliged to believe in the Buddha as next in the succession of prophets. A corollary of such a view would imply that the New World was bereft of its own prophets during the dispensations of Christ and Muhammad.

'Abdu'l-Bahá on Native Messengers of God

In his compendium of Bahá'í teachings, *'Amr va khalq* ("Command and creation"), Fádil Mázandarání refers to a tablet of 'Abdu'l-Bahá addressed to a certain Amir Khan of Tehran. The gist of this piece is this: in times past, the Call of God (*nidáy-i iláhí*), referring to ancient messengers of God, had assuredly been raised among the people of North America (*ahl-i amrík*), though most of the teachings have been forgotten. As to translation, the Universal House of Justice has provided the following authorized translation of the central portion of the text:

> In ancient times the people of America were, through their northern regions, close to Asia, that is, separated from Asia by a strait. For this reason, it hath been said that crossing had occurred. There are other signs which indicate communication.

> As to places whose people were not informed of the appearance of Prophets, such people are excused. In the Qur'an it hath been revealed: "We will not chastise them if they had not been sent a Messenger." (Q. 17:15)
>
> Undoubtedly in those regions the Call of God must have been raised in ancient times, but it hath been forgotten now[70] (*al-battih dar án afahát níz dar azmanih-yi qadímih*[71] *vaqtí nidá-yi iláhí buland gashtih va-lákin hál farámúsh shudih ast*[72]).

In this particular context, the expression "Call of God" (*nidáy-i iláhí*) is a transparent reference to prophets of God. The expression, the "Call of God," is a stock allusion to revelation, as in Bahá'u'lláh's poetic description of the Báb's revelation: "The divine call (*nidáy-i iláhí*) of the Celestial Herald from beyond the Veil of Glory."[73] Adduced in the text translated above is a quranic verse which 'Abdu'l-Bahá cites indicating that God would not judge a people unto whom no messenger (*rasúl*; *Amr va Khalq* 2:46) had come. Knowledge of God, according to Bahá'í doctrine, is necessarily mediated by chosen Revealers. This coded validation of Native messengers of God might suggest a separate and distinct spiritual history in a world far removed from Abrahamic tradition.

However, at the present time, the language of this tablet is not specific enough to warrant an explicitly positive statement from the House of Justice, which writes:

> The Bahá'í Teachings do not explicitly confirm, nor do they rule out, the possibility that Messengers of God have appeared in the Americas. In the absence of a clear Text the Universal House of Justice has no basis for issuing the kind of statement you propose which would confirm, "in principle, that God sent Manifestations to the indigenous peoples of the Americas."[74]

Universalizing Universalism

What is the status of this particular pronouncement, which admittedly exists in splendid isolation? Its implications are clear, and in relation to the paradigm bias of semiticentrism, the statement is profound. This Bahá'í validation of native messengers of God suggests a separate and distinct spiritual history in a world far removed from Abrahamic tradition. Thus, a Bahá'í pamphlet incorporating such a position might look something like the figure below:

Progressive Revelation

* Messengers of God to First Nations
Abraham
Krishna
Moses
Zoroaster
Buddha
Jesus
Muhammad
The Báb
Bahá'u'lláh

*Sacred tradition names such messengers as Deganawida, Quetzalcoátl, and Viracocha (Iroquois, Toltec, Inca traditions in North, Central, and South America).

From silence, we conclude that the question of the authenticity of native spirituality was not explicitly addressed during Shoghi Effendi's ministry as Guardian of the Bahá'í Faith. Though the Bahá'í stricture against adding names to the succession of prophets attested in Abrahamic scriptures would inevitably frustrate any Bahá'í attempt to enshrine a native culture hero who must be accepted by all Bahá'ís as a Manifestation of God, such a list might be open-ended with respect to principle. Native traditions pose their own difficulties in attestation, especially where accounts vary and when such traditions betray Christian influence and, more recently, Euroamerican influence at the hands of anthropologists and the press as well.[75] It could be argued that such historical uncertainties are no worse than problems surrounding the historicity of Krishna, for example.

At issue here is not the question of the *existence* of other messengers of God not attested to and listed in the Bahá'í writings, but the problem of designating them by name. In principle, a Bahá'í can certainly affirm that messengers of God have been sent to all peoples, according to Bahá'í belief, but that there is simply no authoritative way to attest the historicity of legendary culture heroes individually. Thus, Bahá'í authorities may consider adding the *category* of (rather than *names* of) messengers of God to First Nations, or messengers of God to indigenous peoples. The problem now is no longer the *principle*, but rather the question of *names*.

Deganawida presents a unique case for Bahá'ís because there is evidence for his historicity, as reflected in a scholarly consensus. This is not to say that the "historical Deganawida" is possible to recover. The fact that Deganawida may have appeared after Muhammad chronologically poses no difficulty, since native spirituality has had no historical connection with the Abrahamic stream of revelation. Diffusionist theories may explain the transmission of some vestiges of ancient native spirituality, but such diffusion does not predetermine subsequent developments. Though Islam is a universal religion and was always so potentially, its presence in the New World is late. Bahá'ís cannot expect Amerindians to have accepted Islam when they had no knowledge of it. Therefore, the existence of Native American prophets must be recognized in principle. Hence, although the Bahá'í Faith cannot claim Deganawida as its own, it can recognize the place of Iroquois spiritual genius within the world's sacred history.

Notes

Christopher Buck, author of *Paradise and Paradigm* (State University of New York Press, 1999), *Symbol and Secret* (Kalimát Press, 1995) teaches at Michigan State University.

1. "To the warring tribes 700-800 years ago there came an astonishing Prophet of Peace—Deganawidah united five, later six, mutually hostile tribal groups in a federal union based on democracy, the first in the Western Hemisphere. He cemented this union with a "Great Law of Peace," a constitution which propounded one expansive human family. And thus, in God's Plan, with Benjamin Franklin and Thomas Jefferson as perceptive mediators, the Bill of Rights and the Constitution were vital steps (after the War of Independence,

1775-83) toward realising in America the Iroquois concept of the primacy of individual rights as superior to property and power. And of course the Iroquois foreshadowed, in their Longhouse of sky and earth, the planetary message of the Bahá'í Faith for today." (David S. Ruhe, "A New Evolution: Religious Bonding for World Unity," *Journal of Bahá'í Studies*, Vol. 6, no. 4 [1994-1995] pp. 45-57).

2. John Arthur Gibson, *Concerning the League: The Iroquois League as Dictated in Onondaga*, newly elicited, edited and translated by Hanni Woodbury in Collaboration with Reg Henry and Harry Webster on the Basis of A.A. Goldenweiser's Manuscript. Memoir 9 (Winnipeg: Algonquian and Iroquoian Linguistics, 1992) pp. 36-41.
3. On Canadian native peoples, see R. Snyder-Penner, "A Select Bibliography on Indigenous Peoples in Canada," *The Conrad Grebel Review,* Vol. 9 (Spring 1991) pp. 171-78. On native spirituality generally, see Armin W. Geertz, "Native North American Religions," in *A New Handbook of Living Religions*, ed. J. R. Hinnells (Oxford: Blackwell, 1997) pp. 514-46.
4. *Canadian Bahá'í News*, Vol. 5, no. 9 (1993) p. 13.
5. The Universal House of Justice formally approved this initiative (*Bahá'í Canada*, Vol. 6, no. 3 [1993] p. 23).
6. *The Right to An Identity* (Toronto: Canadian Bahá'í Committee, n.d.). The time frame within which publication of this pamphlet must have occurred (1967-1976) is ventured by W. Collins, *Bibliography of English Language Works on the Bábí and Bahá'í Faiths 1844-1985* (Oxford: George Ronald, 1990).
7. National Spiritual Assembly of the Bahá'ís of Canada, "A Submission to the Joint Committee of the Senate and the House of Commons on Indian Affairs," in *Minutes of Proceedings and Evidence, No. 4. May 18, 1960* (Canada Senate and House of Commons, 24th Parliament, 3rd Session; Joint Committee of the Senate and the House of Commons on Indian Affairs, 1960). Also in French. Cited in Abler, *A Canadian Indian Bibliography 1960-1970* (Toronto: University of Toronto Press, 1974) pp. 148-49 (entry 720).
8. Abstracted in Abler, *A Canadian Indian Bibliography,* pp. 51-52 (entry 262).
9. Jacqueline Left Hand Bull, "Bahá'í," in *Parliament of Souls: In Search of Global Spirituality. Interviews with 28 Spiritual Leaders from Around the World*, ed. M. Tobias, J. Morrison, B. Gray (San Francisco: KQED Books, 1995) p. 22.
10. From an academic perspective, the Quetzalcoátl prophecies are best treated by David Carrasco, *Quetzalcoátl and the Irony of Empire: Myths and Prophecies in the Aztec Tradition* (University of Chicago Press, 1982) pp. 148-204; idem, "Quetzalcoátl's Revenge: Primordium and Application in Aztec Religion," *History of Religions*, Vol. 19 (1980) pp. 296-320. For a translation of one of the native Quetzalcoátl traditions, see J. Bierhorst, *Four Masterworks of American Indian Literature: Quetzalcoátl/The Ritual of Condolence/ Cuceb/The Night Chant* (Toronto: Doubleday, 1974) pp. 17-105.

11. Latin literature purportedly transcribed from hieroglyphic texts. One of the "Sacred Books of the Jaguar Priests" has been translated by M. S. Edmonson, *The Ancient Future of the Itza: The Book of Chilam Balam of Tizimin* (Austin, Texas, 1982); cf. R. Roys (tr.), *The Book of Chilam Balam of Chumayel* (University of Oklahoma Press, 1967). Several Naturegraph publications, including pamphlets by the late Vinson Brown who established Naturegraph, have appealed to such traditions.
12. M. Jansen, "The Art of Writing in Ancient Mexico: An Ethno-iconological Perspective," in *Visible Religion* (Leiden: Brill, 1986). In the sixteenth century, as Spaniards further explored Mesoamerica, they found eighteen different systems of writing. See also O. Dickason, *Canada's First Nations: A History of Founding Peoples from Earliest Times* (Toronto: McClelland and Stewart, 1992) p. 432, n. 34.
13. Photograph in *The Bahá'í World: An International Record*, Vol. 16 (Haifa: Bahá'í World Centre, 1978) p. 445. The sign in Spanish reads: "Bahá'u'lláh el retorno Viracocha." The caption states: "This sign says that Bahá'u'lláh is the return of Viracocha, a divine being of Indian tradition."
14. Phenomenologically, the figure of Bahá'u'lláh has been associated with various messianic traditions:

(1): **Bábí tradition:**	*	Him Whom God Shall Manifest; the Báb remanifest.
(2): **Shí'í Islam:**	*	Imám Husayn *redivivus.*
(3): **Zoroastrianism:**	*	Sháh Bahrám Varjávand.
(4): **Judaism:**	*	Ancient of Days; Glory of God; Everlasting Father.
(5): **Christianity:**	*	Christ returned; the Comforter/Spirit of Truth.
(6): **Sunní Islam:**	***	Return of Jesus Christ
(7): **Hinduism:**	**	Kalki Visnuyasas; the Tenth Avatar; return of Krishna.
(8): **Buddhism:**	**	Maitreya, the Fifth Buddha.
(9): **Indigenous:**	****	Viracocha's return (Quechua Inca tradition).

Legend:	*Period during which messianic identification was made:*
*	During Bahá'u'lláh's ministry.
**	During 'Abdu'l-Bahá's ministry.
***	During the Guardian's ministry. Earlier attestation uncertain.
****	Possibly as early as the Guardian's ministry.

15. See also Tony Shearer, *Lord of the Dawn: Quetzalcoátl, the Plumed Serpent of Mexico* (Healdsburg, CA: Naturegraph, 1971).
16. Dickason, *Canada's First Nations,* pp. 440-41, n. 11.
17. *The Bahá'ís: A Profile of the Bahá'í Faith and Its Worldwide Community* (London: Bahá'í Publishing Trust, 1992) is a publication of the Bahá'í International Community (a non-governmental organization [NGO] with consultative status at the United Nations), Office of Public Information.
18. Native religious traditions, it is true, are suffused with ecological referents. For the modern native Canadian, what may have once qualified as animism

has been considerably psychologised. Myth is now appreciated as heritage and is found to be replete with meaning, sending its own message to an ecologically endangered industrial society.

19. For a relevant discussion of the why such terms are so theologically freighted, see James L. Cox, "The Classification 'Primal Religions' as a Non-Empirical Christian Theological Construct," *Studies in World Christianity*, Vol. 2, no. 1 (1996) pp. 55-76.
20. As pointed out to me by Stephen Bedingfield, personal communication, 28 December 1995. It should be noted that Newfoundland joined the Canadian federation in 1949.
21. [No author cited], "30 Years of Pioneering on Tyendinaga Honored," *Tekawennake* [Brantford, Ontario] Vol. 5, no. 4 (1979). The present writer has not accessed this article.
22. Willie Wiloya and Vinson Brown, *Warriors of the Rainbow: Strange and Prophetic Dreams of the Indian Peoples* (Healdsburg, CA: Naturegraph, 1962) pp. 42-48; Vinson Brown, *Voices of Earth and Sky* (Stackpole, 1979).
23. On the development of Bahá'í universalism, see my article, "A Unique Eschatological Interface: Bahá'u'lláh and Cross-cultural Messianism," in *In Iran. Studies in Bábí and Bahá'í History*, Vol. 3, ed. by Peter Smith (Los Angeles: Kalimát Press, 1986) pp. 157-79.
24. From a letter written on behalf of Shoghi Effendi dated 10 October 1950, *Lights of Guidance: A Bahá'í reference file*, comp. H. Hornby, 2nd ed. (New Delhi: Bahá'í Publishing Trust, 1988) p. 503.
25. From a letter written on behalf of Shoghi Effendi dated 13 March 1950, *Lights of Guidance,* p. 503.
26. From a letter written on behalf of Shoghi Effendi dated 5 March 1957, *The Compilation of Compilations: Prepared by the Universal House of Justice 1963-1990* (Maryborough, Victoria: Bahá'í Publications Australia, 1991) Vol. 1, p. 23.
27. 'Abdu'l-Bahá accepted both Buddha and Krishna as Manifestations of God. Evidence of Bahá'u'lláh's estimation of Krishna is found in Vol. 7 of Ishráq-Khávarí, ed., *Má'iday-i ásmání* (Tehran: Mu'assisa Mabu'át Amrí, 129 Badí' [1972]).
28. In an obituary for the Iroquois Bahá'í pioneer James Loft, Deganawida is spoken of as a prophet in a purely referential way: "It is perhaps significant that Tyendinaga is the birthplace of Deganawida, the fifteenth century figure whom tradition regards as the founder of the Iroquois Confederacy. Regarded as a prophet by the Indian people, Deganawida, who was Huron by birth and Mohawk by adoption, united various tribes under one law and devoted his life to establishing peace, righteousness and civil law . . . His grave marker —within the shadow of the monument erected to the revered Deganawida— bears the simple legend, *Alfred "Jim" Loft—Bahá'í Pioneer* and is engraved with the Indian thunderbird symbol and a nine-pointed star" (Evelyn Loft Watts and Charles Jardine, "Alfred James Loft 13 July 1908-22 May 1973," in *The Bahá'í World,* Vol. 16, pp. 515-16).
29. Ruhe, "A New Evolution," p. 45.

30. Delahunt, "Bahá'í," in *A Parliament of Souls*, p. 22.
31. Richard Pilant, "An Address to Iroquoian Studies," McMaster University, Hamilton, Ontario, Canada, 6 April 1960; *apud* G. Reaman, *The Trail of the Iroquois Indians: How the Iroquois Nation saved Canada for the British Empire* (Toronto: Peter Martin Associates, 1967).
32. See J. Tuck, "Iroquois Confederacy," *Scientific American*, Vol. 224, no. 2 (1971) pp. 32-42.
33. A distinction drawn by D. Richter, "Ordeals of the Longhouse: The Five Nations in Early American History," in *Beyond the Covenant Chain: The Iroquois and Their Neighbors in North America, 1600-1800* (Syracuse University Press, 1987) pp. 11-27.
34. A. Parker, "The Traditional Narrative of the Origin of the Confederation of the Five Nations Commonly Known as the Iroquois," in *Parker on the Iroquois*, ed. by W. Fenton (Syracuse University Press, 1968) Vol. 3, no. 64, n. 2.
35. The year A.D. 1390 is given in J. Myers, *The Fitzhenry and Whiteside Book of Canadian Facts and Dates* (Richmond Hill, Ontario: Fitzhenry and Whiteside, 1991) p. 17. No documentation is adduced to support such a date. It has now entered the popular domain as a "fact."
36. A drawing of Deganawida appears in Dickason, *Canada's First Nations*, p. 72.
37. Whether "Heavenly Messenger" is the actual meaning of, or is simply an epithet for, Deganawida is not specified in Dickason, *Canada's First Nations*, p. 71.
38. Two critical treatments of the Deganawida cycle deserve mention here: D. Richter, "Ordeals of the Longhouse," pp. 11-27; C. Vecsey, "The Story and Structure of the Iroquois Confederacy," *Journal of the American Academy of Religion*, Vol. 54, no. 1 (1986) pp. 79-106; reprinted in *Imagine Ourselves Richly: Mythic Narratives of North American Indians* (New York: Crossroad, 1988) pp. 94-117.
39. Tooker, "The United States Constitution and the Iroquois League," pp. 113-14.
40. *The Code of Dekanahwideh together with The Tradition of the Origin of the Five Nations' League,* "Prepared by the committee of chiefs appointed by the Six Nations' Council of Grand River, Canada, and adopted by Council of Chiefs, July 3, 1900," in W. Fenton, ed., *Parker on the Iroquois* (Syracuse University Press, 1968) Vol. 3, no. 62.
41. For this the reader is referred to the work of Vecsey, *Imagine Ourselves Richly*, pp. 98-106, 115-17.
42. P. Wallace, *The White Roots of Peace* (Philadelphia: University of Pennsylvania Press, 1946) pp. 13-14. On the six principles that Deganawida explains to the Mother of Nations, see Vecsey, *Imagine Ourselves Richly*, pp. 113-15.
43. Fenton, *Parker on the Iroquois*, Vol. 3, no. 15.
44. Ibid., Vol. 3, no. 16.
45. See L. Ceci, "The Value of Wampum among the New York Iroquois: A Case Study in Artifact Analysis," *Journal of Anthropological Research*, Vol. 38, no. 1 (1982) pp. 97-107.

46. Fenton, *Parker on the Iroquois*, Vol. 3, no. 3.
47. This epitome of the Deganawida cycle was for the most part based on Vecsey's much longer and carefully documented summary in, "The Story and Structure of the Iroquois Confederacy," pp. 82-90. Vecsey is to be consulted for the important variants in the retelling of the saga in its several versions and for his penetrating analysis of the legend as a whole.
48. Bonnefoy, *Mythologies*, Vol. 2, no. 1161.
49. Sherman Ward Seldon, *The Legend, Myth and Code of Deganaweda and their Significance to Iroquois Culture History* (Ph.D. Thesis, Folklore Program, Indiana University). Available from University Microfilms. Abstracted in Abler, *A Canadian Indian Bibliography,* pp. 656-57 (entry 2959).
50. Vecsey, "Story and Structure," p. 80, n. 3.
51. *Apologies to the Iroquois,* pp. 163-64.
52. Vecsey, "Story and Structure of the Iroquois Confederacy," p. 90.
53. Fenton, *Parker on the Iroquois,* Vol. 3, p. 105.
54. Peterson, "Deganawidah: Peacemaker of the Iroquois," in *Native American Prophecies,* pp. 62-89. Mad Bear's prophecy is reprinted on pp. 77-79.
55. G. Schaaf, "The American Indian Peace Movement: Past and Present," *Interculture,* Vol. 18, no. 4 [no. 89, English ed.] (1985) pp. 2-13; reprinted from *Akwesane Notes,* Vol. 17, no. 5 (1985). Schaaf highlights recent achievements by Amerindian leaders to promote peace.
56. B. Johansen, *Forgotten Founders: Benjamin Franklin, the Iroquois and the Rationale for the American Revolution* (Ipswich, MA: Gambit, 1982).
57. L. Labaree, ed., *The Papers of Benjamin Franklin* (New Haven: Yale University Press, 1961) Vol. 4, pp. 118-19. Cited by Tooker, "The United States Constitution and the Iroquois League," p. 110.
58. Tooker, pp. 115, 121.
59. See "Iroquois Great Law of Peace and the United States Constitution: How the Founding Fathers ignored the Clan Mothers," *American Indian Law Review,* Vol. 16 (1991) pp. 497-531; cf. P. A. Levy, "Exemplars of Taking Liberties: The Iroquois Influence Thesis and the Problem of Evidence," *William and Mary Quarterly,* Vol. 53, no. 3 (July 1996) pp. 588-604; S. B. Payne, "The Iroquois League, the Articles of Confederation, and the Constitution," *William and Mary Quarterly,* Vol. 53, no. 3 (1996) pp. 605-620; D. A. Grinde, A Sauce for the Goose: Demand and Definitions for Proof regarding the Iroquois and Democracy," *William and Mary Quarterly,* Vol. 53, no. 3 (1996) pp. 621-36.
60. Ibid., p. 100, translator's note.
61. See my "The Identity of the Sabian: An Historical Quest," *The Muslim World,* Vol. 74 (1984) pp. 172-86.
62. From a letter written on behalf of Shoghi Effendi dated 10 November 1939, *Compilation of Compilations,* Vol. 1, p. 20.
63. Bahá'u'lláh identifies the Sabians so: "After the martyrdom of the son of Zachariah [John the Baptist], some of His followers did not turn unto the divine Manifestation of Jesus, the Son of Mary, and removed themselves

from the Faith of God, and until this day they have continued to exist in the world, being known to some as the Sabians. These people consider themselves to be the community of John" (*Qamus-i Iqan,* Vol. 2, p. 987, cited in *World Order,* Vol. 10 [1975] p. 3). In another passage, Bahá'u'lláh speaks of the followers of John the Baptist as those "who are even now still on the earth and are known as the Sabians" (*Asrar al-Athar,* Vol. 4, p. 233, cited in *World Order,* Vol. 10 [1975-76] p. 11).

64. In a letter to "Mrs. Russell," dated 28 July 1936, Shoghi Effendi wrote: "The number nine, which in itself is the number of perfection, is considered by the Bahá'ís as sacred, because it is symbolic of the perfection of the Bahá'í Revelation which constitutes the ninth in the line of existing religions, the latest and fullest Revelation which mankind has ever known. The eighth is the religion of the Báb and the remaining seven are: Hinduism, Buddhism, Zoroastrianism, Judaism, Christianity, Islám, and the religion of the Sabeans. These religions are not the only true religions that have appeared in the world but are the only ones still existing." *Bahá'í News,* No. 105 (1937) p. 2.
65. "The Guardian feels that with intellectuals and students of religion the question of exactly which are the 9 existing religions is controversial, and it would be better to avoid it" (letter dated 28 Oct. 1949 on behalf of the Guardian to an individual believer, originally published in *Bahá'í News,* No. 228 [1950] p. 4). See *Lights of Guidance,* p. 415.
66. In *The Bahá'ís,* the Bahá'í International Community publication referred to earlier, this particular significance attached to the number nine is completely omitted (p. 52).
67. Memorandum dated 24 May 1988, "Questions Relayed by the Spiritual Assembly of Mitcham," p. 2.
68. 'Abdu'l-Bahá, "Seven Candles of Unity," in Shoghi Effendi, *World Order of Bahá'u'lláh* (Wilmette: Bahá'í Publishing Trust, 1974) p. 38.
69. Memorandum dated 24 May 1988, "Questions Relayed by the Spiritual Assembly of Mitcham," p. 3.
70. Research Department Memorandum, dated 16 May 1996.
71. I have slightly amended the text here due to a misplaced *hamza* above *qadíma*. The *hamza* must surely have been intended for *azmanih*. The transliteration here reflects modern Tehran pronunciation, instead of *azmina*. See H. Wehr, *Arabic-English Dictionary* (Ithaca, New York: Spoken Language Services, 1976) p. 382.
72. 'Abdu'l-Bahá, *apud* Fádil-i Mázandarání, *Amr va Khalq,* Vol. 2 (Germany: Bahá'í-Verlag, 1985) p. 46.
73. Bahá'u'lláh, *The Kitáb-i-Íqán: The Book of Certitude*, tr. Shoghi Effendi (Wilmette: Bahá'í Publishing Trust, 1931 [1970]) p. 239; Persian text, Bahá'u'lláh, *Kitáb-i-Íqán: Book of Certitude* (Bahá'í Verlag, 1980) p. 186, line 3.
74. From a letter written on behalf of the Universal House of Justice dated 16 May 1996.
75. See Jordan Paper, "Methodological Controversies in the Study of Native American Religions," *Studies in Religion / Sciences Religieuses,* Vol. 22, no. 3 (1993) pp. 365-77.

THE NEW YORK STOCK EXCHANGE

Bahá'í Approaches to Economics

Bryan Graham

This essay reviews some of the secondary literature on the Bahá'í Faith and economics. The Bahá'í writings include important teachings on the spiritual dimensions of work, distributive justice, industrial relations, and the importance of cooperation in commerce. A survey and critique is provided of published articles. This review also discusses some important issues of methodology.[1]

> The ideas of economists and political philosophers, both when they are right and when they are wrong, are more powerful than is commonly understood. Indeed, the world is ruled by little else. — John M. Keynes[2]
>
> Be anxiously concerned with the needs of the age ye live in, and center your deliberations on its exigencies and requirements. — Bahá'u'lláh[3]

That Bahá'ís are concerned with economic issues should not be surprising. The Bahá'í Faith includes many social teachings, and economics is, after all, a social science. Issues of economic justice and development are among the key social teachings of the religion. In his "World Order" letters, Shoghi Effendi notes that Bahá'u'lláh has "provided for the essentials of a Divine Economy,"[4] and later in the same letter he calls this Divine Economy Bahá'u'lláh's "inestimable gift to mankind."[5] Economic issues are at the heart of Bahá'í conceptions of social justice, suggesting the existence of a constructive role for Bahá'í economists to play. However, it is important to define what this role entails.

Exploration of Bahá'í teachings on economics has occupied an important place in the Bahá'í community for many years. Indeed, it was the social teachings of the Faith that formed the basis of many of 'Abdu'l-Bahá's talks in the West. However, for most of the last century the Bahá'í community, while utilizing the social teachings of the Faith in its proclamation and teaching activities, did little to develop and articulate them beyond the level of quotation of 'Abdu'l-Bahá or Shoghi Effendi. The phrase "spiritual solutions to economic problems," is included in most Bahá'í "principles" lists and introductory pamphlets, yet many Bahá'ís would have difficulty articulating the exact nature of these "spiritual solutions." Clearly, there is a need for further scholarship in this field.[6]

Fortunately, this pattern of negligence is eroding. The Universal House of Justice's 1983 call for renewed emphasis on social and economic development, the publication of *The Promise of World Peace*, and the activities of the Bahá'í International Community at the United Nations have increased awareness of the Faith's social teachings. This increased awareness is reflected in the expansion of scholarly work on the Faith. This article reviews some of the more recent articles written by Bahá'ís on economics.[7]

Selecting articles to include in a review is an inherently subjective task. The rationale employed below is as follows: First, only essay and journal articles have been reviewed. Second, only materials published since 1975 have been included. Third, only materials that are relatively easy to obtain have been used. In practice, this means that only articles published in books or in readily available journals have been reviewed. Finally, a somewhat narrow interpretation of "economics" has been adopted.

Anyone who begins to explore this literature will soon realize that while existing materials are limited, the range of topics discussed is vast. The use of a narrow definition has resulted in some significant holes in the review. For example none of the several articles on Marxism are discussed. However, the approach allows for a more in-depth treatment of several key topics in the literature. This review has sought to extract those themes which emerge as "key" in the literature and discuss them more thoroughly in recognition of their centrality.

The articles reviewed are necessarily preliminary in nature. Indeed, all of their authors emphasize that the discussions are largely speculative as "Bahá'í" economics would only occur within the context of a Bahá'í commonwealth—an as yet unrealized stage of human development. As Huddleston puts it: "Bahá'í economic views acquire real meaning only when considered in the context of a Bahá'í civilization."[8] Furthermore, it is important to keep in mind Shoghi Effendi's statement that "Bahá'u'lláh did not bring a complete system of economics to the world."[9] Therefore, in an important sense, there is no such thing as "Bahá'í" economics, at least not when understood as a narrow set of "orthodox" normative and positive principles.

The Bahá'í writings include teachings that have a bearing, indeed sometimes a critical bearing, on our conceptions of what constitutes an ideal economic system or the "divine economy" discussed by Shoghi Effendi, but they do not constitute an economic system unto themselves. Therefore, "Bahá'í economics" is somewhat of a misnomer. Economics, as an academic discipline, is a social science that employs a set of analytical, theoretical, and empirical tools developed over the past two hundred years. Bahá'ís have a vital role to play in the development of this discipline, but this role does not include supplanting "secular" economics with a poorly constructed "Bahá'í" paradigm. Indeed, Shoghi Effendi repeatedly emphasized that Bahá'ís must keep up with the cutting edge of knowledge and current affairs in order to correlate the Bahá'í teachings with modern thinking.[10] With this in mind, we might modestly define a Bahá'í economist as nothing more than an economist whose normative framework is informed by the Bahá'í teachings.

Two issues have significant bearing on the task of a Bahá'í economist. First, we must remember that, according to Bahá'u'lláh, the fundamental purpose of religion "is to safeguard the interests and promote the unity of the human race."[11] Second, we must remember Shoghi Effendi's warning "that many [economic] issues at present baffling the minds of the world are not even mentioned" in the Bahá'í writings, and therefore we cannot view the few technical teachings on economics found in the writings as anything approaching a comprehensive "Bahá'í" system. These two statements at once define the basic objectives and parameters of the Bahá'í economist: to breathe life into an existing shell of the economics discipline and thereby transform it; to apply the spiritual to the material.

Broadly speaking, all of the articles surveyed below operate within the framework outlined above. The lack of a clearly formulated Bahá'í system of economics is, indeed, an advantage. As Dahl notes in "Evolving toward a Bahá'í Economic System," the lack of technical teachings on economics in the writings means that "Bahá'ís can thereby hope to avoid narrow orthodoxy, which has been a stifling influence on so many intellectual disciplines."[12] There is clearly room for constructive disagreement.

The approach adopted below is as follows: Themes common to all the articles, or a significant subset of them, serve as the basic organizing principle of the review. The areas discussed are: (1) the spiritual and ethical dimensions of work; (2) distributive justice; (3) industrial relations; and (4) issues of cooperation and competition. Where appropriate, material from the mainstream economic literature on these topics is included. In addition to the topics outlined above a few clarifying and critical remarks on Bahá'í attitudes towards "economics" and "capitalism" are included. Finally, areas for further research are outlined.

The Spiritual and Ethical Dimensions of Work

One theme that underlies all Bahá'í scholarship on economics is the notion that the spiritual and material dimensions of existence are connected, are mutually reinforcing, and are indeed reflected in one another. All of these articles proceed from the premise that "the material and spiritual worlds are closely interlinked."[13] William Hatcher most forcefully articulates the implications of this notion in his article "Economics and Moral Values." Hatcher argues that the interconnectedness of the spiritual and material worlds implies that "our economic system is simply an external and concrete reflection of our collective inner life."[14] Shahruz Mohtadi in "Economic Justice in the

New World Order" makes a similar argument, noting "that among the fundamental causes of economic injustice are such attitudes of selfishness, greed, competitiveness, and apathy."[15] The implication is that today's material impoverishment is merely a reflection of our collective spiritual impoverishment.

The close relationship between the material and spiritual worlds suggests that there are significant material gains to improvements in the moral fabric of society; reciprocally, moral decadence is costly. One way this link is nurtured in the Bahá'í Faith is through the "spiritualization" of work. Work is a "calling" and a divine injunction: "The best of men," writes Bahá'u'lláh, "are they that earn a livelihood by their calling and spend upon themselves and upon their kindred for the love of God."[16] Work becomes a spiritual act, and thereby becomes imbued with virtue: honesty, hard work, and a spirit of service come to characterize our actions.[17]

The literature of the economics of asymmetric information gives one illustration on the economic implications of a virtuous society. Information, its accuracy and flow, is a critical determinant of market efficiency. Therefore, the quality of information we use to make our decisions directly affects the ability of the market to meet society's collective material needs.

For example, consider the market for used cars; this market is dominated by what is known as the "used car salesman," a caricature of dishonesty. The used car salesman is interested solely in selling a car at the highest price possible. In order to achieve this goal, he is willing to lie; that is, to give the potential car-buyer inaccurate information about the quality of the car (e.g., not disclose full maintenance records). In this case, the used car salesman is using bad information to extract (i.e., steal) money from the buyer—money that the buyer would not willingly part with if he had all relevant information at his disposal.[18] Society as a whole loses because if the transaction had been open and honest the car-buyer would have paid a "fair" price (i.e., the true market value of the car) and the exchange would have been mutually beneficial instead of asymmetrically exploitative.[19]

The notion of honesty and its economic implications was of concern to the classical economists. Adam Smith argued in his *Theory of Moral Sentiments* that a well functioning society was dependent on adherence to what he called a "code of honor."[20] These concerns have often been lost in the mathematical abstraction of modern economics, but they are increasingly of concern to economists.[21] The 1997 *World Development Report*, produced by the World Bank, argues that public service and business sector "corruption" (i.e., the pervasive absence of Smith's "code of honor") are serious barriers to sustained social and economic development in the developing world.

Bahá'ís have a great opportunity to bring Smith's "code of honor" back into the mainstream of the economics discipline. This process is started in a few of the articles (e.g., Sabetan provides a simple game theory analysis of how the Bahá'í "ethical position of selfless service" leads an optimal outcome), and its continued development is crucial because the social and economic implications of a spiritually imbued "sense" of work are profound.[22] The Bahá'í teachings are rich on this subject; charity, voluntary giving to the fund, Huqúqu'lláh, and honesty are all areas of potential further analysis.

Dahl, in his earlier *World Order* article, outlines the implications of the Faith's emphasis on voluntary giving. He envisions a world that will experience "a simultaneous process of transformation, as inward-looking, self-centered lives become more outward-looking and society-conscious, and the economic structure of society shifts from a preponderance of personal consumption, to the provision of more services and 'public goods.' "[23] Today, public goods such as schools, roads, and parks are government provided; however, in the context of a Bahá'í civilization, private provision of public goods would alleviate some of the current strain placed on governments.[24]

The economic implications of voluntary giving, as opposed to involuntary giving (i.e., taxation), are profound. Voluntary sharing of wealth does not result in a distortion of incentives nor does it compromise the work ethic. Therefore, there may be significant social returns to a world where voluntary giving is a significant source of revenue for the provision of public needs. Huddleston, in his *World Order* article, points out that the Bahá'í community is funded by voluntary donations, and so it provides a concrete example of a volunteer-funded system.

Another area where the spiritual teachings of the Faith would have a concrete impact on the economic organization of society is in the functioning of a firm. Huddleston, in "Principles of Economic Justice" points out that "at a minimum . . . a business should be conducted with compete honesty and trustworthiness."[25] However, Huddleston notes that the Faith's teachings on work as service suggest that Bahá'í businesses would focus on providing goods and services that "contribute to the . . . creation of a noble race of men."[26] In economic jargon, this implies a harmonization of concerns about private and social returns in economic decision making. For example, the private returns to an entrepreneur might be the same for two alternative ventures. The first might be opening up a strip bar next to a prestigious university. The second might be opening up an academic bookshop in the same area. The Bahá'í entrepreneur, recognizing the disparity of social "returns" between these two possible ventures, would opt for the bookshop. There is a well developed analytical framework in the economics literature for evaluating the relationships between private and social returns. Bahá'í economists might do well to explore the social welfare implications of a Bahá'í "bias" towards work activities with high rates of social return in the context of this literature.

In summary, the implications of recognizing the close link between the spiritual and material dimensions of life are profound. Bahá'í teachings regarding work as service, voluntary giving, and the importance of honesty all have potentially important implications for the economic structure and material welfare of society. Some of these topics are beginning to be discussed again in the economics literature, and Bahá'í economists would do well to explore this literature as a way to articulate and evaluate Bahá'í teachings on economics.

Distributive Justice

> The basest of men are they that yield nothing on earth . . .
>
> — Bahá'u'lláh[27]

> When we see poverty allowed to reach a condition of starvation it is a sure sign that somewhere we shall find tyranny. — 'Abdu'l-Bahá[28]

Bahá'í writings have a great deal to say about justice. Bahá'u'lláh calls justice "the light of men,"[29] while in the Epistle to the Son of the Wolf he predicates "the establishment of . . . the tranquillity of the nations" on justice.[30] Issues of justice are discussed in all of the articles under review here, however, it is in the pair of articles included in *Toward the Most Great Justice* that they are discussed most thoroughly.[31]

Shahruz Mohtadi in "Economic Justice in a New World Order" begins his article by arguing that the foundation of a Bahá'í world order will be "a new and universal standard of justice."[32] Mohtadi goes on to say that the principle of reward and punishment is central to understanding the Bahá'í standard of justice: "The trainer of the world is justice, for it consists of two pillars: reward and retribution."[33] This concept has important distributional implications.

Bahá'u'lláh clearly affirms the importance of work as a means of securing material welfare in the Kitáb-i Aqdas, writing: "Waste not your hours in idleness and sloth but occupy yourself with what will profit you and others."[34] Bahá'u'lláh emphasizes that the reasons behind this injunction are "to earn the means of a livelihood."[35] Shoghi Effendi elucidates the distributive implications of this teaching, writing that "wages should be unequal . . . and [people] should receive wages that correspond to their varying capacities and resources."[36]

The Bahá'í system does not, to use economic jargon, sever the wage-productivity link. Neo-classical theories of distribution emphasize that efficiency, and thus welfare, is maximized when wages are equated with the marginal productivity of labor. That is, a wage earner should be paid an amount equal to the contribution he or she will make to an enterprise. Therefore, wages in the Bahá'í system are earned.

The theoretical elegance of the unmodified neo-classical paradigm breaks down in the real world. There are many examples where wages and productivity are not closely linked. The severing of the ties between productivity and labor generally occurs because the market does not embody complete and perfect information, or simply because people deliberately usurp its functioning.[37] Put simply, there are many examples of exploitation in the world; whether it is a senior executive exploiting corporate shareholders, or a local landowner exploiting peasants. To refer to the passage quoted above: "When we see poverty allowed to reach a condition of starvation it is a sure sign that somewhere we shall find tyranny."[38]

The writings clearly envision these circumstances, and while emphasizing the principle of reward and retribution—the link between net pay and net contribution—they do not espouse any brutal form of social Darwinism. There are factors over which people have little or no control. In the Bahá'í system, no one "earns" tyranny and a flood is not some sort of retribution for a farmer's laziness. "O Children of Dust! Tell the rich of the midnight sighing of the poor . . . To give and be generous are attributes of Mine; well is it with him that adorneth himself with My virtues."[39] Therefore, in the Bahá'í system, there is an element of basic social provision which modifies justice's primary principle of reward and punishment.

Dahl interprets the modifying principle of "poverty as tyranny" as implying that "every human being has the right to a reasonable level of personal welfare," a belief echoed by Sabetan and Fish in their call for the meeting of basic needs.[40] Mohtadi emphasizes that the Bahá'í teachings on voluntary giving, progressive taxation, huqúqu'lláh, and *zakát* would all operate in such a way as to eliminate extremes of wealth in society. Huddleston highlights similar teachings and identifies the elimination of extreme differences in per capita wealth as one "of the main economic functions of the world government."[41] The Bahá'í system, therefore, combines voluntary and mandatory means for the elimination of the extremes of wealth, operating within a framework where wages are conceived as just rewards. The Bahá'í world would be more equal, but not absolutely equal.

While all of these articles accurately and adequately summarize the Bahá'í teachings on distributive justice, a major shortcoming is that they fail to draw creative links between the Bahá'í teachings and other theories of justice. Mohtadi gives a brief summary of other theories of justice, but does not connect them to the Bahá'í teachings—other than to say that they have common features and important differences.[42] Sabetan provides an interesting, though confusing, critique of utilitarianism. His emphasis on the more philosophical dimensions of the school (he questions the adequacy of viewing humans as "seats of utility") is useful but obfuscates some of the more positive dimensions of the approach. For example, under the relatively standard economic assumption of diminishing marginal returns to consumption, a theory of distribution based on utilitarianism implies a more equitable distribution of income—an important Bahá'í teaching. That is, transferring resources from the rich to the poor "helps" the recipients more than it "hurts" the donors, therefore net social welfare is raised. Exploring the limits of these links would be useful.[43] The other articles give at best passing reference to alternative theories of distributive justice. This is unfortunate.

There is tremendous scope for synergy between theories of distributive justice and the Bahá'í teachings, and Bahá'ís have both a great deal to learn from and a great deal to contribute to these theories. In particular, the utilitarian theory of Jeremy Bentham and John Stuart Mill might provide fruitful frameworks in which to evaluate statements from 'Abdu'l-Bahá such as:

> If a few have inordinate riches while the rest are impoverished, and no fruit or benefit accrues from that wealth, then it is only a liability to its possessor.[44]

And perhaps most strikingly, 'Abdu'l-Bahá's description of the nature of belonging to a Bahá'í society:

> It means to consider the welfare of the community as one's own. It means, in brief, to regard humanity as a single individual.[45]

These statements share a great deal with the basic premises of utilitarianism. However, the Bahá'í emphasis on reward and punishment, for example, signals significant departures from any crude formulation of utilitarianism. The teachings of reward and punishment might be usefully analyzed in the context of libertarianism, and the writings of John Locke, Adam Smith, Thomas Jefferson, and modern day neo-classical economics. Bahá'í economists would find it fruitful to explore these avenues.

A second area where discussion would have been useful is on the complementarity of distributive goals with other social and economic goals. In the popular press, issues such as economic growth, fiscal sustainability, and distributive justice are often portrayed as working at cross-purposes. Huddleston in "Principles of Economic Justice" alludes to these tensions, noting that the growth-equity tension lies at the heart of the ideological debate in economics and informs the "capitalism-socialism" divide. On the other hand, the Bahá'í view emphasizes that progress and justice are intimately linked, and are not mutually exclusive goals. Huddleston does a good job of sketching the ideological contours at play but does not make use of the growing literature on the relationship between equity and development. None of the other articles even get as far as Huddleston does. Bahá'í scholars would find that this literature lends significant empirical support to many of the normative principles found in the Bahá'í writings.

This empirical literature is new, and the theoretical structures informing the empirics are often quite crude. However, these features in some ways increase the scope for constructive contributions by Bahá'ís. For example, Harvard economist Robert Barro in a path-breaking study on the determinants of democracy finds that the level of female education is the single strongest determinant of stable democracy, after per capita income, across a worldwide sample of developing and industrialized nations.[46] The result goes almost unmentioned in his article. The Bahá'í scholar has at his or her disposal the necessary normative and positive principles needed to understand and illuminate the implications of this result. The writings note that "until the reality of the equality between man and woman is fully attained, the highest social development of mankind is not possible," and furthermore that the remedy to inequity is education.[47]

Much of the recent work in development economics underscores the complementarity, as opposed to the mutual exclusiveness, of key social and economic goals. Roberto Perotti of Columbia University finds that income equality, a teaching at the heart of Bahá'í economic views, is positively related to political stability and stable democracy. Furthermore, he finds synergy between education, equity, and growth.[48] Notions of complementarity resonate well with the Bahá'í perspective. By utilizing this growing literature, Bahá'í scholars can both enhance their own understanding of the Faith's teachings on economic issues and contribute to the normative and spiritual underpinnings of this expanding empirical work.

Unfortunately, none of the articles make anything but passing use of mainstream economics literature; and references to this literature, when made, are often dismissive. The implications of these issues are explored more fully below.

---

*See, for example, the paper by Geeta Kingdon, "Women, Education, and Development" in this volume, pp. 231-43.

Industrial Relations

When 'Abdu'l-Bahá visited the West, the process of widespread unionization was just starting to occur. The labor shortages induced by the First World War gave new power to organized labor. The Great Depression of the 1930s saw the institutionalization of many of the demands of organized labor throughout the United States and the countries of Western Europe. Prior to this period, labor surpluses kept wages and employment opportunities for unskilled labor low, much as David Ricardo had envisioned over fifty years before.

Anecdotes of foreman and plant-manager brutality and exploitation against the first generation of industrial workers abound. Threats of arbitrary dismissal were used to "induce" employees to work unpaid overtime, to abuse workers physically and sexually, and to cultivate a sense of servitude and fear. One illustrative example of the psychological and emotional conditions that urban industrial workers lived under at the turn of the century is given by the case of the foreman who would toss an apple into the throngs of unemployed outside the factory gate. Whoever caught the apple was given a job. Destitution was at times so thick that people lined up to be treated like dogs.

As 'Abdu'l-Bahá traveled through London, New York, and Chicago, issues concerning strikes and unions were in the newspapers. He often touched upon issues of industrial relations in his talks during the period. While he generally condemned the adversarial nature of unions and strikes, he did recognize their root cause, noting that "the principle cause of these difficulties [strikes] lies in the laws of the present civilization; for they lead to a small number of individuals accumulating incomparable fortunes, beyond their needs, while the great number remain destitute, stripped and in the greatest misery."[49]

This passage signals one way in which industrial strife would be alleviated in a Bahá'í world: through a more equitable distribution of income. However, the Bahá'í teachings on this matter are much more sophisticated than this simplistic solution. Huddleston, in his most recent article, emphasizes the teachings on profit sharing and consultation as two ways in which employer-employee relations could be improved.[50] He makes similar points in his earlier *World Order* article. Dahl, in both of his articles, emphasizes the need to move from confrontational to cooperative approaches in worker-management relations.[51] Mohtadi again makes references to profit sharing.[52] He also emphasizes that profit sharing allows workers to be "partners in every work."[53]

While recognizing the sources of industrial strife, Bahá'í writings articulate unique approaches to their resolution. 'Abdu'l-Bahá recognized that the strike and the "resort to force . . . is manifestly wrong and destructive of human foundations."[54] Confrontational approaches to industrial relations are focused on commanding as large a share of existing resources as possible. The Bahá'í alternative moves away from this zero-sum approach by recognizing the shared interests of workers and management and the gains to be realized from cooperation. These approaches have also been emphasized in recent academic literature. The 1997 *World Development Report* highlights the gains from consultative decision-making in the context of national and local governance, while recent management theory incorporates insights that are shared with the Bahá'í approach. One unique feature of the Bahá'í approach, emphasized by Mohtadi, is that a firm which operates along Bahá'í principles not only conducts worker-management relations in a cooperative spirit, but also structures the firm around both the profit and the service motive. Indeed, the service motive runs deep in virtually every component of the "Bahá'í" system.

All of the articles do summarize well the basic teachings on profit sharing and consultation as they relate to industrial relations. However, their one shortcoming is the unquestioning linking of the profit motive with greed. Mohtadi emphasizes that the profit maximization motive leads employers to treat labor like a commodity, while Hatcher emphasizes a manipulative approach to human relations that is characteristic of modern society. In their condemnation of the profit motive they ignore a critical result of organizing economic production along profit driven lines: efficiency. This shortcoming stems primarily from their treatment of cooperation and competition.

Cooperation vs. Competition?

Many of the articles place great emphasis on the shift from competitive economic structures to cooperative economic structures that would characterize the emergence of a Bahá'í civilization. Hatcher argues that a cooperation-centered society is a natural corollary of the service motive. He writes: "Cooperation rather than competition implies a less selfish kind of relationship between groups."[55] Mohtadi cites "competitiveness" as a fundamental cause of economic injustice.[56] These statements are not problematic on the surface, but without further elucidation they could be.[57]

Competitiveness and competition have become highly misunderstood and politicized terms. In economic terms, they imply nothing more than structuring an economy along efficiency lines, that is, along the principle of comparative advantage. Organizing economic production according to comparative advantage maximizes aggregate welfare and efficiency. As Adam Smith wrote in *The Wealth of Nations*:

> The shoemaker does not attempt to make his own clothes, but employs a tailor . . . What is prudence in the conduct of every private family, can scarce be folly in that of a great kingdom. If a foreign country can supply us with a commodity cheaper than we ourselves can make it, better buy it off them with some part of the produce of our own industry, employed in a way in which we have some advantage.[58]

Mohtadi and Hatcher would have done well to qualify more of their statements on the benefits of cooperation and be less dismissive of the benefits of competition. Would anyone pay $50 for a banana? No, that is why we import them from Costa Rica instead of growing them in heated greenhouses in the Yukon.

Both Sabetan and Huddleston make the key point: "Opportunities to cooperate should be pursued, as a matter of principle, so long as the intent and result is not a reduction in the quality of service to the public."[59] That is, cooperation can have welfare-reducing implications. For example, a country could unite behind a failing industry, perpetuating its existence and inefficiency. Perhaps the best example of this is the common agricultural policy of the European Union. Two-thirds of the EU budget is spent saving a mythical French countryside and impoverishing developing-country farmers by denying them fair market access; similar policies exist in the United States. Collusion is another form of destructive cooperation as the OPEC oil shock and the de Beers diamond cartel have illustrated.

In sum, cooperation is beneficial, and there are many areas of human endeavor, economic and non-economic, where its greater application could result in significant gains. However, there are many cases where pursuing what on the surface appears to be a cooperative economic strategy can have larger negative welfare effects. In the future, Bahá'í economists should qualify what they mean by cooperation. Failure to do so will lead to the same sort of gross distortions and misunderstandings that surround the concept of competition today. Furthermore, Bahá'í scholars have an opportunity to qualify and deepen the parameters underscoring constructive competition.

Competition, in the economic sense, is nothing more than a situation characterized by the equation of marginal costs with marginal benefits. Is a concept where the price of a product is a function of its costs so alien to the Bahá'í teachings? Equating competition with destructive behavior is as simplistic as it is dangerous. For example, Sabetan describes "perfect competition" as a situation where "innumerable producers compete so vigorously with each other that no one producer can possibly charge a higher price than the other."[60] It is an accurate definition but nonetheless somewhat misleading. Another approach, highlighted above, would be to emphasize that perfect competition is a state characterized by the equation of marginal costs with price; that is, a market structure where price does not exceed the costs of production, or alternatively a situation where the merchant does not, and can not, cheat the buyer—a situation that is clearly advantageous.

Competition is not a celebration of immorality or dishonesty. Adam Smith was quite clear about the qualifications which constrained the exchange relationship. Man is free to pursue his own interest in his own way "as long as he does not violate the laws of justice."[61] Smith, as a moral philosopher, was interested in what types of social structure lead to a harmonization between private and social goals, not in the sanctification of "self-interest" as Fish and Sabetan assert. Sabetan is particularly forceful, arguing that self-interest is "perhaps the single element most destructive of well-being."[62] In fairness to both Fish and Sabetan, their assertion of an almost monomaniacal obsession with "rational self-interest" in modern economics contains a large element of truth, and, as both authors argue, Bahá'ís have an important role to play in extending the definition of "economic man." What is disconcerting, however, is the failure to summarize fairly the teachings of the classical economists themselves.

A close reading of Smith leads to a much more balanced view of the foundations of modern economics. Richard F. Teichgraeber, one of the foremost historians of economic thought, argues that "we impoverish Smith if we see his case for economic freedom as argued mainly on the grounds that the fundamental explanation of man's conduct can be found in the rational, pursuit of self-interest."[63] Bahá'ís, instead of dismissing the foundations of modern economic thought, might more fruitfully focus their attention on helping modern economists see the foundations of their own discipline more clearly. Economics is a discipline, after all, that began as a branch of moral philosophy.

The Bahá'í conception does not dismiss Smith's basic formulation, but rather deepens it. In the Bahá'í world, integrity and honesty are bare minimums: service and generosity are the highest goals. However, these are spiritual and social goals and not systemic or legal ones. When Bahá'ís approach a technical discipline, terminology is critical and underlying assumptions must be clearly stated. The right question to ask is not "competition" versus "cooperation," but rather under what conditions are competition and cooperation socially constructive? When are they destructive? As noted above, Huddleston briefly alludes to this matter, without really exploring it. The other articles fail to even allude to the question.

Attitudes Towards "Economics" and "Capitalism"

There is a pervasive anti-economics and anti-capitalism attitude in all of these articles. Dahl begins his *World Order* article with a two-paragraph discussion of the shortcomings of economists, who "prefer to take refuge in self-consistent theoretical worlds . . . comprehensible only to themselves."[64] Hatcher begins his article with the following statement: "There is a pervasive modern sentiment that economics and morality are peculiarly incompatible."[65] These statements are as inaccurate as they are unconstructive.

Since the beginning of their discipline, economists have devoted their energies to the underlying ethical and moral issues of human endeavor. Adam Smith set the tone for the discipline in his *Theory of Moral Sentiments* writing:

> And hence it is, that to feel much for others and little for ourselves, that to restrain our selfish, and to indulge our benevolent affections, constitutes the perfection of human nature; and can alone produce among mankind that harmony of sentiments and passions in which consists their whole grace and propriety.[66]

This hardly seems to indicate an incompatibility between economics and moral values. Indeed Smith's comment compares favorably with 'Abdu'l-Bahá's question, asking:

> . . . [Is it] possible that, seeing one of his fellow-creatures starving, destitute of everything, a man can rest comfortably in his luxurious mansion?[67]

There are serious problems with modern economics, not the least of which is 1996 Nobel Prize winner William Vikrey's statement that his prize-winning paper was one of his few "digressions into abstract economics" and at best of "minor significance in terms of human welfare."[68] However, in many respects, Vikrey's observation is an anomaly both in terms of his own work and that of the discipline in general.

Jeffrey Sachs, whom *Time* magazine referred to "as the world's best known economist," identified the overwhelming motive in his professional life through asking the question: "What makes for a good society?"[69] Economists from ideological backgrounds as diverse as those of Hayek and Friedman, to the recent work of Krugman, have taken great pains to explain economic issues to the wider educated public. Bahá'ís have a great deal to learn from economists, in many ways, and to take a dismissive posture towards economics, either implicitly or explicitly, is not conducive towards creating the necessary dialogue.

Attitudes towards "capitalism" in the Bahá'í literature are, at times, equally as conflated as those pertaining to the discipline of economics. The confusion generally arises from failing to separate analytically the concept of a "market system" from that of a "consumer society." Capitalism is necessarily a system where the market is the principal allocative mechanism. It does not follow, however, that consumerism is an inevitable by-product of the capitalist system.[70]

The origins of capitalism have been traced in detail by sociologists such Max Weber and, more recently, Daniel Bell. What Weber noted in the beginning of the century was that the rise of capitalism resulted from the creation of an "elective affinity" between character and work, or, according to Bell:

> In the Protestant worldview, all work (from the highest to the lowest) was a "calling" and thus sanctified, as against the [Catholic] view that work was a punishment for man's sin of disobedience. The idea of a calling, then—which Weber argued did not exist in previous religious or ethical codes—is a moral obligation that projects religious behavior onto the everyday world.[71]

Bahá'ís would do well to remember that capitalism's rise to prominence was largely the result of a worldview not dissimilar to our own. Furthermore, capitalism has been associated with the most massive reduction in poverty in world history, in the United States and Western Europe in the last century; and in East Asia and other places in this century. Indeed, impoverishment has more often been associated with abandoning the market system than participating in it, as the Soviet Union, Albania, Tanzania, Cuba, and a host of other examples indicate.[72]

Where capitalism is probably incompatible with Bahá'í ideals is in its historical, though not inevitable, tendency to give rise to consumerism, which as Bell points out, is in fact an erosion of the original motive force behind the Protestant ethic of restraint. Consumerism is clearly incompatible with the Bahá'í teachings. Consumerism infects virtually every arena of thinking in the industrialized world. Think how often we misuse the word *need:* "I need a new sweater," "We need a new car," etc. Perhaps the biggest spiritual cost of affluence is a complete loss of understanding about what constitutes necessity. Modern society has tried to compensate for this moral contradiction by creating what Bell calls a "culturati" of consumerism. Fashion becomes "art." Gillette becomes the best a man can get; women's magazines tie notions of self-esteem with certain products and consumer habits; "SAFARI" by Ralph Lauren becomes a "post-modern fragrance" and is associated with "Living without boundaries."[73]

Bahá'í ideals of charity and the oneness of humankind necessarily imply a movement away from "the best a man can get" to giving something to someone who needs it. Indeed, there is nothing wrong with the market as an allocative principle. What is lacking is the moral backbone in society to constructively guide and set is parameters. It is in this regard that Bahá'ís have a great deal to say. However, crude equations of "markets=capitalism=consumerism" are inaccurate and unconstructive. Bahá'ís would do well to recognize more explicitly the differences as well as the connections between these concepts and incorporate this understanding into their research.

Areas for Further Research

There are many areas where valuable analysis could be undertaken. One area in particular is in the economics of gender. Notions of gender increasingly inform research across the social sciences and economics is no exception. The scope for Bahá'í contributions to this area is immense. For example, the teaching in the Aqdas that female education should be given priority in the presence of scarce resources is potentially radical, given that cross-country measurements of the social returns to education are almost universally higher for women. According to the economics literature, investment in women is economically efficient and socially advantageous, a finding which corresponds to Bahá'í notions.[74]

Another area that might be constructively explored is in the economics of crime, morality, and peace. Dahl alludes to the potential returns to "peace" in his discussion of defense budgets. Indeed the numbers are staggering: "defense" spending in the United States is greater than the entire gross domestic product of Australia. For a fraction of the United States' defense budget the cities of Sydney, Melbourne, or Brisbane, or a few national highways, or a score of universities could be maintained. Extending discussions of the "peace dividend" to the economics of "law and order" would be fruitful. The costs of crime in today's world are immense. Whole industries revolve around crime: prisons, security, locks. The social and economic returns to a world with less crime are potentially gigantic. Bahá'ís, with a positive vision of humankind, could be at the forefront of sketching out the economic implications of something as simple as pervasive worldwide honesty.

In sum, it is in exploring the implications of evolving personal and social priorities associated with the Bahá'í writings that Bahá'ís have a potentially significant role to play. What are the economic consequences of a reduction in corruption? Of peace? Of a highly educated society? Of good governance? These are the questions that Bahá'í economists can usefully ask.

Conclusion

This review has been somewhat aggressive in its critique, and perhaps because of this posture it has been overly reductive in its treatment of the reviewed articles. However, it is hoped that this strategy has helped to sketch the limits of Bahá'í scholarship on economics thus far, even if at the sacrifice of some of the subtlety and variety of the articles themselves. There is tremendous scope for Bahá'ís to contribute to the social sciences, and economics is no exception. The nine articles reviewed above, despite their shortcomings, are truly admirable starting points for further research on the economic implications of the revelation of Bahá'u'lláh and should inspire further research.

Several themes emerge from these articles:

- The main Bahá'í teaching on economics is that a human being's material activities must be imbued with a sense of spiritual purpose. While the idea than an individual's economic activities should reflect more fundamental spiritual and moral obligations dates at least as far back as Smith and the North American Puritans, the Bahá'í formulation is important in its emphasis on service to humanity.

- Bahá'u'lláh's emphasis on justice extends to the realm of economics in the form of teachings on the distribution of wealth and on industrial relations. Employer-employee relationships should be characterized by a cooperative spirit of partnership.

- Cooperative modes of production are favored. However, as discussed above, the parameters of this statement need to be more fully explored and qualified.

Two main problems emerge from the efforts of Bahá'í scholars on economics thus far:

- A near universal failure to utilize existing social science literature.
- A pervasive undercurrent of hostility towards the social sciences as currently practiced.

These are serious problems, and they need to be addressed in any future work done by Bahá'ís. Anyone involved in the Bahá'í community soon comes to realize that a great number of our activities are either explicitly or implicitly informed by a triumphalist worldview.

While I do not suggest that Bahá'ís suppress the magnitude of the vision articulated by Bahá'u'lláh, there are more constructive ways to frame it. The current dismissive posture towards other forms of knowledge in the Bahá'í community today, which is matched by an equally strong belief that "everything is in the writings," is perhaps the best way to cut-off dialogue between Bahá'ís and "leaders of thought" outside the community. The best way to bring Bahá'í teachings on social issues to non-Bahá'ís is for Bahá'ís to remember they have just as much to learn as they have to give.

NOTES

BRYAN GRAHAM completed an M.Phil. in Economics at the University of Oxford as a Rhodes Scholar, and is currently a doctoral candidate in the Department of Economics, Harvard University.

1. I have provided a bibliography rather than complete references in the footnotes so that interested readers can more easily refer to my sources.
2. Keynes, *The General Theory,* p. 383.
3. Bahá'u'lláh, *Gleanings,* p. 213.
4. Shoghi Effendi, *World Order of Bahá'u'lláh,* p. 19.
5. Ibid., pp. 23-24.
6. The "neglect" of the development of the Bahá'í teachings on economics in the first two-thirds of this century was a function of several factors. Shoghi Effendi commented to the national spiritual assembly of the United States during the Great Depression that the "time is not right for such activities," suggesting that the community's priorities lay elsewhere during this period.

Furthermore, the statement indicates Shoghi Effendi's concern that "scholarship" on the economic teachings of the Faith be rigorous. He continues in the same letter, writing that "we have to study the economic teachings of the Faith in the light of modern problems more thoroughly . . . " cited in Badi'i, *The True Foundation*, p. 20.

7. A list of the reviewed articles is found in the bibliography.
8. Huddleston, "World Commonwealth."
9. Shoghi Effendi, *Directives,* p. 19.
10. Shoghi Effendi, *The Individual and Teaching,* p. 28.
11. Bahá'u'lláh, *Gleanings,* p. 216.
12. Dahl, "Economic System," p. 2.
13. Ibid., p. 1.
14. Hatcher, "Economics," p. 14.
15. Mohtadi, "Justice," p. 163.
16. Bahá'u'lláh, *The Hidden Words,* #82 from the Persian.
17. For an interesting historical parallel consider the following statement by G. A. Rowntree in reference to the Quakers in the nineteenth century: "Is it not merely a coincidence or is it a consequence that the lofty profession of spirituality made by the Friends has gone hand in hand with shrewdness and tact in the transaction of mundane affairs? Real piety favours the success of a trader by insuring his integrity and fostering habits of prudence and forethought" Cited in Baran, *Political Economy*, pp. 48-49.
18. The economic term for this "extra" money is monopolistic rent; where the used car salesman exercises monopoly power in information.
19. It is important to note that dishonesty is just one among many factors leading to imperfect or incomplete information. Uncertainty is an unalterable characteristic of this world and the "problem" of imperfect information is unlikely ever to be fully resolved.
20. Adam Smith was a moral philosopher first and an economist second; a fact that is often forgotten by both the public and economists.
21. I am grateful to a referee of this paper who reminded me that most mathematical models either operate on certain assumptions regarding information or directly incorporate these issues in their structure. Historically, however, information issues have not been at the forefront of modern economics. This is changing, as are many other aspects of the discipline. A quick search for articles on "incomplete information" in Econlit turned up 500 references. For a reference on the economics of honesty see Nyberg, "Honest Society."
22. Sabetan, "Exploration," p. 65.
23. Dahl, "Overview," p. 24.
24. There are many possible examples of how this would work in practice. Dahl in his *World Order* article (1975, p 24) gives some. Additional examples might include public access to privately owned beaches and voluntary private contributions to public schools. Private provision of public goods is not a new idea as Andrew Carnegie (who was praised by 'Abdu'l-Bahá for his philanthropy) and others illustrate. The Bahá'í "system" envisions that this

process will become more widespread. Of course there would still be extensive scope and need for government provision of public goods and services, such as schools, hospitals, roads, and other infrastructure.

25. Huddleston, "Economic Justice," p. 145.
26. Ibid., p. 145.
27. Bahá'u'lláh, *The Hidden Words,* #81 from the Persian.
28. 'Abdu'l-Bahá, *Paris Talks,* p. 159.
29. Bahá'u'lláh, *Tablets,* p. 66.
30. Bahá'u'lláh, *Epistle,* p. 28.
31. The two respective articles are: John Huddleston, "Principles of Economic Justice" and Shahruz Mohtadi, "Economic Justice in a New World Order."
32. Mohtadi, "Justice," p. 153.
33. Bahá'u'lláh as cited in Huddleston, "World Commonwealth," p. 40.
34. Bahá'u'lláh, *Aqdas,* p. 30.
35. Bahá'u'lláh, *Gleanings,* p. 202.
36. Shoghi Effendi as cited in Mohtadi, "Justice," p. 157.
37. Huddleston, in "World Commonwealth," acknowledges these types of "market failures" writing: "It is inconceivable that in a Bahá'í society there would be a continuation of the present extreme and nonsensical differences which exist between those who do the dirtiest and most dangerous tasks for society and those who are able to exploit their position and power to extract greatly inflated payments for their services," p. 40.
38. 'Abdu'l-Bahá, *Paris Talks,* p. 159.
39. Bahá'u'lláh, *The Hidden Words,* #49 from the Persian.
40. Dahl, "Overview," p. 23, Sabetan, "Exploration," p. 53, and Fish, "Economic Prosperity," p. 6.
41. Huddleston, "Economic Justice" and "World Commonwealth," p. 40. (Quote from 1975 article).
42. Mohtadi, "Justice," p. 155.
43. Sabetan, "Exploration," pp. 48-51.
44. 'Abdu'l-Bahá, *Civilization,* p. 25.
45. Ibid., p. 39.
46. Barro, "Democracy."
47. 'Abdu'l-Bahá, *Promulgation,* pp. 76 - 77.
48. Perotti, "Income Distribution."
49. 'Abdu'l-Bahá, *Some Answered Questions*, p. 273.
50. Huddleston, "Economic Justice," p. 146.
51. Dahl, "Economic System," p 7, and "Overview," p. 24.
52. Mohtadi, "Justice," p. 163.
53. 'Abdu'l-Bahá, cited in Badi'i, *True Foundation,* p. 129.
54. 'Abdu'l-Bahá, *Promulgation,* p. 238.
55. Hatcher, "Economics," p. 21.
56. Mohtadi, "Justice," p. 163.
57. I will leave aside the some of the implications of these and other associated

statements until the section on "Bahá'í Attitudes Towards Economics and Capitalism" below.

58. Smith, *Wealth*.
59. Huddleston, "Economic Justice," p. 146. Sabetan, "Exploration," makes the point that "cooperation should not be confused with oligopolistic and collusive behaviour." p. 64.
60. Sabetan, "Exploration," pp. 60-61.
61. Smith (*Wealth*, p. 618 of the 1937 edition). It should be pointed out that Smith is among the most abused economists of all time and unfortunately his name is invariably associated with conservatism. This assignment is misleading and Smith should be read on his own terms and in the context of the historical time period in which he wrote. It is interesting to consider that in 18th century Scotland Smith, as a non-landowner, was unable to vote.
62. Sabetan, "Exploration," p. 59.
63. Teichgraeber, *Free Trade*, p. 124.
64. Dahl, "Overview," p. 19.
65. Hatcher, "Economics," p. 14.
66. Smith, *Theory*, p. 32.
67. 'Abdu'l-Bahá, *Some Answered Questions,* p. 277.
68. Cited in Cassidy, "Decline," p. 50.
69. Cited in Graham, "Interview."
70. One point I am trying to make here is that Bahá'ís (and the academic community in general) need to de-politicize terms like capitalism, liberalism etc., or make a clearer distinction between their positive and normative dimensions. Capitalism, as I am using it above, is an economic system where markets play the leading role in the allocation of goods. It is not exploitation, imperialism, sweat-shops etc. The fact that these destructive forces are often associated with capitalism is a separate question.
71. Bell, *Contradictions*, p. 288.
72. There is a very extensive literature of the relationship between market institutions, economic growth, and economic distribution. Many authors have argued that the rise of the "west" to ascendancy was not a product of the organizational, social, and technological transformations inherent in the market system but of exploitive economic practices such as slavery and imperialism (see, for example, A. Gunder, 1969). While the question of the exact determinants of growth is a never-ending debate, the historical facts do not support the belief that imperialism was the source of the west's wealth. If anything imperialism was an unfortunate by-product of growing European wealth. The question of economic growth is discussed very thoroughly in Nathan Rosenburg's *How the West Grew Rich*. For a good summary of the modern literature see Jeffrey Sachs and Andrew Warner's 1995 Brookings Paper on the process of global integration.
73. See Bell, *Contradictions*, for a more complete discussion.
74. For a discussion of the economics of education see any recent reference by George Psacharopoulos of the World Bank or Paul Schultze of Yale University. (See also the article by Kingdon in this volume, pp. 229-43.)

Works Cited

(a) Reviewed Articles

Dahl, Gregory C. "Economics and the Bahá'í Teachings: An Overview;" *World Order*, Vol. 10, no. 1 (1975) pp. 19-40.

Dahl, Gregory C. "Evolving toward a Bahá'í Economic System," *Journal of Bahá'í Studies*, Vol. 4, no. 3 (1991) pp. 1-15.

Fish, Mary. "Economic Prosperity: A Global Imperative," *Journal of Bahá'í Studies*, Vol. 7, no. 3 (1997) pp. 1-16.

Hatcher, William S. "Economics and Moral Values," *World Order*, Vol. 9, no. 2 (1974/5) pp. 14-27.

Huddleston, John. "The Economy of a World Commonwealth," *World Order*, Vol. 9, no. 4 (1975) pp. 37-43.

________. "Towards a World Economy," *Journal of Bahá'í Studies*, Vol. 3, no. 3 (1991) pp. 21-34.

________ "Principles of Economic Justice," in *Toward the Most Great Justice: Elements of Justice in the New World Order*, ed. by C. Lerche. London: Bahá'í Publishing Trust, 1996, pp. 137-52.

Mohtadi, Shahruz. "Economic Justice in a New World Order," in *Toward the Most Great Justice: Elements of Justice in the New World Order*, ed by C. Lerche. London: Bahá'í Publishing Trust, 1996, pp. 153-170.

Sabetan, Farhad. "An Exploration into the Political Economy of Global Prosperity," *Journal of Bahá'í Studies*, Vol. 7, no. 4 (1997) pp. 43-68.

(b) Additional Bahá'í References

'Abdu'l-Bahá. *The Secret of Divine Civilization.* Wilmette: Bahá'í Publishing Trust, 1975.

________. *The Promulgation of Universal Peace.* Wilmette: Bahá'í Publish-ing Trust, 1982.

________. *Some Answered Questions*. Wilmette: Bahá'í Publishing Trust, 1985.

________. *Paris Talks: Addresses Given by 'Abdu'l-Bahá* (12th Ed.). London: Bahá'í Publishing Trust, 1995.

Badi'i, Hooshmand. *The True Foundation of All Economics (A Compilation)* 2nd rev. ed. Canada: Webcom, 1996.

Bahá'u'lláh. *Gleanings from the Writings of Bahá'u'lláh.* Wilmette: Bahá'í Publishing Trust, 1938.

________. *Epistle to the Son of the Wolf.* Wilmette: Bahá'í Publishing Trust, 1988.

________. *The Kitáb-i-Aqdas.* Haifa: Bahá'í World Centre, 1992.

________. *Tablets of Bahá'u'lláh revealed after the Kitáb-i-Aqdas.* Wilmette: Bahá'í Publishing Trust, 1993.

Shoghi Effendi. *Directives from the Guardian.* New Delhi: Bahá'í Publishing Trust, 1973.

________. *The World Order of Bahá'u'lláh.* Wilmette: Bahá'í Publishing Trust, 1974.

________. *The Individual and Teaching.* Wilmette: Bahá'í Publishing Trust, 1977.

(c) Non-Bahá'í References

Baran, Paul A. *The Political Economy of Growth.* New York: Monthly Review Press, 1957.

Barro, Robert. "Democracy and Growth," *Journal of Economic Growth* Vol. 1, no. 1 (1996) pp. 1-27.

Bell, Daniel. *The Cultural Contradictions of Capitalism.* Rev. ed. New York: Basic Books, 1996.

Cassidy, John. "The Decline of Economics," *The New Yorker* (December 2,1996) pp. 50-60.

Frank, Andre Gunder. *Latin America: Underdevelopment or Revolution.* New York: Monthly Review Press, 1969. See especially pp. 162-74.

Graham, Bryan S. "An Interview with Jeffrey Sachs," *Hemispheres: Tufts Journal of International Affairs.* Vol. 19, no. 1 (1997) pp. 100-111.

Keynes, John M. *The General Theory of Employment, Interest and Money.* London: Macmillan, 1936.

Nyberg, S. "The Honest Society: Stability and Policy Considerations," *Journal of Public Economics* Vol. 64, no.1 (1997) pp. 83-99.

Perotti, Roberto. "Growth, Income Distribution and Democracy: What the Data Say," *Journal of Economic Growth* Vol. 1, no. 2 (1996) pp. 149-87.

Rosenberg, Nathan and L.E. Birdzell. *How the West Grew Rich: The Economic Transformation of the Industrial World.* New York: Basic Books, Inc., 1986.

Sachs, Jeffrey D. and Andrew M. Warner. "Economic Reform and the Process of Global Integration," *Brookings Papers on Economic Activity*, Vol. 1 (1995) pp. 1-95.

Smith, Adam. *The Wealth of Nations*, 1776.

________ *The Theory of Moral Sentiments.* London: Cadell and Davies, 1812.

Teichgraeber, Richard F. *'Free Trade' and Moral Philosophy: Rethinking the Sources of Adam Smith's Wealth of Nations.* Durham: Duke University Press, 1986.

The World Bank. *World Development Report 1997: The State in a Changing World.* Oxford University Press, 1997.

Bahá'í World Center

BAHÁ'Í DEVELOPMENT PROJECT—INDORE, INDIA
Bahá'í Vocational Institute for Rural Women, November 1995

Women, Education, and Development

Geeta Gandhi Kingdon

This essay presents the findings of some recent research on the social and the economic benefits of the education of women and considers the pathways through which women's schooling leads to social gains. These findings may provide insights as to why Bahá'u'lláh stressed the importance of women's education.

In the Bahá'í teachings, there are two extraordinary statements about the education of women. First, that women's education is of greater importance than men's education; and, second, that not until the equality of opportunity in education between the sexes is established will the foundations of war be removed.[1] These challenging ideas deserve study in order for us to understand better their meaning and ramifications.

The principle of sexual equality in education—one facet of the general principle of the equality of the sexes—was revolutionary in the mid-1800s.[2] It was proposed by Bahá'u'lláh more than half a century before Western thought added sexual equality to its list of rationally based moral principles of relevance to political life—such as democracy, secularism, and the rights of the individual—and long before it became enshrined in numerous national and international documents as a universal value.

Signs of the rapid convergence between certain ideas of the secular world and teachings of the Bahá'í Faith are abundant. In the political and economic spheres, for example, this is conspicuous in the enthusiasm for global governance among thinkers, academics, and international institutions.[3] It can also be seen in the acceptance, among many influential opinion-makers, of the need for a world currency and for international economic policy coordination.[4] Many other ideas and institutions prescribed by Bahá'u'lláh in the last century have been embraced by the world in the past few decades. The recognition of the wisdom of the Bahá'í emphasis on women's education is a recent addition to the list of areas of convergence.

Women's Status

Women account for roughly half the world's population, perform two-thirds of the hours worked, receive one-tenth of the world's income, and have less than one-hundredth of the world's property registered in their names.[5] Female deprivation is particularly acute in developing countries with high levels of poverty, though in affluent nations women also suffer low status due to conservative attitudes.

The most dramatic and telling statistic of women's status is the sex-ratio in the population, that is, the number of females per 100 males. It is a well-known fact that life-expectancy at birth favors females. This appears to be a biological constant. Yet, the proportion of females to males varies greatly across different regions of the world. For example, the proportion of females is 52.5% in the industrialized world, but in sub-Saharan Africa women account for only 51% of the population. The figures are 48% of the population in East Asia and less than 47% in South Asia. From figures such as these, economist Amartya Sen[6] has estimated that there are 100 million women "missing" in the world. Sen describes the fate of these women as "one of the more momentous problems facing the contemporary world." This is a moral as well as a development-related problem.

The overwhelming reason why 100 million women are missing in the world is excess female mortality. In the developed world, women outlive men by an average of six years; by contrast, in large parts of South Asia, men can expect to live longer than women.

Differential mortality is only the most dramatic manifestation of systematic discrimination against females. Women and girls are more likely to be impoverished than men and boys. Also, studies have found that girls are fed less than their brothers and that their illnesses are less likely to be treated. It should come as no surprise then that, in most regions of the world, female literacy and education fall far short of male literacy and education, as shown in Table 1. While poverty and cultural factors must surely influence the extent of female deprivation, they do not explain it entirely. For example, sub-Saharan Africa is one of the poorest regions of the world, but the problem of excess mortality of females is much less severe there than in South Asia.

Table 1
Male-Female Gaps in education, 1998
(Index: Males = 100)*

Region	Adult Literacy	Primary enrollment	Secondary enrollment
OECD Countries	-	100	98
All Developing Countries	80	94	83
Least Developed Countries	67	83	66
Arab states	66	91	85
East Asia	83	100	88
Latin America and Caribbean	98	98	102
South Asia	64	86	-
SE Asia and the Pacific	92	99	95
Sub-Saharan Africa	76	85	72

Source: UNDP, Human Development Report 2000 (New York: Oxford University Press, 2000), table 28, p. 258.
Notes: The figures relate to women's education in relation to men's, the index for men being 100. Thus, for example, in least developed countries, the adult literacy rate for women was only 67% that of men, while in Latin America and in the Caribbean, it was 98% that of men.

*A dash indicates that no information was available.

The Economic and Social Gains from Female Education

Equality of the sexes—in terms of men and women's command over resources, their access to education and health, and in terms of freedom to develop their potential—has an intrinsic value in its own right. The equal treatment of the sexes for intrinsic reasons is, in the parlance of welfare economics, the equity reason for reducing gender imbalances. A second important reason in favor of reducing gender imbalances is what might be termed the instrumental reason, that is, the gains to be had from granting equality. For example, if with equal education, women's contribution to economic development (or to other desirable goals) is comparable to men's, then reducing gender imbalances in education will enhance women's capacity to contribute to economic progress. This is the efficiency reason for reducing gender inequality in areas where women are currently deprived. Both the intrinsic (equity) and instrumental (efficiency) based reasons for gender equality are emphasized in the teachings of Bahá'u'lláh.[7]

Economic Efficiency

Human capital theory suggests that just as physical capital (i.e., machines) augments economic productivity, so human capital acquired through education improves the productivity of individuals. Studies of the sources of economic growth demonstrate persuasively that education plays a major role as a factor in the rise of output per worker. The new growth theories in economics place education and human resource development at the center of their explanation for long-term economic growth.[8] Confidence has grown in the belief that education affects economic growth because many studies have shown the positive correlation between a country's educational effort and its economic status, and causality has been attributed to education. Prominent examples of this are the so-called "miracle" economies of East Asia.

If female schooling raises human capital, productivity, and economic growth as much as male schooling does, then women's disadvantage in education is economically inefficient. Research worldwide shows that, in general, the economic benefits from women's education—calculated as the economic rate of return to education—are comparable to those from men's education.[9] Thus, from the point of view of economic efficiency, the gender gap in education is undesirable.

Social Efficiency

While the economic benefits of educating girls are similar in size to the economic benefits of educating boys, recent findings suggest that the social benefits from investing in female education are far greater than those from investing in male education. Specifically, female education has powerful effects on the total fertility rate (and hence on population growth), the infant mortality rate,[10] the female disadvantage in child survival, and on child health and nutrition. By contrast, statistical analyses show that male schooling has relatively much smaller effects on these important social outcomes.[11]

For example, a study by Subbarao and Raney[12] using national aggregate data from 72 countries regressed the total fertility rate of 1985 on the male and female secondary school enrollment rates lagged by ten years, i.e. on the enrollment rates of 1975. The objective was to examine the effect of education on fertility, controlling for a number of other factors such as family planning service provision and per capita income. The results show that female secondary school enrollment (lagged by ten years) is inversely correlated with the total fertility rate, but that male secondary school enrollment shows no strong correlation. Similarly, a regression of the 1985 infant mortality rate on ten-year lagged male and female secondary school enrollment rates shows that while female education is associated with lower infant mortality, male education has no statistically significant effect.

A similar exercise by Murthi, Guio, and Drèze[13] for India using district level aggregated data shows that whereas the district female literacy rate had a strong inverse correlation on the district average total fertility rate, on under-five child mortality rate, and on the female disadvantage in child survival, the district male literacy rate had no significant effect on any of these outcomes. Moreover, district per capita income, urbanization, and the spread of medical facilities were not statistically significant determinants of total fertility rate. While these latter three variables do have positive effects on child survival levels, their effects were relatively small compared with the powerful effect of female literacy.

Numerous studies have been carried out using household-level data that confirm the findings from studies using aggregated data. To cite one example, an examination of the determinants of fertility in fourteen countries of sub-Saharan Africa by Ainsworth, Beegle, and Nyamete[14] using household survey data shows an inverse correlation between female schooling and fertility in virtually all of the countries, though the relationship is non-linear: female primary schooling has an inverse relation with fertility in only about half of the countries, but female secondary schooling is universally associated with lower fertility, and the strength of the correlation increases with increasing years of schooling. Among women ever married, husband's schooling has no significant relation with fertility in about one-third of the countries. Moreover, in cases where both women's and men's schooling matter, women's schooling exerts a much larger negative effect on fertility than men's schooling.

Simulations show that the benefits of reduced family size from expanding female education are far greater than the benefits from other public interventions, such as improving family planning service provision or increasing the number of physicians in the population. For example, Subbarao and Raney found that a doubling of the 1975 average secondary school enrollment ratio in the 72 sample countries from 19% to 38% would have reduced the average number of births in 1985 by 29%, compared to the actual number in 1985, whereas a doubling of the family planning provision would have reduced the number of births by only 3.5%.

The gains in terms of deaths averted are also striking. Simulations predict that doubling the female secondary school enrollment ratio from 19% to 38% in 1975 reduces infant deaths in 1985 by 64%, while doubling the number of physicians reduces the number of infant deaths by a mere 2.5%. Surprisingly, doubling per capita income from the average of $650 in the 72 sample countries to $1300 would have no effect at all on the number of infant deaths.

Subbarao and Raney also reported data on desired family size from the World Fertility Survey for 37 countries. Econometric analysis of this data suggested that after controlling for per capita income, female secondary school enrollment was a highly significant determinant of desired family size (and therefore of the total fertility rate and population growth rate). Male school enrollment ratio, however, had no impact on desired family size.

Finally, a large body of microeconomic evidence shows that increases in women's education generally lead to increases in their labor force participation, as well as in increases to their earnings.[15] Educated women's greater participation in labor market work and their higher earnings are thought to be good for their own status (economic models say "bargaining power") within the household; and they are good for their children because it appears that a greater proportion of women's income than men's is spent on child goods.[16] On the down side, it may be thought that educated women's greater labor force participation takes them away from their children for longer periods of time (than is the case for uneducated or less-educated women), and this may disadvantage educated women's children through neglect. At present this is a relatively unresearched issue. However, limited evidence suggests that children whose mothers work have just as good or better educational outcomes than children whose mothers do not work.

The findings in the studies cited above are corroborated by international as well as national studies. They demonstrate the powerful role of women's agency and women's educational empowerment in reducing desired family size, fertility, population growth, child morbidity, child mortality, and gender-bias in child mortality, while at the same time showing that men's education mattered comparatively less to these important social outcomes.

Pathways Through Which Education Affects Social Outcomes

Why should education of females significantly reduce the fertility and mortality rates and improve child health? What are the pathways through which girls' education leads to these social gains? Bahá'ís have tended to focus importantly, though not exclusively, on the value of an educated woman for the upbringing and education of her offspring. This benefit is now prominently recognized outside the religion.

Economists tend to focus on the role of incentives as a way of understanding phenomena. They reason that female education lowers the fertility rate by reducing desired family size, and that this, in turn, is because education raises the value of women's economic activities by raising the labor market rewards for going out of the home for work. In other words, the opportunity-cost of staying at home for child bearing and rearing increases as women become more educated, and so educated women desire smaller families. Education may also change women's preferences about the quantity versus the quality of children, with educated women choosing fewer children but of better "quality." Moreover, as mentioned earlier, recent research suggests that a greater proportion of women's cash income than men's is spent on child goods. So women's education and the consequent increase in women's income would appear to have particular benefits for child quality.

Education of women improves child health because of the educated mother's greater knowledge of the importance of hygiene and of simple remedies. All this lowers infant mortality, which in turn means that a family does not need to have a large number of children in order to hedge against the possibility of the premature death of some children. Further, it appears that education of females increases the age at marriage (or at cohabitation) and through this delay, lowers the total fertility rate, (i.e., number of children ever born to a woman).[17]

Finally, some studies find that mother's education has a greater impact on the educational attainment and school achievement of children than father's education. This is plausible given the greater interaction between mother and children in most families since, in most countries, fathers are usually the main earners in the household. In this way, education of females contributes more significantly (than the education of males) to increases in human capital, productivity, and economic growth not only in their own generation but also in the next generation.

Gender Equality in Education: A Universal Value?

It appears that there is an increasing challenge to the principle of gender equality, and not only from religious fundamentalists. A broader current, particularly in Asia, questions the universality of the principle, contesting it as a "Western value." For example, when a 1993 study found that Pakistan had forgone much economic growth between 1970 and 1985, because of its large-scale failure to invest in the education of its females,[18] a large group of angry Pakistani economics academics called education of females a "Western value" and argued that education of females had led to increased incidence of divorce, family breakdown, and social problems in Western countries. Fred Halliday, professor of International Relations at London School of Economics, suggests that perhaps the most pervasive and difficult of all the moral issues confronting the world is that of universal versus particular values.[19]

Indeed, the Pakistani detractors who questioned the usefulness of women's education and claimed that it had wrought family breakdown in Western countries might have a valid argument. Access to education per se is not sufficient. The content of education is also important, as emphasized in the Bahá'í writings. Could recognition that content of education is fundamentally important be the next stage in the convergence of secular and Bahá'í thinking?

The Way Forward

In order to see how more girls can be educated, it is essential to ask what holds them back from gaining education currently. There are many reasons why women's education seriously lags behind men's education, particularly in developing countries, as seen in Table 1. The most commonly cited is that in certain societies parents continue to envisage a strict gender division of labor. If for most of her adult life a daughter will be a housewife, it seems pointless to educate her. The immense contribution that education can make to women's efficiency in child rearing and in domestic tasks is insufficiently recognized. In some countries, societal norms such as early-age marriage or the dowry system militate against girls' education. But, most importantly, when people live on low incomes—as in rural areas of all developing countries—it is the mismatch between the costs and benefits of girls' schooling that causes the gender gap in education to persist. In most developing countries, where typically there is no social security or state pension, male children still provide old age support to their parents. But female children do not; any benefits of a daughter's education are reaped by her in-laws. Thus the expenditure on boys' schooling results in benefits for the parents, but not expenditure on girls' schooling. In other words, there is an asymmetry in parental incentives to educate sons and daughters.

These explanations of the gender gap in schooling have important policy implications. First, they suggest the need for public education about the intrinsic and instrumental value of women's education. Such a policy step would aim to change conservative attitudes towards girls' schooling. Secondly, they suggest that public policy should compensate for the asymmetry in parental incentives to educate girls and boys by giving extra subsidies for girls' schooling. This makes sense because many of the benefits of girls' education are public benefits. They accrue not only to the educated individual and her family, but also to society in general—for example, lower infant mortality and fertility rates.

One further policy suggestion is that governments should improve the economic incentives for women's education by attempting to reduce job and wage discrimination against women in the labor market (for example, through stricter labor legislation). This would raise the economic returns to women's education. Evidence suggests that cultural inhibitions can be overcome if the labor market (i.e., economic) incentives for acquiring education are strong enough.

Summary and Conclusions

In this paper I have summarized the findings of recent research showing that the social gains from female schooling are generally far greater than those from male schooling. These findings have led, in recent years, to a widespread recognition of the importance of women's education, though the principle still faces challenges from certain quarters. International agencies that provide development assistance to economically less developed countries have come to realize the momentous advantages of expanding girls' access to schooling and are now enthusiastically championing the cause.[20] This convergence of secular and Bahá'í thinking on a key issue like education is welcome indeed.

The main policy prescriptions of this paper are that governments and other organizations should attempt to educate people about the equity and efficiency benefits of female education and that public policy should encourage girls' access to schooling by extra subsidies in order to compensate for the asymmetry in parental incentives to educate sons and daughters in poor societies. I have also argued that education per se is not sufficient. It is clear that societies which have achieved universal education are currently extremely deficient socially despite their economic prosperity. The next step in the evolution of secular thinking will, it is hoped, be in the important area of the content of education.

Notes

Geeta Kingdon is a Research Officer at the Department of Economics, University of Oxford, with interests in education and labor economics.

1. "The education of women is more important than the education of men . . . When all mankind shall receive the same opportunity of education and the equality of men and women be realized, the foundations of war will be utterly destroyed. Without equality, this will be impossible." ('Abdu'l-Bahá, *The Promulgation of Universal Peace* [Wilmette: Bahá'í Publishing Trust, 1982] p. 175).
2. Indeed, the early Bahá'ís of Iran suffered persecution partly for their belief in this principle. For example, analyzing the causes of the persecution of Bábís and Bahá'ís, Lord Curzon, a British diplomat in Tehran in the 1880s, notes that "the charge of immorality [against Bábís and Bahá'ís] seems to have arisen partly from the malignant invention of opponents, [and] partly from the much greater freedom claimed for women by the Báb, which in the oriental mind is scarcely dissociable from profligacy of conduct." (quoted in Shoghi Effendi, *God Passes By* [Wilmette: Bahá'í Publishing Trust, 1944]

and taken from *Persia and the Persian Question* by Lord Curzon of Kedleston).

3. For example, see Paul Streeten's paper "Global Institutions for an Interdependent World," *World Development*, Vol. 17, no. 9 (1989) pp. 1349-59. Also, see "Global Governance for Human Development," Occasional Paper No. 4, Human Development Report Office, United Nations Development Program, 1992.
4. For example, see the lead article "Get Ready for World Currency," *The Economist* (9 Jan 1988). See also contributions by Rupert Pennant-Rea (then deputy Governor of Bank of England) and Fred Bergsten (Director of the Institute for International Economics) in "The Future Surveyed," *The Economist* (11 Sept 1993). Both authors believe in the inevitability of a world currency and in the idea that global cooperative economic management will become the norm in the twenty-first century.
5. Janet Momsen, *Women and Development in the Third World* (London: Routledge, 1991) pp. 1-2.
6. Amartya Sen, "Women's Survival as a Development Problem," *Bulletin of the American Academy of Arts and Sciences,* Vol. 43 (1989) pp. 14-29. Also see, A. Sen, "Missing Women," *British Medical Journal*, Vol. 304 (1992) pp. 587-88.
7. For instance, 'Abdu'l Bahá underlines the equity argument when he states that "men and women are equal in the sight of God and that there is no distinction to be made between them." (*Promulgation of Universal Peace*, p. 174) The instrumental benefits of female education are also elaborated in many Bahá'í writings. For example, there is a strong focus on the beneficial effects of mother's education for the quality of her children.
8. The new or "endogenous" growth theories initially set forth by P. M. Romer, "Increasing Returns and Long-run Growth," *Journal of Political Economy,* Vol. 94 (1986) pp. 1002-37; and R.E. Lucas, "On the Mechanics of Economic Development," *Journal of Monetary Economics*, Vol. 22 (1988) pp. 3-42. See also the subsequent vast literature sparked by these major contributions to economic growth theory. For example, see the *Economic Journal* (June 1996) for a collection of relevant papers.
9. See review of studies in T. P. Schultz, "Returns to women's education," Ch. 2 in E. King and M. Hill, eds., *Women's Education in Developing Countries* (Washington D.C.: Johns Hopkins Press for the World Bank, 1993).
10. The total fertility rate (TFR) is simply the number of children ever born to a woman. In aggregated national data, the TFR of a country is the average number of children born per adult woman in the country. The infant mortality rate (IMR) is the number of children—per thousand born alive—that die before reaching the age of one.
11. See J. Strauss and D. Thomas, "Human Resources: Empirical modelling of household and family decisions," in J. Behrman and T. N. Srinivasan, eds., *Handbook of Development Economics*, Vol III (1995).
12. K. Subbarao and L. Raney, "Social Gains from Female Education: A Cross-National Study," *Economic Development and Cultural Change*, Vol. 44, no. 1 (1995) pp. 105-128.

13 M. Murthi, A. Guio, and J. Drèze, "Mortality, Fertility, and Gender Bias in India," in J. Drèze and A. Sen, eds., *Indian Development: Selected Regional Perspectives*, (Delhi: Oxford University Press, 1997).
14. M. Ainsworth, K. Beegle, and A. Nyamete, "The Impact of Women's Schooling on Fertility and Contraceptive Use: A Study of Fourteen Sub-Saharan African Countries," *World Bank Economic Review*, Vol. 10, no. 1 (1996) pp. 85-122.
15. For a recent example of such a study, see Geeta Gandhi Kingdon, "Does the Labour Market Explain Lower Female Schooling in India?" *Journal of Development Studies*, Vol. 35, no. 1 (1998) pp. 39-65.
16 For example, see John Hoddinott and Lawrence Haddad, "Does Female Income Share Influence Household Expenditures?" *Oxford Bulletin of Economics and Statistics*, Vol. 57, no. 1 (1995) pp. 77-96. This study finds that, in the Ivory Coast, raising wives' share of cash income increases the budget share of food and children's and adults' clothing, and reduces the budget share of alcohol and cigarettes.
17. For example, see Simon Appleton, "How Does Female Education Affect Fertility? A Structural Model for Cote D'Ivoire," *Oxford Bulletin of Economics and Statistics*, Vol. 58, no. 1 (1996) pp. 139-66. It may be thought that education of females would cause them to recognize the advantages of choosing breast rather than bottle-feeding, or to increase the duration of breast-feeding, thereby suppressing fertility during the period of breast-feeding. However, Appleton found that, in the Ivory Coast, educated women chose shorter duration of breast-feeding, leading to increased fertility.
18. N. Birdsall, D. Ross, and R. Sabot, "Underinvestment in Education: How Much Growth Has Pakistan Forgone?" *Pakistan Development Review*, Vol. 32, no. 4 (1993) pp. 453-92.
19. Fred Halliday, "The New World and its Discontents," Discussion Paper No. 4, Centre for the Study of Global Governance, London School of Economics, 1993.
20. For example, Lawrence Summers stated "educating girls quite possibly yields a higher rate of return than any other investment available in the developing world." ("The Most Influential Investment," *Scientific American* [August 1992] p. 108). Similar statements appear in many World Bank documents.